PONDEROSA PINE GROVE,
YOSEMITE VALLEY, 1986.

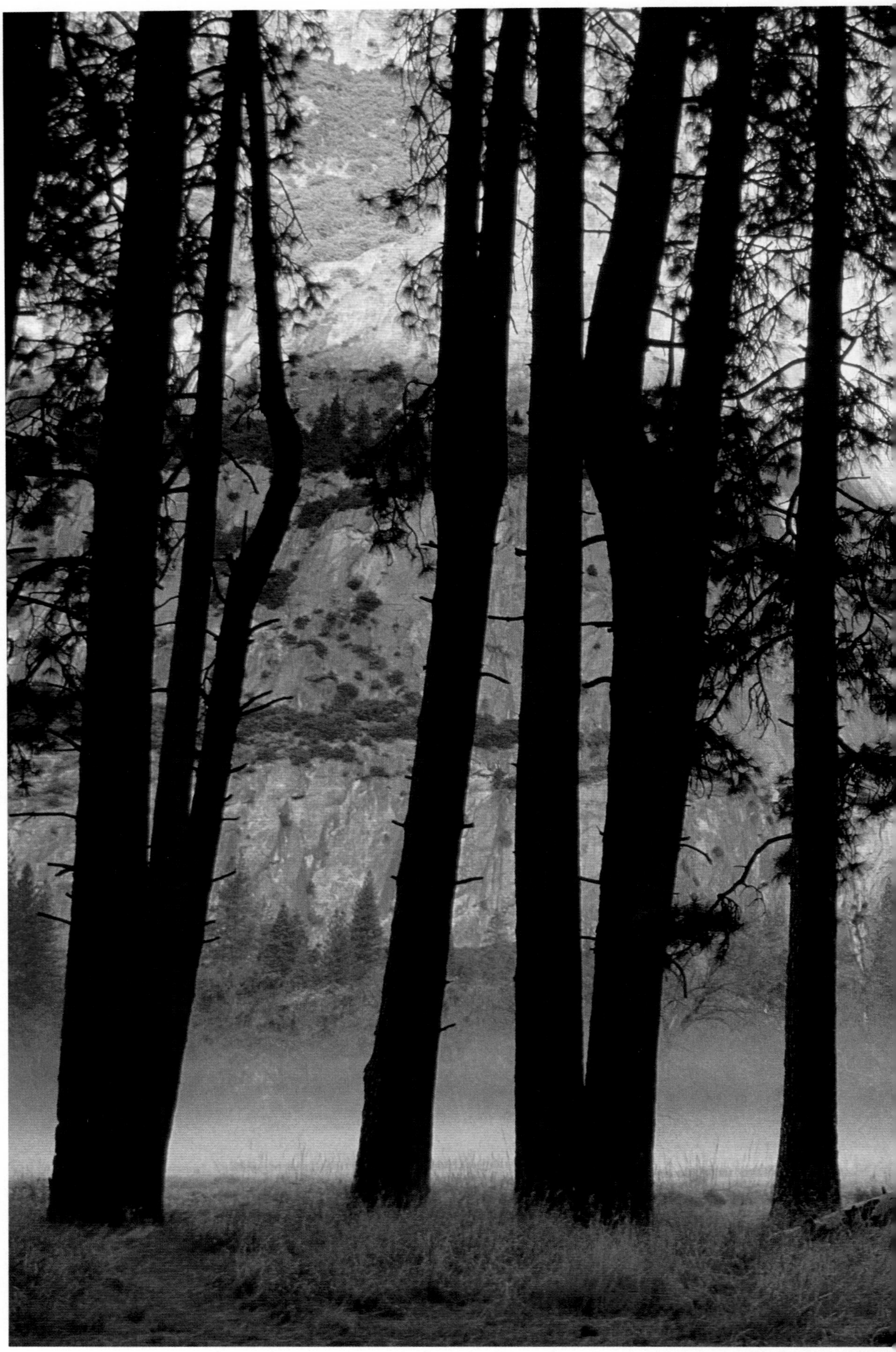

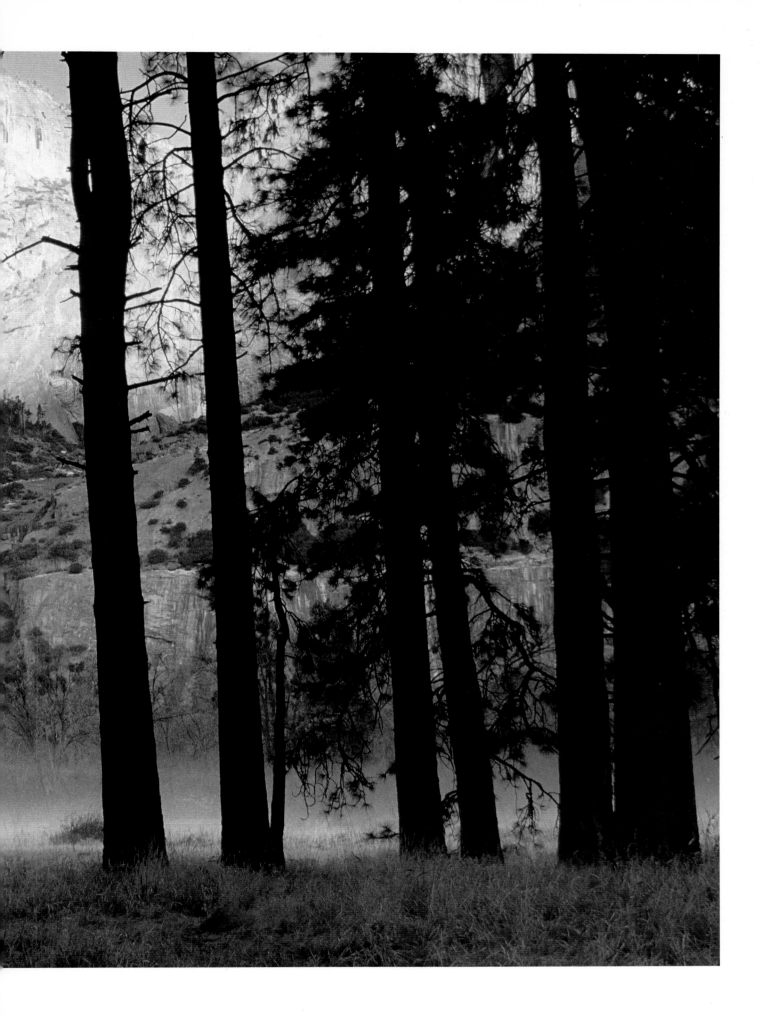

MERCED RIVER BELOW VERNAL
FALL, 1985.

# THE YOSEMITE

*The original* JOHN MUIR *text
illustrated with photographs by* GALEN ROWELL
*each photograph accompanied by an excerpt
from the works of John Muir and an
annotation by Galen Rowell*

INTRODUCTION BY THE PHOTOGRAPHER

A YOLLA BOLLY PRESS BOOK PUBLISHED BY
## SIERRA CLUB BOOKS
San Francisco

A YOLLA BOLLY PRESS BOOK

*The Yosemite* was produced in association with
the publisher at The Yolla Bolly Press, Covelo,
California, under the supervision of James and
Carolyn Robertson. Editorial and design
staff: Barbara Youngblood, Diana Fairbanks,
Nancy Campbell. Composition by Wilsted
& Taylor, Oakland, California.

The Sierra Club, founded in 1892 by John Muir, has devoted itself to the study and
protection of the earth's scenic and ecological resources—mountains, wetlands,
woodlands, wild shores and rivers, deserts and plains. The publishing program of
the Sierra Club offers books to the public as a nonprofit educational service in
the hope that they may enlarge the public's understanding of the Club's basic
concerns. The point of view expressed in each book, however, does not necessarily
represent that of the Club. The Sierra Club has some sixty chapters coast to coast,
in Canada, Hawaii, and Alaska. For information about how you may participate in
its programs to preserve wilderness and the quality of life, please address inquiries
to Sierra Club, 730 Polk Street, San Francisco, CA 94109.

LIBRARY OF CONGRESS CATALOGING-IN-PUBLICATION DATA

Muir, John, 1838–1914.
   The Yosemite: the original John Muir text.

   "A Yolla Bolly Press book."
   Bibliography: p.
   1. Yosemite National Park (Calif.) 2. Yosemite
Valley (Calif.) 3. Yosemite National Park (Calif.)—
Pictorial works. 4. Yosemite Valley (Calif.)—
Description and travel—Views. I. Rowell, Galen A.
II. Title.
F868.Y6M92   1989        979.4′47        88-34919
ISBN 0-87156-587-0

*Printed and bound by*
*Dai Nippon Printing Company, Ltd.,*
*Hong Kong*

10   9   8   7   6   5   4   3   2   1

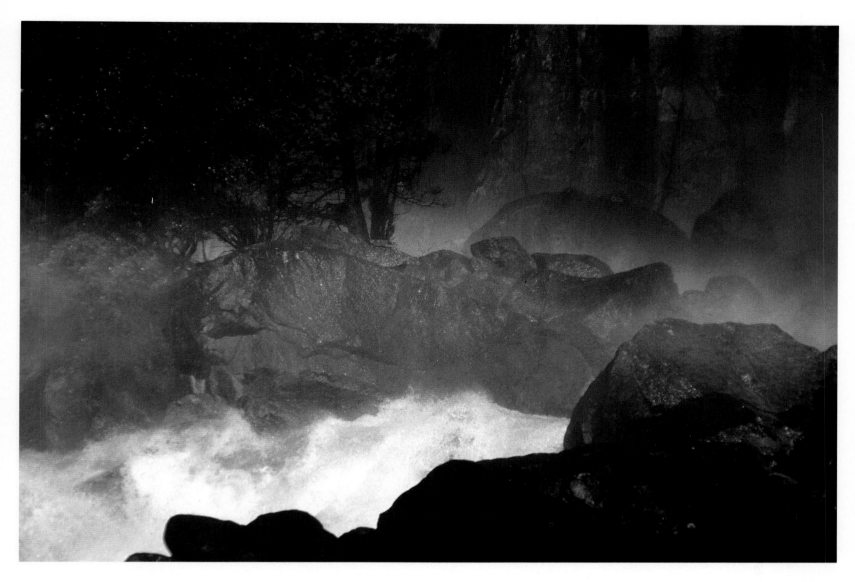

RAINBOW AT BASE OF LOWER
YOSEMITE FALL, 1986.

For my mother, Margaret Avery Rowell, whose lifelong passion for Yosemite
started with a visit by open touring car in 1916.

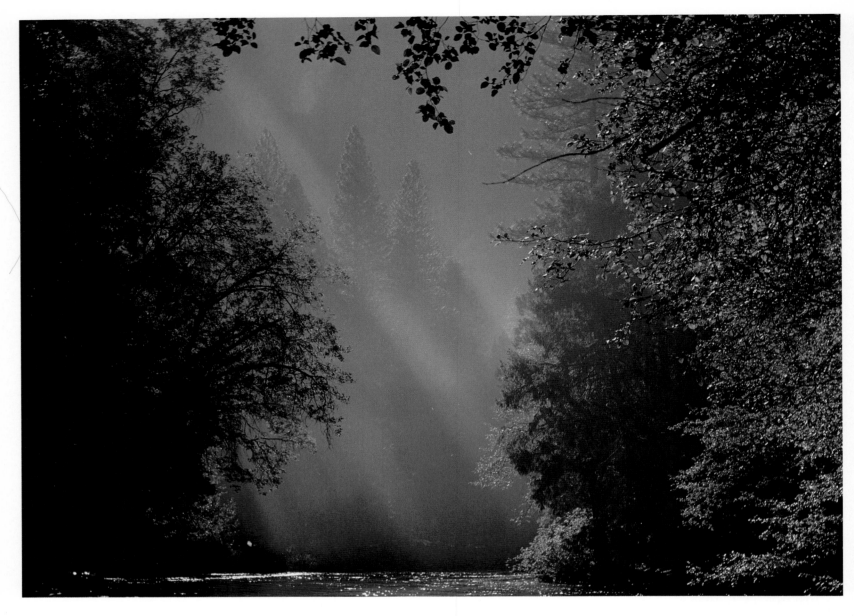

MISTY SUMMER MORNING,
MERCED RIVER, 1986.

# Contents

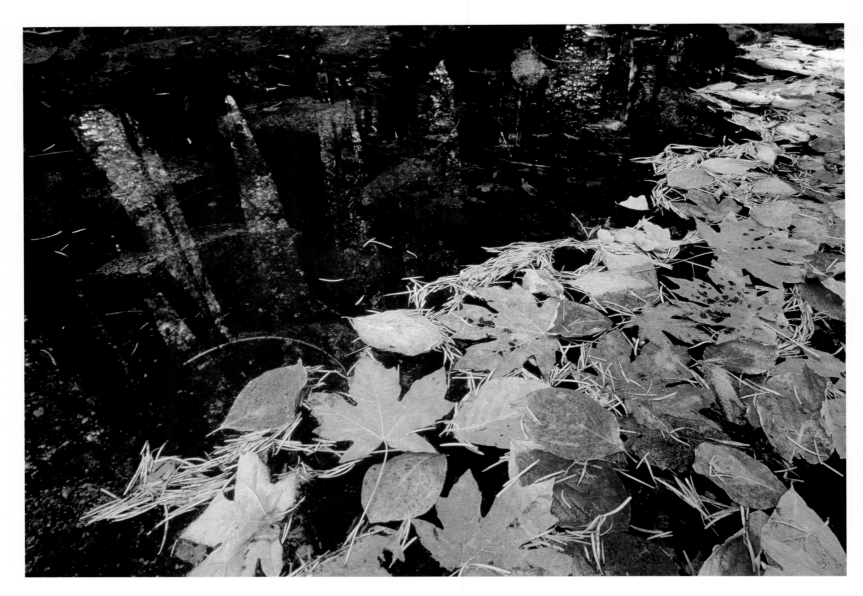

LEAVES IN FERN SPRING,
YOSEMITE VALLEY, 1987.

# List of Photographs

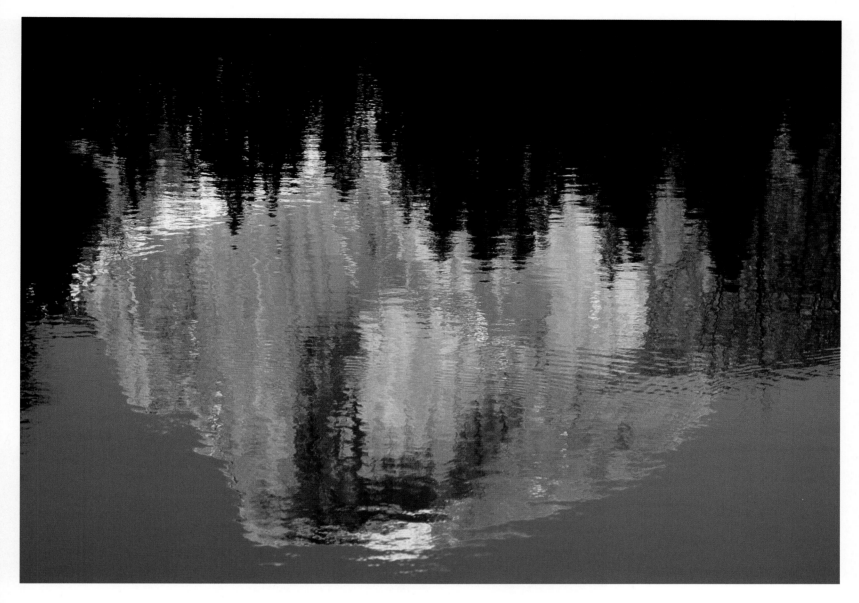

REFLECTION OF HALF DOME IN
MERCED RIVER, 1986.

GATES OF THE VALLEY ON A
SUMMER AFTERNOON, 1987.

"The Valley, comprehensively seen,
looks like an immense hall or
temple lighted from above. But no
temple made with hands can
compare with Yosemite. Every rock
in its walls seems to glow with life.
Some lean back in majestic repose;
others, absolutely sheer or nearly so
for thousands of feet, advance
beyond their companions in
thoughtful attitudes."

*I've found this view from a classic
roadside turnout beside the Merced
River to be the most consistently
fine of any in Yosemite Valley. So
much rock, water, and meadow are
visible at so close a range that
unusual lighting effects are
unnecessary to produce a dramatic
photograph. On an average summer
day a remarkably similar vision
presents itself in late afternoon
light, especially from a low camera
position close to the water, so that
the sky becomes a distant window
behind El Capitan and the
Cathedral Rocks instead of a major
component of the vista.*

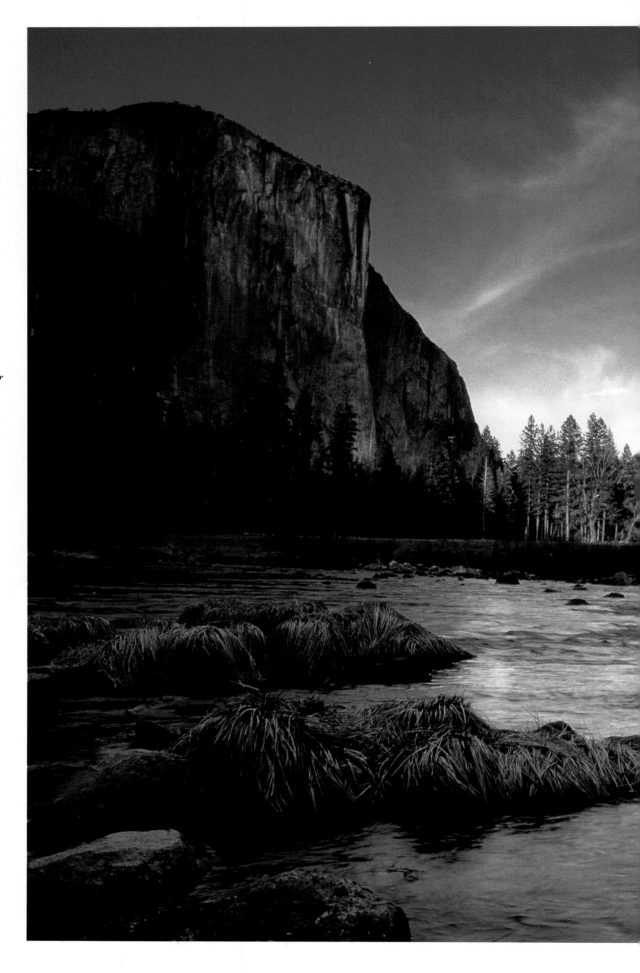

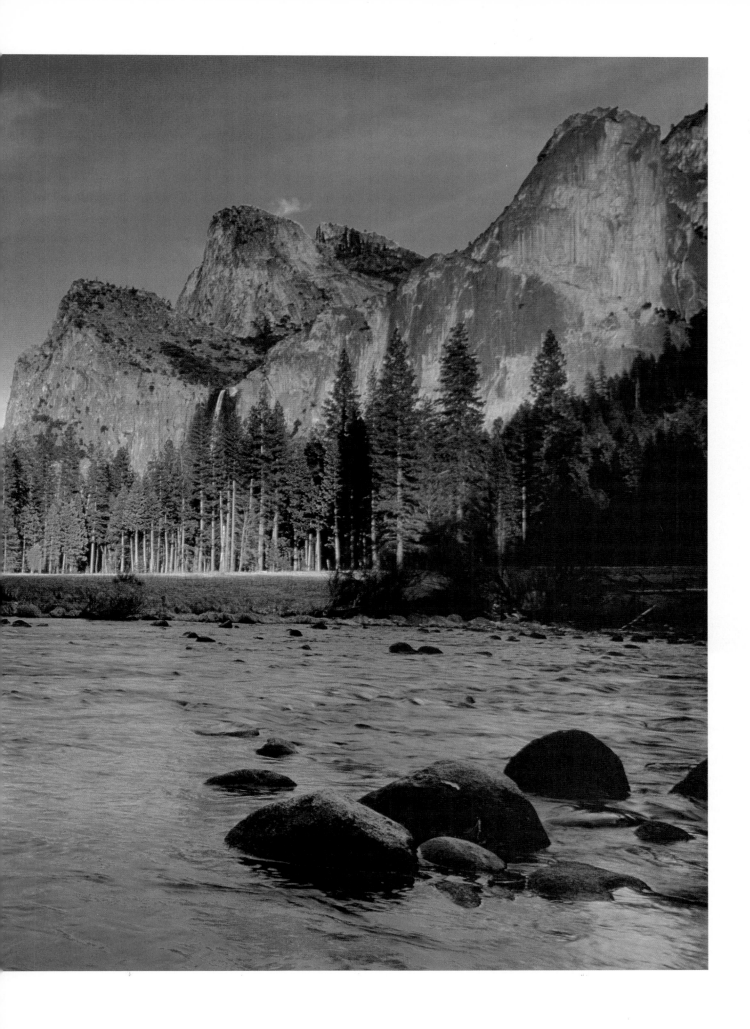

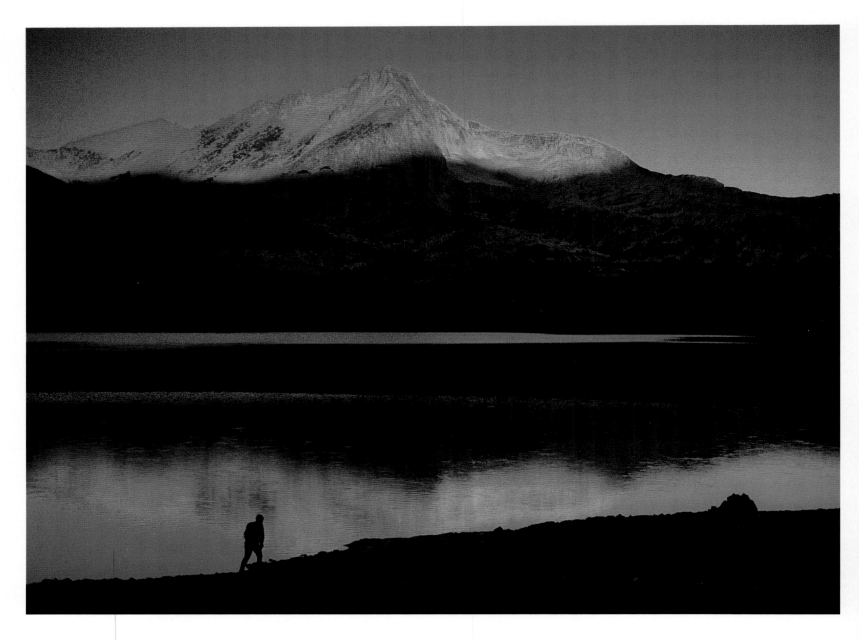

DAWN ON NORTH PEAK, TIOGA
PASS REGION, 1987.

"I drifted enchanted . . . gazing afar
over domes and peaks, lakes and
woods, and the billowy glaciated
fields. . . . In the midst of such
beauty . . . one's body is all one
tingling palate. Who wouldn't
be a mountaineer!"

*Claude Fiddler begins a day hike at
dawn beside Saddlebag Lake en
route to traverse the Sierra Crest
from North Peak and Tioga Pass.
Today Claude is neither a
backpacker nor a technical climber.
He plans to scramble over miles of
high-altitude terrain without the
burden of a sleeping bag, a pot, or a
tent because he intends to return
before nightfall. He carries no ropes
or hardware, limiting himself to
climbing what he can without such
equipment, even though he has
made hundreds of technical ascents
in Yosemite Valley. In the Muir
tradition, Claude revels in a day of
Sierra scrambling to awaken his
senses to the high country.*

# Introduction

WHEN I FIRST read *The Yosemite* at age sixteen, the book had a profound effect upon me. I had just hitchhiked home from Yosemite after the most Muiresque adventure of my young life. The meaning of my own journey became forever entwined with Muir's words and philosophy. His descriptions of Yosemite travels continue to trigger my imagination as unwaveringly as a whiff of burning pine brings forth an image of a campfire. Today, more than thirty years later, I can't separate his words from my own mental images of walking sixty miles across the Sierra en route to my first roped climb in Yosemite.

My goal in this volume is to use the powerful connection between Muir's words and my images to celebrate the one hundredth anniversary of the creation of Yosemite National Park in 1890. This connection goes well beyond the personal and the coincidental. I was neither the first nor will I be the last to find myself living both in the physical world Muir wrote about and in his thought world. At first I didn't question why my experience so closely matched his in a previous century. Why shouldn't I walk the same paths, climb the same peaks, think the same thoughts?

Since then I have come to appreciate that my modern experiences in Yosemite are not a given, but rather a direct consequence of John Muir's life. I know this firsthand after traveling through lands written about by some of Muir's contemporaries. In Mark Twain's Old West and in Rudyard Kipling's India, I have found the connection to be far weaker because the worlds they wrote about are all but gone. The modern ghost town of Virginia City only faintly echoes Mark Twain's prose, but Yosemite Falls in spring still booms with "the richest, as well as the most powerful, voice of all the falls in the Valley." A narrow footpath follows Muir's route to its top amidst "the rustle of the wind in the glossy leaves of the live-oaks and the soft, sifting, hushing tones of the pines."

Muir's greatness defies a single, simple definition. He operated in at least four dimensions. Muir the explorer rambled through uncharted mountains and made many first ascents. Muir the natural scientist was the first to recognize the major role of glaciers in the formation of Yosemite Valley. Muir the writer produced enduring books that remain in print more than a century after his travels. But the man's greatest legacy goes beyond these considerable physical, scientific, and literary achievements. John Muir was truly a visionary.

Before I continue this line of thought, let me interject a cautionary note. In today's world, *visionary* has two opposing meanings. Webster's first definition is simply "a person who sees visions." The second has what some might consider a negative connotation: "a person who has impractical or fantastic ideas or schemes." Muir's life proved to be unquestionably successful, but even now, a century after the creation of Yosemite National Park, he has not fully risen above this contradiction. On the one hand, some conservationists sanctify Muir as a saint or guru, a figure beyond mortal reproach. On the other hand, hard-fought political battles for parks and wilderness indicate that many Americans view preserving certain public lands forever as one of those "impractical or fantastic ideas" out of step with the times.

Although I see John Muir as a visionary in the best sense of the word, some of his critics rightly point out that much of his philosophy was not original. He borrowed Thoreau's attitude toward wildness as well as Tyndall's use of poetic metaphor to describe glacial action. The real question here is whether it is fair to expect a man of such diversity, or anyone hot on the track of new ideas, to be wholly original in expression. Throughout history great men and women have absorbed the important information of their eras and combined it with their own personal visions to create something beyond the imagination of their peers.

After Muir became well known to the American public, he applied the weight of his fame and the muscle of his prose to the task of preserving Yosemite as a national park. Later, when he lured Theodore Roosevelt away from the presidential entourage to spend several nights with him alone under the giant sequoias of Yosemite, he didn't stop at complimenting the president for beginning to institute the most sweeping conservation reforms in history. In a gutsy manner Muir went on to chide Roosevelt for not going a major step further.

Muir's visionary conservation ideas charted a fourth dimension well beyond Roosevelt's limited view that protection of wild areas, rather than being an end in itself, was "a means to increase and sustain the resources of the country and the industries which depend on them." Far ahead of its time, Muir's way of thinking presupposed the recent environmental movement. Viewed in historical context, it is not surprising that the little alpine club he founded in San Francisco in 1892 for the expressed purpose of exploring the High Sierra and defending Yosemite emerged from the environmental darkness of post–World War II America as the new Sierra Club, no longer a regional outing society, but an international institution that forced the world to look at the global consequences of dwindling wildness, pollution, and energy use, and what they mean to the quality of life of future generations. Muir already had destiny in his mind's eye when, still in his twenties, he left his family's farm in Wisconsin to walk a thousand miles to the Gulf of Mexico and signed his first journal entry "John Muir, Earth-planet Universe."

To understand how bold Muir's ideas were for his time, we need to imagine having been born 150 years ago into an era when natural history was depicted in terms of static creation rather than in terms of continual change. Darwin's theory of evolution, first published in 1859, 2 years before Muir entered college, was not included in Muir's textbooks, although his favorite professor, Ezra Carr, was aware of its implications. That Muir continued to see God's hand in all creation is not, as some modern readers assume, an indication that he did not fully accept evolution. Listen carefully to the philosophy behind his eloquence: "I used to envy the father of our race, dwelling as he did in contact with the new-made field and plants of Eden; but I do so no more, because I have discovered that I also live in 'creation's dawn.' The morning stars still sing together, and the world, not yet half made, becomes more beautiful every day."

Between the lines, Muir is telling us that he used to believe in a fixed creation of all living things at some time in the past, but he changed his way of thinking to see the world as a place of constant change, where creation is happening right now. His perspective is quite close to that of Darwin's, who also acknowledged a divine author of all living things, but denied the common wisdom of separate acts of creation for each fixed species, especially for the human race itself. What is significant is not that Muir adopted Darwinian thought soon after its inception, but that Muir's own philosophy went a step beyond, creating a new ethic to preserve the state of the earth.

Muir and Darwin share some striking parallels in their lives. Like Darwin, Muir traveled far and wide, personally observing the universal ways of the natural world. Also like Darwin, he waited several decades after his first observations before publishing books. By the time *The Yosemite* first appeared in 1912, Muir had seen considerably more of the world than he had written about in his familiar books. Besides his better-known journeys into Alaska, the High Sierra, and overland from Wisconsin to the Gulf of Mexico, Muir also visited Siberia, Manchuria, Finland, Egypt, India, the Himalayas, Africa, and South America.

Thus the global scope of Muir's thought and his embracing of Darwinian ideas as we find them in the text of *The Yosemite* reflect more than his original experiences there. Field notes made during wilderness journeys as a youth became catalysts for the more clearly stated philosophy of his later life. Darwin's theory evolved in such a strikingly similar way that Loren Eiseley in *Darwin's Century*, his book on the history of nineteenth-century evolutionary thought, ends with a Muiresque scene of a lone man contemplating the meaning of wilderness: "As a young man somewhere in the high-starred Andean night, or perhaps drinking alone at an island where wild birds who had never learned to fear man came down upon his shoulder, Charles Darwin saw a vision. It was one of the most tremendous insights a living being ever had . . . none saw, in a similar manner, the whole vista of life with quite such a sweeping vision."

In 1837, at the age of twenty-eight, Darwin jotted in his notes, "animals . . . may partake of our origin in one common ancestor—we may all be melted together." At twenty-nine, Muir left home to explore the natural world and eventually to express himself even more expansively: "When we try to pick out anything by itself, we find it hitched to everything else in the universe."

Yosemite became to Muir what the Galápagos Islands were to Darwin: a place where personal experience and visionary thought came together to influence broader concepts pursued for decades thereafter in other parts of the world. Both men looked closely at the primordial struggle for existence long observed by others; both saw not something life-threatening and destructive, but rather a creative, life-giving process. Darwin liberated biologists from looking at species as fixed entities. Muir freed first himself, then generations of his disciples, from the venerated tradition of adapting land to human needs, urging instead a new ethic of adapting human behavior toward preserving the natural state of the earth.

I believe that Muir made this leap of faith precisely because he was not pursuing a tangible goal in society, such as a college degree, a homestead, a pioneer trail, or even a national park. He inadvertently put himself into a situation where he spent long periods of time in the wilds without trying to change his surroundings to fit his needs. When he climbed mountains, the essence of his experience was the natural character of the terrain. Applied on a larger scale, the new way of viewing the world he discovered for himself gave birth to the environmental movement as well as to forms of new self-propelled outdoor recreation virtually unknown in his time.

I enjoy speculating about what John Muir would do today if he were to return to Yosemite as the fit young man of his first visits, with modern equipment and

SUNSET FROM THE SUMMIT OF
HALF DOME, 1987.

"The Sierra should be called, not
the Nevada or Snowy Range, but
the Range of Light. And after ten
years of wandering and wondering
in the heart of it, rejoicing in its
glorious floods of light, the white
beams of the morning streaming
through the passes, the noonday
radiance on the crystal rocks, the
flush of the alpenglow, and the
irised spray of countless waterfalls,
it still seems above all others the
Range of Light."

*One hazy summer evening I was
camped in a red fir forest on the
shoulder of Half Dome with several
friends. Forest fires were raging
unchecked through the high country
because of the modern policy of the
park service to let nature take its
course. I almost decided against my
plan to run to the summit to see the
sunset, because I knew the natural
features would be veiled in haze. At
the last minute, however, I put my
camera in a chest pouch, ran all but
the final five minutes of cabled
stairway, and topped out into a
solid-appearing mass of orange
light. The Visor, that great overhang
at the top of the sheer Northwest
Face, seemed to be floating apart
from the world.*

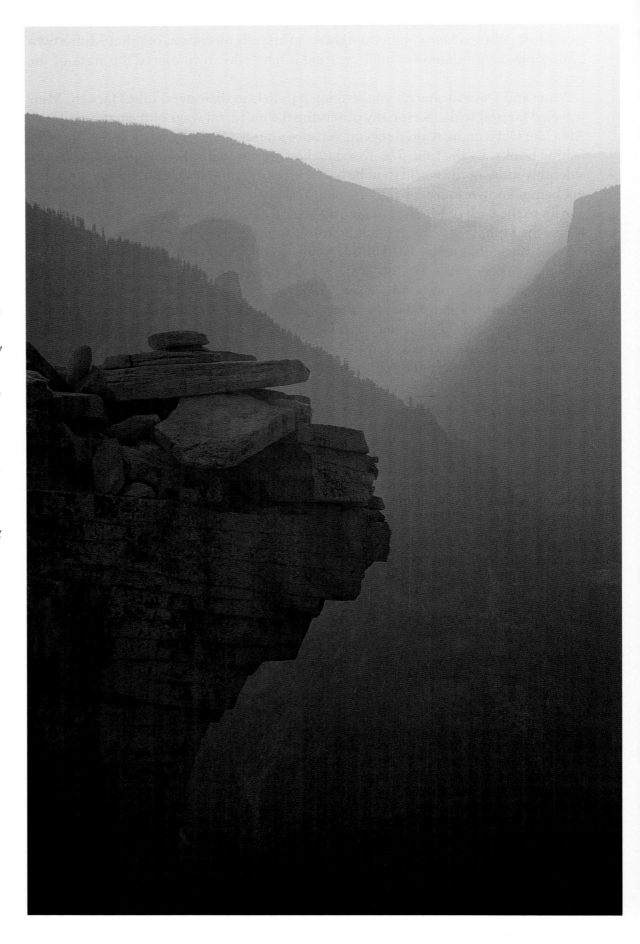

techniques but with his nineteenth-century ethics. I realize that I tread on dangerous ground here by attempting to project how a revered man might behave a century after his time, but dangerous ground was Muir's chosen turf, and the man is
hardly out of his time today except for his obvious physical absence. I admit that
much of my fascination is based on a feeling that Muir and I would share some of
the same activities.

Most nineteenth-century explorers moved through the land at a far slower rate
than do today's wilderness visitors who backpack on modern trails, but Muir was
a notable exception. Frederic Gunsky, editor of *The Yosemite*'s 1962 edition, included the following footnote to Muir's proposed Yosemite hiking itineraries:
"Muir was a prodigy of speed, agility and ascetic devotion to mountain pursuits.
Ordinary hikers, even those who are muscular and experienced, should take his
timetables with a grain of skepticism."

Today we live in an era when overweight, unathletic people don sophisticated
running shoes to walk around the corner to the 7-Eleven. One look at the torturous
footgear of Muir's day makes his trail (and off-trail ) exploits seem all the more
incredible. The man loved speed. After a one-day climb of both Half Dome (before
the present NPS cable path) and Clouds Rest, he "ran home in the moonlight with
firm strides." Given modern shoes and trails, Muir would certainly pick up his pace
and join company with some of today's mountain runners who make the roundtrip
to the summit of Half Dome before breakfast or complete the fifty-mile loop of
Yosemite High Sierra camps in less than a day. If these feats sound improbable,
consider that they were recently achieved by a middle-aged Yosemite waiter with
no early athletic background.

Advances in equipment and technique give today's John Muirs many more wilderness options than were available a century ago. Before we examine these new
possibilities, consider that all of Muir's original exploits are repeatable today by a
fit mountaineer clad only in shorts and running shoes, with the exception of the few
he did in winter or inclement weather. In Muir's Yosemite days, winter travel was
basic survival. Only a decade before Muir came to Yosemite, members of the Don-
ner Party perished in the same Sierra lake basin where crowds now casually gather
for winter recreation.

If Muir were alive today, he would definitely be a cross-country skier. He describes setting out "one fine Yosemite morning after a heavy snowfall, being eager
to see as many avalanches as possible and wide views of the forest and the summit
peaks. . . . Most of the way I sank waist deep, almost out of sight in some places
. . . spending the whole day to within half an hour or so of sundown." Once pro-
ficient on skis, Muir would join the adventurous few each year who wait for perfect
early spring conditions to glide across the entire park from Tioga Pass to Yosemite
Valley with only a day pack. While Muir would ethically disagree with the place-
ment of chairlifts in the Yosemite high country, his love of speed and agility would
probably lead him to getting a lift ticket for Badger Pass, imprisoning his feet in
plastic boots, and skiing as many runs as possible before the lifts closed for the day.

Being one of the best natural rock climbers of his day, Muir would not be able
to resist trying the modern version of the sport with strong nylon ropes, protection
devices that attach to the rock, and special shoes. I wouldn't be surprised to see him
doing multiday new routes up the faces of Half Dome and El Capitan, as well as
the sheer walls of his favorite backcountry peaks. Like modern rock climbers, he

would overstay the legal limit in the campgrounds. In a letter to an old friend, he suggests that he is not a man to blindly obey regulations. He speaks of living "among the sublimities of Yosemite," where he could "forget that ever a thought of civilization or time-honored proprieties came among my pathless, lawless thoughts and wanderings." Undoubtedly, he would be fined time and again, especially for sleeping in his vehicle (and he would have one) on stormy nights, as are many contemporary mountaineers, who never know if the knock on the window by a ranger is a request for them to help rescue a lost or injured person or a $100 citation for sleeping out of bounds.

In 1872 California's largest earthquake in recorded history struck while Muir was in Yosemite Valley. He described running out of his cabin shouting, "A noble earthquake! A noble earthquake!" He perceived creation, not destruction, as Eagle Rock, a rather large formation on the south wall, "gave way and I saw it falling in thousands of the great boulders I had so long been studying." What he did next was, for him, the obvious thing to do: "Eager to examine the new-born talus I ran up the Valley in the moonlight and climbed upon it before the huge blocks, after their fiery flight, had come to rest. They were slowly settling in their places, chafing, grating. . . . The air was filled with the odor of crushed Douglas spruces."

In 1987, when a large slide fell in almost the same spot, I saw an opportunity to match another Muir experience with a modern photograph. The road remained closed three weeks later, and two hundred yards from the slide was a ribbon with the words "Area closed by order of the Superintendent." While working as a photojournalist I have often seen police ribbons abandoned at a site weeks after an event, and I thought little of walking past the ribbon to take a picture, until rangers with bullhorns came at me from both sides. I was cited and ordered to appear that very day before a federal magistrate. A stern National Park Service prosecutor recommended "possible custody" because I had flagrantly risked not only my life, but also the lives of the rangers who had *had* to come get me. The magistrate gave me the choice of accepting a $100 fine on the spot or allowing him time to take the matter under consideration. Four months later I was fined $250.

The National Park Service sees a very different Yosemite from the one Muir describes within these covers. The agency works hard to execute its original 1916 mandate of preserving parks from the impact of too many people while at the same time providing for their enjoyment, but its efforts are being partially paralyzed by an acute phobia of public liability lawsuits. Had the slide on the Yosemite road occurred in a Third World country such as Nepal or Pakistan, traffic would have resumed within the first hour or two, but in Yosemite the road remained closed and expensively guarded for months, until resource specialists were convinced that the most feared event—a lawsuit stemming from a secondary slide—was unlikely.

On my first assignment for the *National Geographic Magazine* in 1973, I was overjoyed at the opportunity to organize, climb, and photograph the first attempt to ascend the Northwest Face of Half Dome entirely without pitons. In my wildest dreams I never imagined that anyone would try to prevent me from documenting the climb: photography for editorial publication is a First Amendment right. Nevertheless, a small group of Yosemite activists plotted to sabotage my photography to "save" Yosemite from being exploited in ten million copies of the magazine. They recruited a sympathetic pair of climbers and talked them into blocking the route up the face by purposely going very slowly right in front of us on the climb, ham-

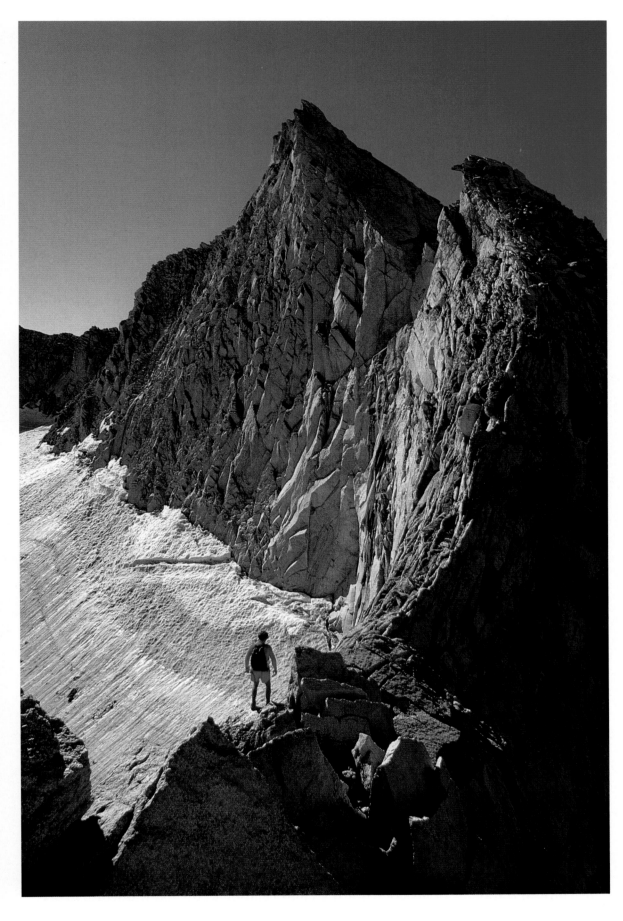

GLACIER BELOW MOUNT
CONNESS, 1987.

"Glaciers, back in their white
solitudes, work apart from men,
exerting their tremendous energies
in silence and darkness. Outspread,
spirit-like, they brood above the
predestined landscapes, work on
unwearied through immeasurable
ages, until, in the fullness of time,
the mountains and valleys are
brought forth . . . basins made for
lakes and meadows . . . soils spread
for forests and fields; then they
shrink and vanish like
summer clouds."

*Although the original glacier Muir
discovered on Red Mountain in
1872 has long since ceased to move
and has begun to vanish like a
cloud, the conditions that created it
remain nearly intact. A slight
change in annual temperature or
moisture could give it rebirth. The
Conness Glacier, on the other hand,
is more favorably positioned in the
greater shadow of a higher, colder
mountain. Even though its icy
bones are completely exposed in
this late summer scene, the yawning
crevasses that it displays speak well
of its current health.*

pering our climb and the photography. Once both parties were on the cliff, however, the culprits confessed the entire ruse. After our successful ascent, we learned that a letter falsely claiming that we were not actually climbing without pitons had already been written and mailed to an international climbing magazine. The letter, signed by a park ranger, was later retracted.

I mention this personal incident for two reasons. First, it had a deep emotional effect on me that in the long run changed my life for the better. At that time I had never been on a foreign expedition or traveled overseas. The Half Dome incident stopped me in my tracks, souring me about doing further innovative climbing in Yosemite Valley. I never again attempted a first ascent of a Valley rock face, and I began to set my sights farther afield. Today, after thirty-five mountain expeditions to such places as the Himalayas, Alaska, and Patagonia, I am able to return to Yosemite and to say with the authority of extensive personal experience how truly unique the park is. I have found nothing like it in the rest of the world, no place where so many virtues of beauty, fine weather, ease of cross-country travel, biological diversity, and wilderness come together to form such a complete mountain paradise.

I am especially fond of the words Mike Borghoff, a climbing partner of mine during the 1960s who was eventually rousted from the park for repeatedly overstaying the camping limit, wrote to describe the Valley's uniqueness: "Look well about you, wanderer! There is but one Yosemite on the face of the earth, and through the myriad moods, the shifting cyclic patterns, will always sound your need, simple joy and certitude, the face of life itself."

The second reason for mentioning the Half Dome incident is that it is a classic example of the chasm between two philosophies of environmental preservation. Some people believe that the way to preserve wildlands is to leave them alone and not publicize them or the adventures that take place in them. They believe that stories in books and magazines bring additional people, who harm the environment and detract from the wilderness experience. And that is what the group of Yosemite activists was trying to prevent by thwarting our climb. The other school, to which John Muir clearly belongs, believes that the salvation of wild places is rooted in public awareness. Muir wrote book after book, article after article, which brought new people into the wilds, but which also helped create an informed electorate with greatly increased awareness of conflicts over natural values.

After my cover story on Half Dome ran in the June 1974 *National Geographic Magazine*, I have no doubt that climbing traffic increased in Yosemite, and especially on Half Dome's Northwest Face. But the story also had a strong positive effect by promoting the new climbing ethic of avoiding piton use so as not to damage the rock. Mass public exposure to the new technique helped change the old ways much more quickly than they would have changed with grassroots methods—years of climbers' chats over beers, and letters written to the editors of specialty mountain magazines.

Between the lines of Muir's flowery prose are two conflicting emotions that are revealed more clearly in his notes and letters than in his polished books. On the one hand, he used language to cleverly bias descriptions of his experiences away from the cultural trappings of his era toward an appreciation of the natural world apart from human influence. Thus his writings live on today because they reflect the slower pace of evolving species and landscapes, rather than the frantic pace of individual human lives. On the other hand, he disliked writing and distrusted language. "Bookmaking frightens me," he wrote to his lifelong friend Jeanne Carr. "It demands so much artificialness. . . . You tell me that I must be patient and reach out and grope in lexicon granaries for the words I want. But if some loquacious angel were to touch my lips with literary fire, bestowing every word of Webster, I would scarcely thank him for the gift, because most of the words of the English language are made of mud."

While writing one of his books he took time out to write to his sister Sarah, "My life these days is like the life of a glacier, one eternal grind, and the top of my head suffers a weariness. . . ." Once he even stated, "I have a low opinion of books; they are but piles of stones set up to show coming travelers where other minds have been. . . . No amount of word-making will ever make a single soul to *know* these mountains. As well seek to warm the naked and frostbitten by lectures on caloric."

Muir tried other ways to record the immediacy of what he saw. Confiding in Jeanne Carr again, he said, "Oftentimes when I am free in the wilds I discover some rare beauty in lake or mountain form, and instantly seek to sketch it with my pencil, but the drawing is always enormously unlike reality . . . in word sketches . . . there is the same infinite shortcoming. The few hard words make but a skeleton, fleshless, heartless, and when you read, the dead bony words rattle in one's teeth."

With considerably more optimism, Muir wrote: "See how willingly Nature poses herself upon photographers' plates." One may question why Muir did not become a mountain photographer. In Europe, for example, mountain-lover and artist John Ruskin had laid down his sketch pad in the 1840s to make the earliest known photographs of the Alps. By the time Muir first visited Yosemite in 1868, the most famous photographers of the day, Eadweard Muybridge and Carlton Watkins, had already come to make stunning photographs.

Given today's 35mm cameras and color films, John Muir would certainly try photography. Given his artistic talent, his firm grasp of mechanics so evident in his early inventions, and his obvious passion for the wilderness, his results might well expand the present horizons of the art. But John Muir forsook photography because at the time it did not fit with his solitary, speedy, self-propelled lifestyle.

Consider the difference between his visits and mine to Muir Gorge, more than a century apart. The gorge is a trailless one-mile section of the Grand Canyon of the Tuolumne River where vertical cliffs confine the rushing waters to a width of twenty feet in places. Even today it is passable only in the late summer of low-snow years, and then only to experienced rock scramblers willing to swim long, cold pools walled by water-polished sheer granite. In July 1872 Muir and Galen Clark made the first passage. In August 1987 I ventured through the gorge with two companions to make a photograph for this book. I used a standard Nikon 35mm camera with three plastic Ziploc bags to seal the camera while I swam. Total weight: three pounds.

Were he alive today, Muir might well have joined us as we ran thirty-two miles of trail, swam the gorge, and photographed our adventure, all in a single day. The camera hardly intruded on the primary experience, fulfilling my desire to make images from the point of view of a participant in the natural world rather than of a remote observer of the landscape and other people's actions.

Muir did not have this option. In his day a "small" camera for landscape photographs used 8-by-10-inch glass plates that had to be developed almost immedi-

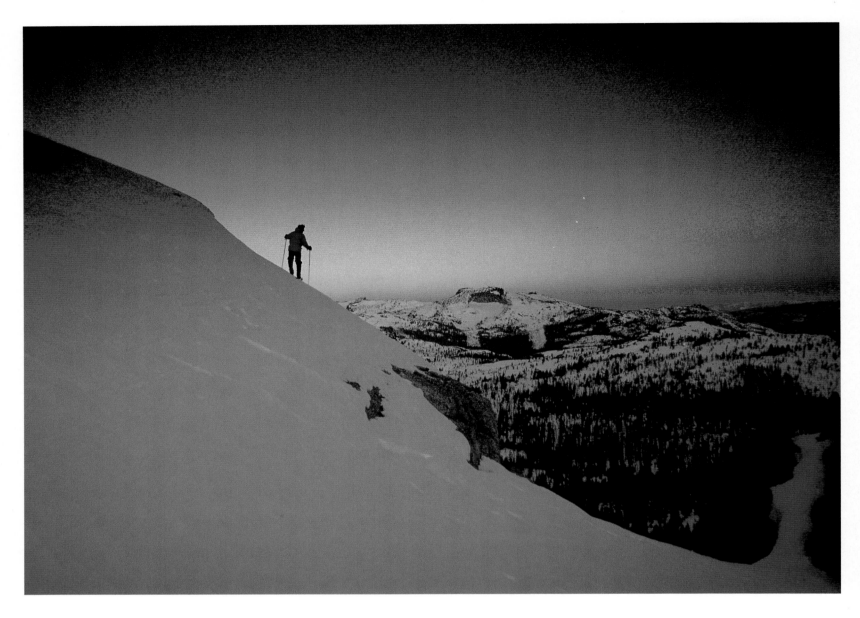

SKIER ON CATHEDRAL PASS AT
DAWN, 1988.

"The last days of this glacial winter
are not yet past, so young is our
world. I used to envy the father of
our race, dwelling as he did in
contact with the new-made fields
and plants of Eden; but I do so no
more, because I have discovered
that I also live in 'creation's dawn.'
The morning stars still sing
together, and the world, not yet half
made, becomes more beautiful
every day."

*On the final day of a 220-mile ski
tour along the John Muir Trail,
David Wilson watches a February
dawn in the Yosemite high country.
He sees not the gentle wilderness
the summer visitor sees, but the
rugged, icy land of the Pleistocene
epoch, a look into that era of snows
and silence before human beings
ruled the range. He traveled 160
miles on skis with two companions
before seeing another human being.*

ately. During the same year Muir made the first traverse of the gorge, William Henry Jackson was busy photographing Yellowstone to help create the nation's first national park. A look at Jackson's equipment shows why he was able only to make photographs and not to do the sort of original explorations that were Muir's penchant. Jackson brought not only his cumbersome camera but also two hundred pounds of necessary gear carefully packed on a mule named Hypo, hand-picked as the least likely of his breed to shatter his master's glass plates and dreams. Jackson's life necessarily centered around photography.

Muir was not a man to compromise his many interests for photography. He wanted to pursue everything at once. After Muir's death, the naturalist Edwin Way Teale tried to find out from Muir's living contemporaries just what aspect of natural history most fascinated him: "One thought it was trees. Another believed it was geology. A third suggested plants. A fourth, probably the nearest right of all, thought it was the whole inter-relationship of life, the complete, rounded picture of the mountain world." Muir believed that the primary goal of his work was to get his experiences fixed forever into his own being: "That's the thing; not to write about them!" When he did pick up his field notes to complete his first book, he was fifty-six years old. Muir in no way fits Wallace Stegner's whimsical definition of a professional writer: "A body that will go on moving a pen after its heart is cut out."

When Muir did move his pen, he flourished it considerably more than modern nature writers. Flowery Victorian prose was the accepted style of the day, and Muir used coveys of adjectives to give form to an image in his mind's eye. Unlike many of his contemporaries, however, he stopped short of using embellished phrases like snake oil to create false impressions. Clarence King, for example, fills his description of an attempt to climb Mount Whitney with considerably more danger and derring-do than Reinhold Messner's recent account of the first solo climb of Mount Everest without oxygen.

As I followed in Muir's footsteps to make the images in this book, I have continually been reminded how accurate Muir's descriptions are, regardless of their ornamentation. His goal was to create pictures with words for an audience that had not seen Yosemite either in real life or in the multitude of color photographs available today. He needed a profusion of words to create the color, texture, and look of the wild things that meant so much to him.

As I began to work on the idea of combining a set of my modern photographs with Muir's original text, I came to realize just how closely some of his words capture what I seek with my camera: fleeting moments of great beauty and wildness. I believe that it is more than coincidence that ornate descriptiveness fell out of favor in writing at just the time photography began to be widely published. Many factors have influenced the spare style of current nonfiction authors, but the role of photography in this regard has not been given its due. In reviewing early Himalayan literature, which flowered during the same turn-of-the-century period that marks the transition to modern prose, I've been struck by how often the writing style in books with photography is more spare and precise than that in books with sketches or in those with no illustrations.

The text of *The Yosemite* falls on both sides of this divide, combining the suspiciously flowery style of a Victorian writer born in 1838 with the credible lack of embellishment of modern nature writers. Chronology helps explain this disparity. Muir's original field notes were written in the 1860s and 1870s; the final manu-

WINTER SUNSET OVER THE
TUOLUMNE HIGH COUNTRY, 1988.

"Here ends my forever memorable
first High Sierra excursion. I have
crossed the Range of Light, surely
the brightest and best of all the
Lord has built; and rejoicing in its
glory, I gladly, gratefully, hopefully
pray I may see it again."

*This winter view of the domes at
the head of the Grand Canyon of
the Tuolumne is from the summit of
Cathedral Peak. John Muir made
the first ascent of the mountain in
1869. The view from the top
remains essentially unchanged
because Muir, through his
conservation efforts, made it
possible for future generations to
cross the Range of Light and gladly,
gratefully, hopefully pray to
see it again.*

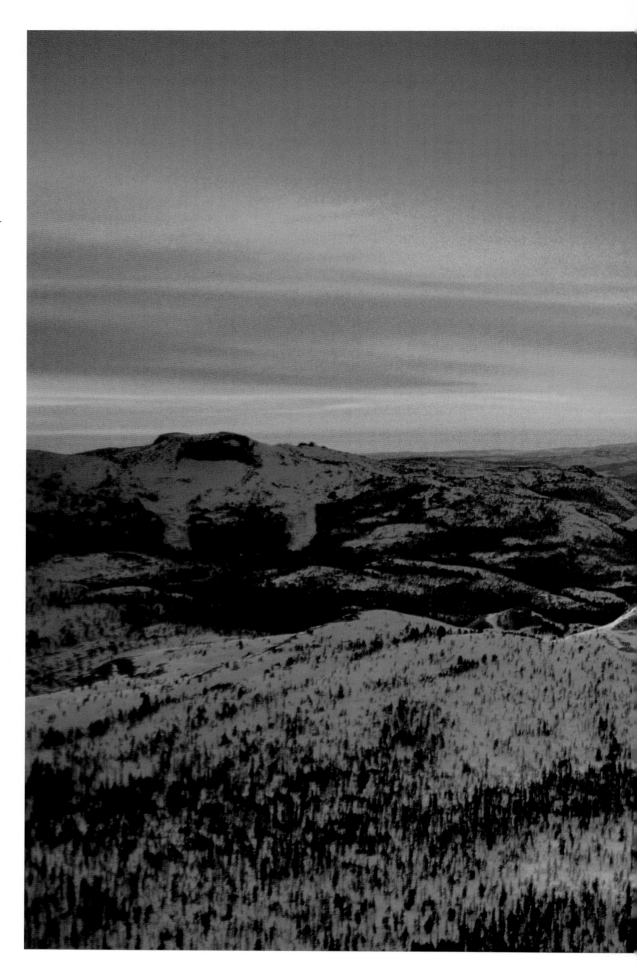

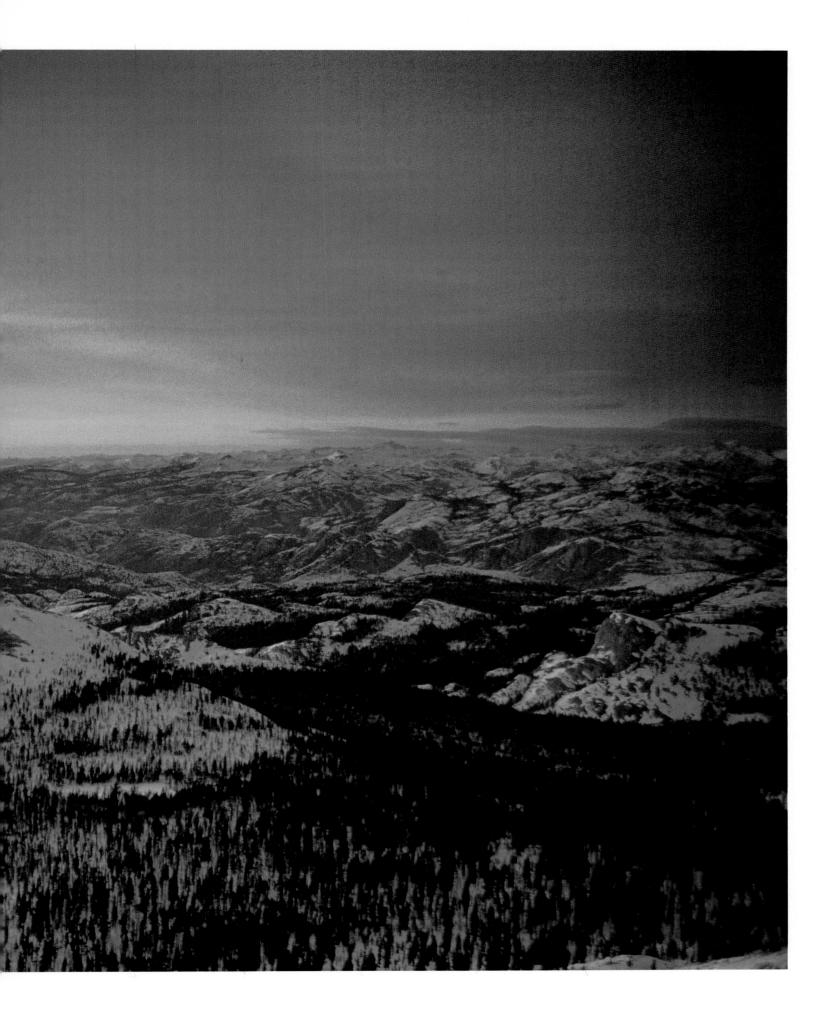

script was rewritten for publication in 1912, just two years before his death. By 1912 Muir had already revised a ninth edition of his best-selling *The Mountains of California*, including "photographs furnished by the author" from his Sierra Club friends, plus many of his own sketches.

Thus Muir had to have anticipated photography as he put together *The Yosemite*. He may never have imagined that his words would ride beside glossy color plates a hundred years after he helped create the park, but he certainly sensed that his audience would "see" much of the same Yosemite he had described many years before in an ever-increasing profusion of those willing natural poses on photographers' plates.

The power of modern photography is not unlike that of old Victorian prose. At its worst, it overwhelms the viewer with visual stimulation that does not truly reflect what the eye of an observer would see or, more important, care to see. At its best, by holding moments still for all time, it shows us something more than our eyes can see. This unswerving ability to hold true to reality while stimulating emotional empathy is not built into the mechanics of the camera, but rather into the heart and soul of its user. This very quality of Muir's prose infects countless visitors to Yosemite with a new appreciation for both the scenes before their eyes and for the man whose vision created such a national park.

The images of Yosemite presented here are by no means intended to document the entire park as it is today. Just as Muir sought to bypass the culture of his time in favor of wildness, I, too, have been highly selective in what I have chosen to publish between these covers. The wild Yosemite that John Muir visited still exists much as he saw it; and unlike many of the cherished places of my youth, Yosemite still remains quite true to my childhood memories. It has changed in only minor ways since that week during World War II—my parents had saved gas-rationing stamps for a year to make the trip—when, as a three-year-old, I first gazed up at El Capitan and Half Dome. Over the years the National Park Service has methodically worked to lessen impact in the Valley by reducing the number of campsites, centralizing facilities, and cancelling events not related to the natural scene (such as the pouring of burning coals over Glacier Point to create the old Firefall). Today visitor numbers are actually lower at peak holiday times than they were thirty years ago, but some disturbing new realities deserve mention here.

In 1984 I again was asked by the *National Geographic Magazine* to photograph Yosemite, this time for a major story. I had already committed to a long assignment in the Himalayas, so I couldn't accept. The *Geographic* selected another photographer, who had worked in the park as a ranger a couple of decades earlier. Because of that old connection, the National Park Service lent him a two-way radio to monitor current events. He produced an accurate but highly controversial behind-the-scenes look at a Yosemite that John Muir could never have imagined: the most serious law enforcement problems in the National Park System.

Although that photographer also covered the backcountry, his story was edited to fit a very different theme from the one that has been playing in my ears ever since I first read *The Yosemite*. Both themes are truthful and meaningful, but neither results in a fair overall impression of the park as it is today.

I thought long and hard about whether to include images of modern problems in this book, but I saw no way of blending the two themes without sacrificing too much of the flavor of wildness that still exists in Yosemite one hundred yards from every park road. I concluded that my goal should be to celebrate Muir's legacy, which includes all the wild places he wrote about as well as past and present methods of wilderness travel to reach them. Thus I decided not to include contemporary people as direct subjects, but only as figures in a broader landscape, to give scale and meaning. Allowing modern visitors to appear as main subjects in my photographs, with their distinctive clothing and modes of travel, would put me face-to-face with the same duality of the old and the new that I have confronted head-on in most of my earlier books by either writing or supplying parallel historical narratives to give my readers deeper insights into the contemporary scene.

This book is a departure from those past works because the focal point is not my modern narrative, but the existing text of Muir's that stands alone except for this introduction, my photographs, and the captions. Because of the great discrepancy of time between Muir's words and my images, I have supplied two captions for each image. The first words are Muir's, selected from the full range of his books, articles, notes, and letters to complement rather than to describe each photograph. My own words follow to impart a feeling of the modern experience and the factors that drew me to the subject matter.

The final interpretation is for you, the reader, to make. If I have succeeded, then something of both Muir's and my own vision will come out of each photograph for you. Photography by itself has little meaning when it is tied only to the singular experience of a photographer. It succeeds only when that experience is re-created in the mind of each viewer. If the eye wanders around searching for a meaning, the photograph fails. When the eye triggers the mind into that wonderful "Ahah!" feeling of instant recognition, then the image has fulfilled its goal of intuitive communication—in this case to bring John Muir's still-living world into the hearts and minds of yet another generation of citizens of "Earth-planet Universe."

GALEN ROWELL
Berkeley, California

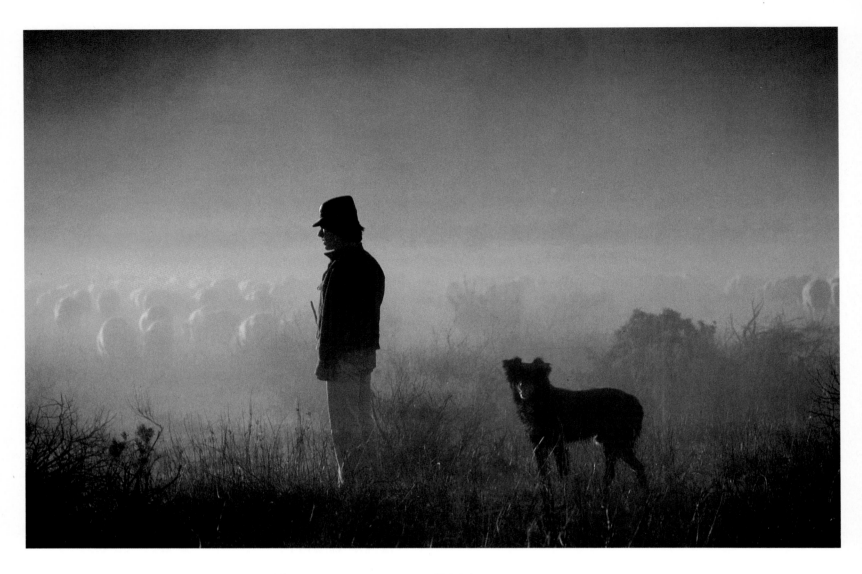

SHEPHERD WITH HIS FLOCK AT
DAWN, EASTERN SIERRA, 1974.

"Sheep, like people, are
ungovernable when hungry.
Excepting my guarded lily gardens,
almost every leaf that those hoofed
locusts can reach within a radius of
a mile or two from camp has been
devoured. Even the bushes are
stripped bare, and in spite of dogs
and shepherds the sheep scatter to
all points of the compass and vanish
in the dust."

*This scene, so reminiscent of Muir's
early days as a shepherd, is
thankfully long gone from within
the boundaries of Yosemite
National Park. Until 1985,
domestic sheep still grazed
meadows just outside the park on
the eastern side of Tioga Pass,
providing a major stumbling block
to the reintroduction of wild Sierra
bighorn into the Yosemite region.
Domestic sheep transmit diseases to
which the wild sheep have no
resistance. In 1985, donors to the
Yosemite Fund provided the capital
to buy up grazing rights and to
transplant a small herd of wild
sheep to Tioga Pass from the two to
three hundred animals that survive
in the Sierra farther south.*

CHAPTER I

# The Approach to the Valley

WHEN I SET OUT on the long excursion that finally led to California I wandered afoot and alone, from Indiana to the Gulf of Mexico, with a plant-press on my back, holding a generally southward course, like the birds when they are going from summer to winter. From the west coast of Florida I crossed the gulf to Cuba, enjoyed the rich tropical flora there for a few months, intending to go thence to the north end of South America, make my way through the woods to the headwaters of the Amazon, and float down that grand river to the ocean. But I was unable to find a ship bound for South America—fortunately perhaps, for I had incredibly little money for so long a trip and had not yet fully recovered from a fever caught in the Florida swamps. Therefore I decided to visit California for a year or two to see its wonderful flora and the famous Yosemite Valley. All the world was before me and every day was a holiday, so it did not seem important to which one of the world's wildernesses I first should wander.

Arriving by the Panama steamer, I stopped one day in San Francisco and then inquired for the nearest way out of town. "But where do you want to go?" asked the man to whom I had applied for this important information. "To any place that is wild," I said. This reply startled him. He seemed to fear I might be crazy and therefore the sooner I was out of town the better, so he directed me to the Oakland ferry.

So on the first of April, 1868, I set out afoot for Yosemite. It was the bloom-time of the year over the lowlands and coast ranges; the landscapes of the Santa Clara Valley were fairly drenched with sunshine, all the air was quivering with the songs of the meadow-larks, and the hills were so covered with flowers that they seemed to be painted. Slow indeed was my progress through these glorious gardens, the first of the California flora I had seen. Cattle and cultivation were making few scars as yet, and I wandered enchanted in long wavering curves, knowing by my pocket map that Yosemite Valley lay to the east and that I should surely find it.

## THE SIERRA FROM THE WEST

Looking eastward from the summit of the Pacheco Pass one shining morning, a landscape was displayed that after all my wanderings still appears as the most beautiful I have ever beheld. At my feet lay the Great Central Valley of California, level and flowery, like a lake of pure sunshine, forty or fifty miles wide, five hundred miles long, one rich furred garden of yellow *Compositæ*. And from the eastern boundary of this vast golden flower-bed rose the mighty Sierra, miles in height, and so gloriously colored and so radiant, it seemed not clothed with light, but wholly composed of it, like the wall of some celestial city. Along the top and extending a good way down, was a rich pearl-gray belt of snow; below it a belt of blue and dark purple, marking the extension of the forests; and stretching along the base of the range a broad belt of rose-purple; all these colors, from the blue sky to the yellow valley smoothly blending as they do in a rainbow, making a wall of light ineffably fine. Then it seemed to me that the Sierra should be called, not the Nevada or Snowy Range, but the Range of Light. And after ten years of wandering and wondering in the heart of it, rejoicing in its glorious floods of light, the white beams of the morning streaming through the passes, the noonday radiance on the crystal rocks, the flush of the alpenglow, and the irised spray of countless waterfalls, it still seems above all others the Range of Light.

In general views no mark of man is visible upon it, nor anything to suggest the wonderful depth and grandeur of its sculpture. None of its magnificent forest-crowned ridges seems to rise much above the general level to publish its wealth. No great valley or river is seen, or group of well-marked features of any kind standing out as distinct pictures. Even the summit peaks, marshaled in glorious array so high in the sky, seem comparatively regular in form. Nevertheless the whole range five hundred miles long is furrowed with cañons 2000 to 5000 feet deep, in which once flowed majestic glaciers, and in which now flow and sing the bright rejoicing rivers.

### CHARACTERISTICS OF THE CAÑONS

Though of such stupendous depth, these cañons are not gloomy gorges, savage and inaccessible. With rough passages here and there they are flowery pathways conducting to the snowy, icy fountains; mountain streets full of life and light, graded and sculptured by the ancient glaciers, and presenting throughout all their courses a rich variety of novel and attractive scenery—the most attractive that has yet been discovered in the mountain ranges of the world. In many places, especially in the middle region of the western flank, the main cañons widen into spacious valleys or parks diversified like landscape gardens with meadows and groves and thickets of blooming bushes, while the lofty walls, infinitely varied in form, are fringed with ferns, flowering plants, shrubs of many species, and tall evergreens and oaks that find footholds on small benches and tables, all enlivened and made glorious with rejoicing streams that come chanting in chorus over the cliffs and through side cañons in falls of every conceivable form, to join the river that flows in tranquil, shining beauty down the middle of each one of them.

### THE INCOMPARABLE YOSEMITE

The most famous and accessible of these cañon valleys, and also the one that presents their most striking and sublime features on the grandest scale, is the Yosemite, situated in the basin of the Merced River at an elevation of 4000 feet above the level of the sea. It is about seven miles long, half a mile to a mile wide, and nearly a mile deep in the solid granite flank of the range. The walls are made up of rocks, mountains in size, partly separated from each other by side cañons, and they are so sheer in front, and so compactly and harmoniously arranged on a level floor, that the Valley, comprehensively seen, looks like an immense hall or temple lighted from above.

But no temple made with hands can compare with Yosemite. Every rock in its walls seems to glow with life. Some lean back in majestic repose; others, absolutely

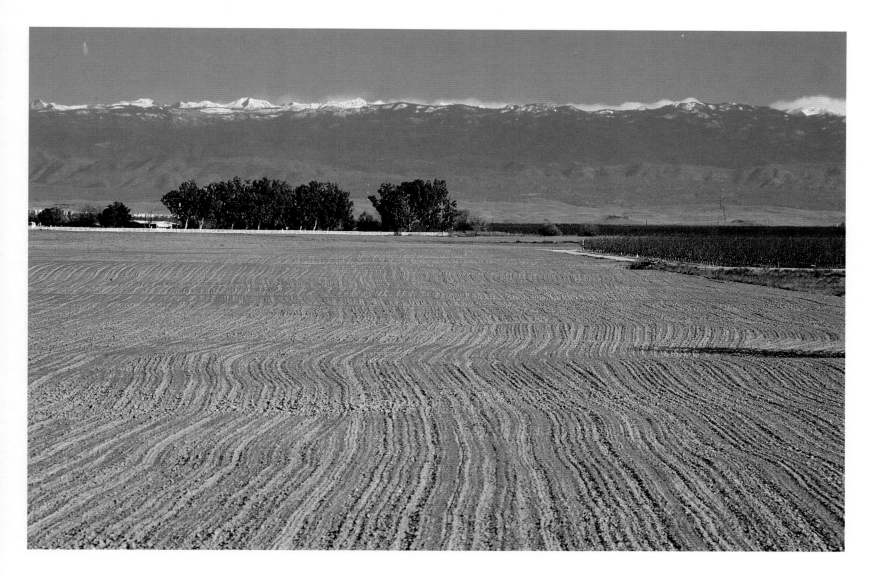

THE HIGH SIERRA FROM THE
CENTRAL VALLEY ON A CLEAR
WINTER DAY, 1988.

"At my feet lay the Great Central
Valley of California, level and
flowery, like a lake of pure
sunshine. . . . And from the eastern
boundary of this vast golden flower-
bed rose the mighty Sierra, miles in
height, and so gloriously colored
and so radiant, it seemed not
clothed with light, but wholly
composed of it, like the wall of
some celestial city."

*Muir's vision of the Sierra over a
lake of flowers is gone, but on cold,
clear days after a storm has
cleansed the increasingly murky
California air, the Range of Light
still appears like an apparition
above the farmed and freewayed
Central Valley. Whenever I see this
sight I am reminded that when
Muir set out for Yosemite in 1868,
California's valleys and mountains
were wilder and less explored than
those of the Himalayas today.*

SPRING WILDFLOWERS NEAR
MARIPOSA, 1987.

"When I first enjoyed this superb
view, one glowing April day, from
the summit of the Pacheco Pass, the
Central Valley, but little trampled
or plowed as yet, was one furred,
rich sheet of golden compositae,
and the luminous wall of the
mountains shone in all its glory."

*I have looked long and hard for a
relic of Muir's vision of the Sierra
from the Coast Range glistening
above a carpet of yellow flowers.
Although this fragment of flowered
foothill near Mariposa lacks a High
Sierra backdrop, it gives a hint of
what Muir beheld, mile after mile,
on his spring journeys
into Yosemite.*

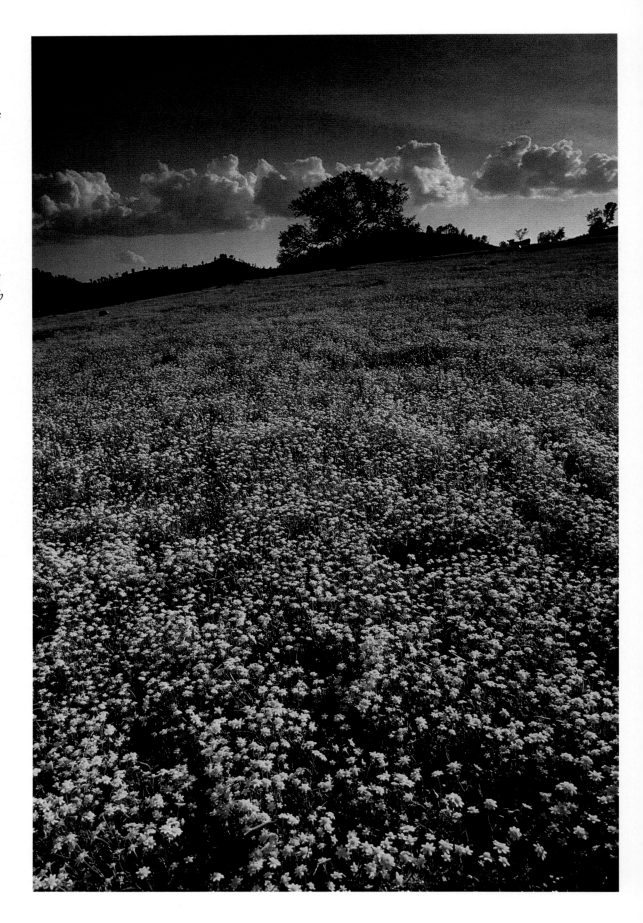

sheer or nearly so for thousands of feet, advance beyond their companions in thoughtful attitudes, giving welcome to storms and calms alike, seemingly aware, yet heedless, of everything going on about them. Awful in stern, immovable majesty, how softly these rocks are adorned, and how fine and reassuring the company they keep: their feet among beautiful groves and meadows, their brows in the sky, a thousand flowers leaning confidingly against their feet, bathed in floods of water, floods of light, while the snow and waterfalls, the winds and avalanches and clouds shine and sing and wreathe about them as the years go by, and myriads of small winged creatures—birds, bees, butterflies—give glad animation and help to make all the air into music. Down through the middle of the Valley flows the crystal Merced, River of Mercy, peacefully quiet, reflecting lilies and trees and the onlooking rocks; things frail and fleeting and types of endurance meeting here and blending in countless forms, as if into this one mountain mansion Nature had gathered her choicest treasures, to draw her lovers into close and confiding communion with her.

## THE APPROACH TO THE VALLEY

Sauntering up the foothills to Yosemite by any of the old trails or roads in use before the railway was built from the town of Merced up the river to the boundary of Yosemite Park, richer and wilder become the forests and streams. At an elevation of 6000 feet above the level of the sea the silver firs are 200 feet high, with branches whorled around the colossal shafts in regular order, and every branch beautifully pinnate like a fern frond. The Douglas spruce, the yellow and sugar pines and brown-barked libocedrus here reach their finest developments of beauty and grandeur. The majestic sequoia is here, too, the king of conifers, the noblest of all the noble race. These colossal trees are as wonderful in fineness of beauty and proportion as in stature—an assemblage of conifers surpassing all that have ever yet been discovered in the forests of the world. Here indeed is the tree-lover's paradise; the woods, dry and wholesome, letting in the light in shimmering masses of half sunshine, half shade; the night air as well as the day air indescribably spicy and exhilarating; plushy fir-boughs for campers' beds, and cascades to sing us to sleep. On the highest ridges, over which these old Yosemite ways passed, the silver fir (*Abies magnifica*) forms the bulk of the woods, pressing forward in glorious array to the very brink of the Valley walls on both sides, and beyond the Valley to a height of from 8000 to 9000 feet above the level of the sea. Thus it appears that Yosemite, presenting such stupendous faces of bare granite, is nevertheless imbedded in magnificent forests, and the main species of pine, fir, spruce and libocedrus are also found in the Valley itself, but there are no "big trees" (*Sequoia gigantea*) in the Valley or about the rim of it. The nearest are about ten and twenty miles beyond the lower end of the valley on small tributaries of the Merced and Tuolumne Rivers.

## THE FIRST VIEW: THE BRIDAL VEIL

From the margin of these glorious forests the first general view of the Valley used to be gained—a revelation in landscape affairs that enriches one's life forever. Entering the Valley, gazing overwhelmed with the multitude of grand objects about us, perhaps the first to fix our attention will be the Bridal Veil, a beautiful waterfall on our right. Its brow, where it first leaps free from the cliff, is about 900 feet above us; and as it sways and sings in the wind, clad in gauzy, sun-sifted spray, half falling,

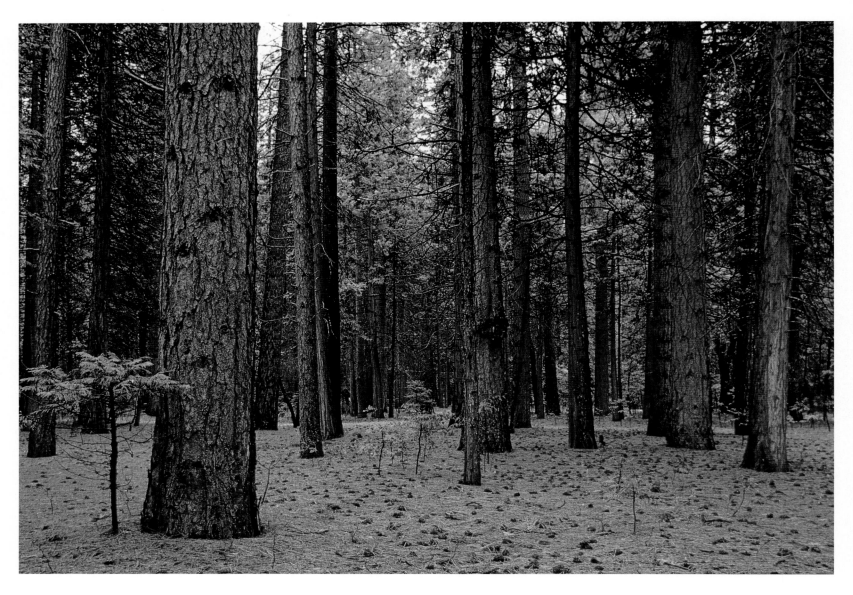

FOREST FLOOR AFTER A
RAINSTORM, YOSEMITE
VALLEY, 1987.

"The inviting openness of the Sierra
woods is one of their most
distinguishing characteristics. The
trees of all the species stand more or
less apart in groves, or in small,
irregular groups, enabling one to
find a way nearly everywhere, along
sunny colonnades and through
openings that have a smooth, park-
like surface, strewn with brown
needles and burs."

*Growing up in California, I made
an incorrect childhood assumption
about mountain forests. Because I
could roam at will through the trees
in Yosemite Valley or any of the
higher forests in the park, I took the
joys of cross-country travel for
granted. Later, when I tried to do
the same thing in the Rockies, in the
Cascades, and in Canada, I was
forced to retreat to the path
most traveled.*

half floating, it seems infinitely gentle and fine; but the hymns it sings tell the solemn fateful power hidden beneath its soft clothing.

The Bridal Veil shoots free from the upper edge of the cliff by the velocity the stream has acquired in descending a long slope above the head of the fall. Looking from the top of the rock-avalanche talus on the west side, about one hundred feet above the foot of the fall, the under surface of the water arch is seen to be finely grooved and striated; and the sky is seen through the arch between rock and water, making a novel and beautiful effect.

Under ordinary weather conditions the fall strikes on flat-topped slabs, forming a kind of ledge about two-thirds of the way down from the top, and as the fall sways back and forth with great variety of motions among these flat-topped pillars, kissing and plashing notes as well as thunder-like detonations are produced, like those of the Yosemite Fall, though on a smaller scale.

The rainbows of the Veil, or rather the spray- and foam-bows, are superb, because the waters are dashed among angular blocks of granite at the foot, producing abundance of spray of the best quality for iris effects, and also for a luxuriant growth of grass and maiden-hair on the side of the talus, which lower down is planted with oak, laurel and willows.

### GENERAL FEATURES OF THE VALLEY

On the other side of the Valley, almost immediately opposite the Bridal Veil, there is another fine fall, considerably wider than the Veil when the snow is melting fast and more than 1000 feet in height, measured from the brow of the cliff where it first springs out into the air to the head of the rocky talus on which it strikes and is broken up into ragged cascades. It is called the Ribbon Fall or Virgin's Tears. During the spring floods it is a magnificent object, but the suffocating blasts of spray that fill the recess in the wall which it occupies prevent a near approach. In autumn, however, when its feeble current falls in a shower, it may then pass for tears with the sentimental onlooker fresh from a visit to the Bridal Veil.

Just beyond this glorious flood the El Capitan Rock, regarded by many as the most sublime feature of the Valley, is seen through the pine groves, standing forward beyond the general line of the wall in most imposing grandeur, a type of permanence. It is 3300 feet high, a plain, severely simple, glacier-sculptured face of granite, the end of one of the most compact and enduring of the mountain ridges, unrivaled in height and breadth and flawless strength.

Across the Valley from here, next to the Bridal Veil, are the picturesque Cathedral Rocks, nearly 2700 feet high, making a noble display of fine yet massive sculpture. They are closely related to El Capitan, having been eroded from the same mountain ridge by the great Yosemite Glacier when the Valley was in process of formation.

Next to the Cathedral Rocks on the south side towers the Sentinel Rock to a height of more than 3000 feet, a telling monument of the glacial period.

Almost immediately opposite the Sentinel are the Three Brothers, an immense mountain mass with three gables fronting the Valley, one above another, the topmost gable nearly 4000 feet high. They were named for three brothers, sons of old Tenaya, the Yosemite chief, captured here during the Indian War, at the time of the discovery of the Valley in 1852.

Sauntering up the Valley through meadow and grove, in the company of these majestic rocks, which seem to follow us as we advance, gazing, admiring, looking for new wonders ahead where all about us is so wonderful, the thunder of the Yosemite Fall is heard, and when we arrive in front of the Sentinel Rock it is revealed in all its glory from base to summit, half a mile in height, and seeming to spring out into the Valley sunshine direct from the sky. But even this fall, perhaps the most wonderful of its kind in the world, cannot at first hold our attention, for now the wide upper portion of the Valley is displayed to view, with the finely modeled North Dome, the Royal Arches and Washington Column on our left; Glacier Point, with its massive, magnificent sculpture on the right; and in the middle, directly in front, looms Tissiack or Half Dome, the most beautiful and most sublime of all the wonderful Yosemite rocks, rising in serene majesty from flowery groves and meadows to a height of 4750 feet.

## THE UPPER CAÑONS

Here the Valley divides into three branches, the Tenaya, Nevada, and Illilouette Cañons, extending back into the fountains of the High Sierra, with scenery every way worthy the relation they bear to Yosemite.

In the south branch, a mile or two from the main Valley, is the Illilouette Fall, 600 feet high, one of the most beautiful of all the Yosemite choir, but to most people inaccessible as yet on account of its rough, steep, boulder-choked cañon. Its principal fountains of ice and snow lie in the beautiful and interesting mountains of the Merced group, while its broad open basin between its fountain mountains and cañon is noted for the beauty of its lakes and forests and magnificent moraines.

Returning to the Valley, and going up the north branch of Tenaya Cañon, we pass between the North Dome and Half Dome, and in less than an hour come to Mirror Lake, the Dome Cascades, and Tenaya Fall. Beyond the Fall, on the north side of the cañon, is the sublime El Capitan-like rock called Mount Watkins; on the south the vast granite wave of Clouds' Rest, a mile in height; and between them the fine Tenaya Cascade with silvery plumes outspread on smooth glacier-polished folds of granite, making a vertical descent in all of about 700 feet.

Just beyond the Dome Cascades, on the shoulder of Mount Watkins, there is an old trail once used by Indians on their way across the range to Mono, but in the cañon above this point there is no trail of any sort. Between Mount Watkins and Clouds' Rest the cañon is accessible only to mountaineers, and it is so dangerous that I hesitate to advise even good climbers, anxious to test their nerve and skill, to attempt to pass through it. Beyond the Cascades no great difficulty will be encountered. A succession of charming lily gardens and meadows occurs in filled-up lake basins among the rock-waves in the bottom of the cañon, and everywhere the surface of the granite has a smooth-wiped appearance, and in many places reflects the sunbeams like glass, a phenomenon due to glacial action, the cañon having been the channel of one of the main tributaries of the ancient Yosemite Glacier.

About ten miles above the Valley we come to the beautiful Tenaya Lake, and here the cañon terminates. A mile or two above the lake stands the grand Sierra Cathedral, a building of one stone, hewn from the living rock, with sides, roof, gable, spire and ornamental pinnacles, fashioned and finished symmetrically like a work of art, and set on a well-graded plateau about 9000 feet high, as if Nature in making so fine a building had also been careful that it should be finely seen. From every direction its peculiar form and graceful, majestic beauty of expression never fail to charm. Its height from its base to the ridge of the roof is about 2500 feet, and among

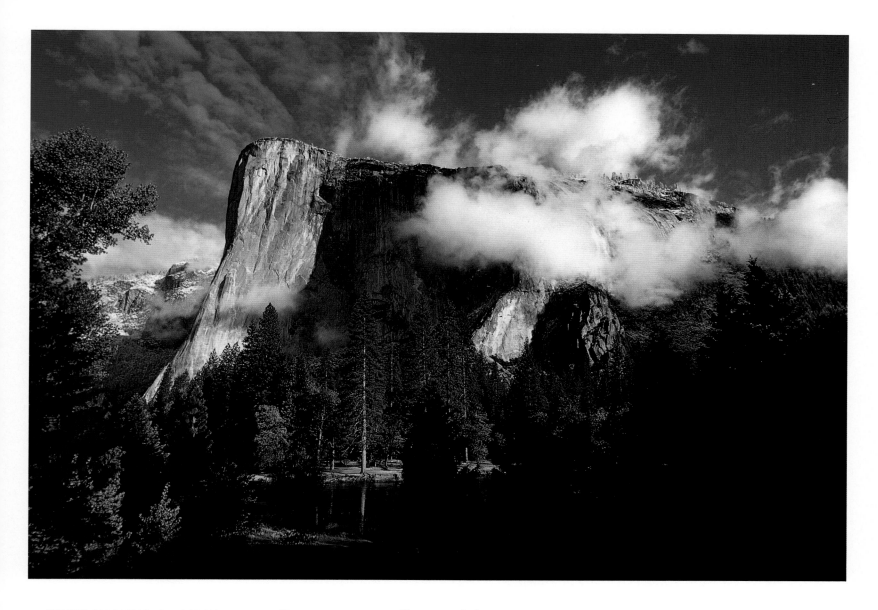

SPRING MORNING, EL CAPITAN, YOSEMITE VALLEY, 1973.

"El Capitan . . . the most sublime feature of the Valley, is seen through the pine groves . . . a plain, severely simple, glacier-sculptured face of granite, the end of one of the most compact and enduring of the mountain ridges, unrivaled in height and breadth and flawless strength."

*On my own ascents, I've marveled at much closer hand than Muir did over the lack of flaws and weaknesses in the face of El Capitan. Other rock walls may appear smooth from a distance, but they almost always provide a climber with an unseen braille-works of handholds and footholds. A few granite walls in Alaska and the Himalayas are larger, but after climbing on them I fully agree with Muir's perfectly qualified assessment that El Cap is "unrivaled in height and breadth and flawless strength."*

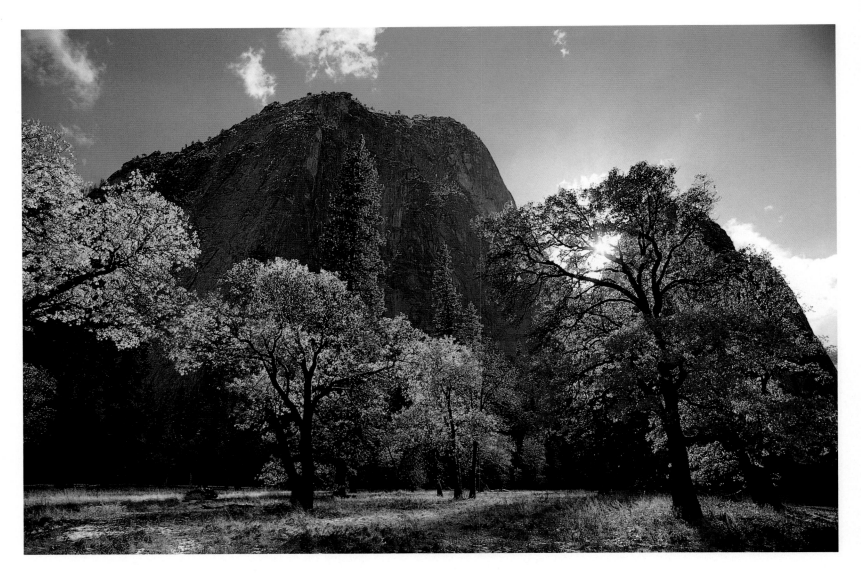

OAK TREES AND CATHEDRAL
ROCKS, 1978.

"In the middle region of the western
flank [of the Sierra Nevada], the
main canyons widen into spacious
valleys or parks diversified like
landscape gardens."

*The lure of Yosemite Valley is as
much due to its absolutely flat,
parklike floor as to its sheer walls.
Here oak trees dominate an open
meadow in the western end of the
Valley. The sun shines late into the
day, allowing lowland grasses and
oaks to lap the bases of the alpine
cliffs. At the same elevation beneath
Glacier Point, the parklike floor is
virtually obscured beneath conifers
that thrive in the deep shade.*

the pinnacles that adorn the front grand views may be gained of the upper basins of the Merced and Tuolumne Rivers.

Passing the Cathedral we descend into the delightful, spacious Tuolumne Valley, from which excursions may be made to Mounts Dana, Lyell, Ritter, Conness, and Mono Lake, and to the many curious peaks that rise above the meadows on the south, and to the Big Tuolumne Cañon, with its glorious abundance of rocks and falling, gliding, tossing water. For all these the beautiful meadows near the Soda Springs form a delightful center.

### NATURAL FEATURES NEAR THE VALLEY

Returning now to Yosemite and ascending the middle or Nevada branch of the Valley, occupied by the main Merced River, we come within a few miles to the Vernal and Nevada Falls, 400 and 600 feet high, pouring their white, rejoicing waters in the midst of the most novel and sublime rock scenery to be found in all the world. Tracing the river beyond the head of the Nevada Fall we are led into the Little Yosemite, a valley like the great Yosemite in form, sculpture and vegetation. It is about three miles long, with walls 1500 to 2000 feet high, cascades coming over them, and the river flowing through the meadows and groves of the level bottom in tranquil, richly-embowered reaches.

Beyond this Little Yosemite in the main cañon, there are three other little yosemites, the highest situated a few miles below the base of Mount Lyell, at an elevation of about 7800 feet above the sea. To describe these, with all their wealth of Yosemite furniture, and the wilderness of lofty peaks above them, the home of the avalanche and treasury of the fountain snow, would take us far beyond the bounds of a single book. Nor can we here consider the formation of these mountain landscapes—how the crystal rocks were brought to light by glaciers made up of crystal snow, making beauty whose influence is so mysterious on every one who sees it.

Of the small glacier lakes so characteristic of these upper regions, there are no fewer than sixty-seven in the basin of the main middle branch, besides countless smaller pools. In the basin of the Illilouette there are sixteen, in the Tenaya basin and its branches thirteen, in the Yosemite Creek basin fourteen, and in the Pohono or Bridal Veil one, making a grand total of one hundred and eleven lakes whose waters come to sing at Yosemite. So glorious is the background of the great Valley, so harmonious its relations to its widespreading fountains.

The same harmony prevails in all the other features of the adjacent landscapes. Climbing out of the Valley by the subordinate cañons, we find the ground rising from the brink of the walls: on the south side to the fountains of the Bridal Veil Creek, the basin of which is noted for the beauty of its meadows and its superb forests of silver fir; on the north side through the basin of the Yosemite Creek to the dividing ridge along the Tuolumne Cañon and the fountains of the Hoffman Range.

### DOWN THE YOSEMITE CREEK

In general views the Yosemite Creek basin seems to be paved with domes and smooth, whaleback masses of granite in every stage of development—some showing only their crowns; others rising high and free above the girdling forests, singly or in groups. Others are developed only on one side, forming bold outstanding bosses usually well fringed with shrubs and trees, and presenting the polished surfaces given them by the glacier that brought them into relief. On the upper portion of the basin broad moraine beds have been deposited and on these fine, thrifty forests are growing. Lakes and meadows and small spongy bogs may be found hiding here and there in the woods or back in the fountain recesses of Mount Hoffman, while a thousand gardens are planted along the banks of the streams.

All the wide, fan-shaped upper portion of the basin is covered with a network of small rills that go cheerily on their way to their grand fall in the Valley, now flowing on smooth pavements in sheets thin as glass, now diving under willows and laving their red roots, oozing through green, plushy bogs, plashing over small falls and dancing down slanting cascades, calming again, gliding through patches of smooth glacier meadows with sod of alpine agrostis mixed with blue and white violets and daisies, breaking, tossing among rough boulders and fallen trees, resting in calm pools, flowing together until, all united, they go to their fate with stately, tranquil gestures like a full-grown river. At the crossing of the Mono Trail, about two miles above the head of the Yosemite Fall, the stream is nearly forty feet wide, and when the snow is melting rapidly in the spring it is about four feet deep, with a current of two and a half miles an hour. This is about the volume of water that forms the Fall in May and June when there had been much snow the preceding winter; but it varies greatly from month to month. The snow rapidly vanishes from the open portion of the basin, which faces southward, and only a few of the tributaries reach back to perennial snow and ice fountains in the shadowy amphitheaters on the precipitous northern slopes of Mount Hoffman. The total descent made by the stream from its highest sources to its confluence with the Merced in the Valley is about 6000 feet, while the distance is only about ten miles, an average fall of 600 feet per mile. The last mile of its course lies between the sides of sunken domes and swelling folds of the granite that are clustered and pressed together like a mass of bossy cumulus clouds. Through this shining way Yosemite Creek goes to its fate, swaying and swirling with easy, graceful gestures and singing the last of its mountain songs before it reaches the dizzy edge of Yosemite to fall 2600 feet into another world, where climate, vegetation, inhabitants, all are different. Emerging from this last cañon the stream glides, in flat, lace-like folds, down a smooth incline into a small pool where it seems to rest and compose itself before taking the grand plunge. Then calmly, as if leaving a lake, it slips over the polished lip of the pool down another incline and out over the brow of the precipice in a magnificent curve thick-sown with rainbow spray.

### THE YOSEMITE FALL

Long ago before I had traced this fine stream to its head back of Mount Hoffman, I was eager to reach the extreme verge to see how it behaved in flying so far through the air; but after enjoying this view and getting safely away I have never advised any one to follow my steps. The last incline down which the stream journeys so gracefully is so steep and smooth one must slip cautiously forward on hands and feet alongside the rushing water, which so near one's head is very exciting. But to gain a perfect view one must go yet farther, over a curving brow to a slight shelf on the extreme brink. This shelf, formed by the flaking off of a fold of granite, is about three inches wide, just wide enough for a safe rest for one's heels. To me it seemed nerve-trying to slip to this narrow foothold and poise on the edge of such a precipice so close to the confusing whirl of the waters; and after casting longing glances over the shining brow of the fall and listening to its sublime psalm, I con-

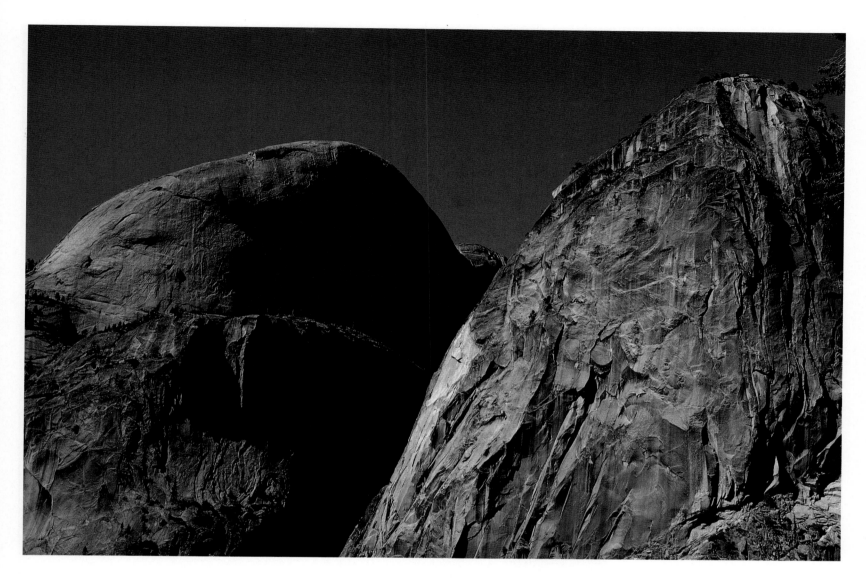

THE CONCENTRIC DOMES OF HALF
DOME, LIBERTY CAP, AND MOUNT
BRODERICK, 1969.

"The Sierra, instead of being a huge
wrinkle of the earth's crust without
any determinate structure, is built
up of regularly formed stones like a
work of art."

*The curved "back sides" of
Yosemite cliffs remained unclimbed
until all of the major faces of the
Valley had been ascended by at least
one route. I made this photograph
as Warren Harding and I were on
our way to attempt the first ascent
of the South Face of Half Dome,
seen here in the background. A year
earlier we had climbed the
Southwest Face of Liberty Cap, the
wall in the middle.*

RIBBON FALL
AMPHITHEATER, 1975.

"Almost immediately opposite the
Bridal Veil, there is another fine fall,
considerably wider than the Veil
when the snow is melting fast and
more than 1,000 feet in height. . . .
It is called the Ribbon Fall or
Virgin's Tears. During the spring
floods it is a magnificent object, but
the suffocating blasts of spray that
fill the recess in the wall which it
occupies prevent a near approach."

*Little-known Ribbon Fall is actually
the highest fall in Yosemite, but
because it dries up each summer it
misses both the record book and the
majority of visitors. When spring
runoff slows enough to permit
entry, the Ribbon Fall Amphitheater
becomes the most auspicious scene
in the Valley. Standing there
surrounded by soft spray with rock
walls towering overhead on three
sides, I feel as if I am perched in a
grand box seat above an unrivaled
stage—the floor of Yosemite Valley.*

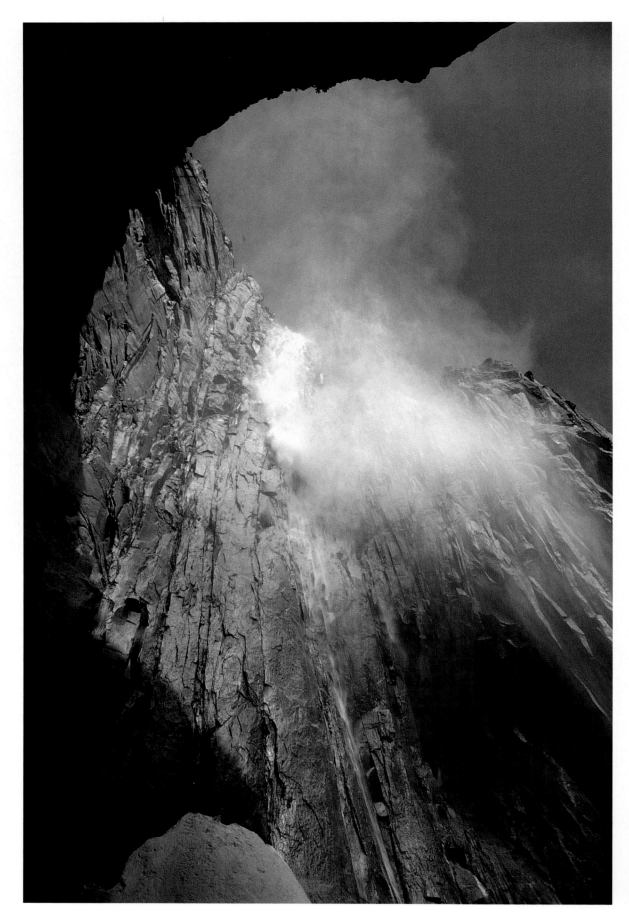

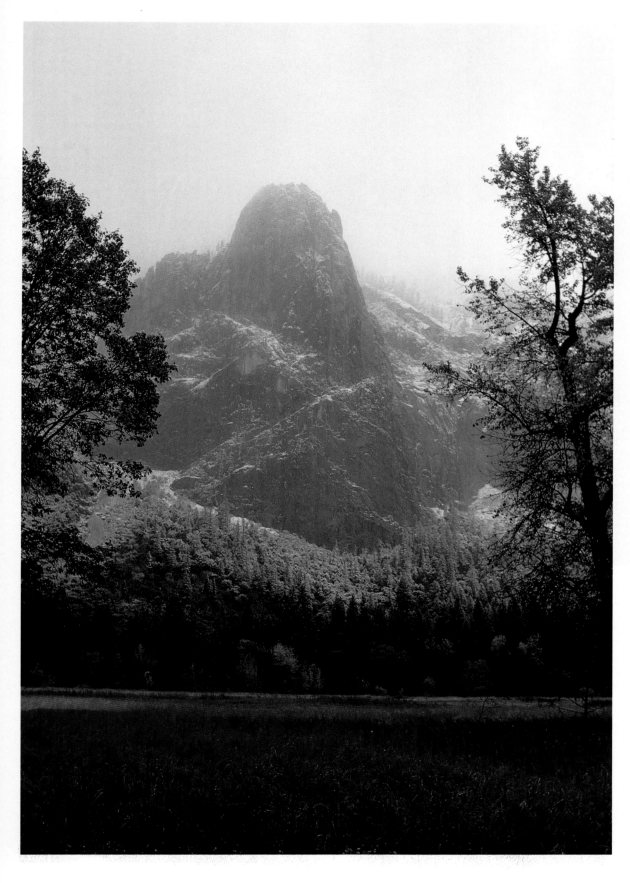

SENTINEL ROCK AND FALL SNOW, YOSEMITE VALLEY, 1978.

"Headlands one by one glowing white out of the shadows hushed and breathless like an audience in awful enthusiasm, while the meadows at their feet sparkle with frost-stars like the sky; . . . clouds in whose depths the frail snow-flowers grow."

*After the fall colors are gone and before the winter snows bring ski crowds, the Valley floor regains much of the hushed wildness of Muir's time. My favorite days for photography are when even, cloudy skies diffuse all the Valley's harsh shadows, allowing the bare brown grasses of the meadows to contrast with features etched into bold relief by early snows. I seek out places where patterns of snow, clouds, or light separate these elements of the landscape and emphasize their juncture.*

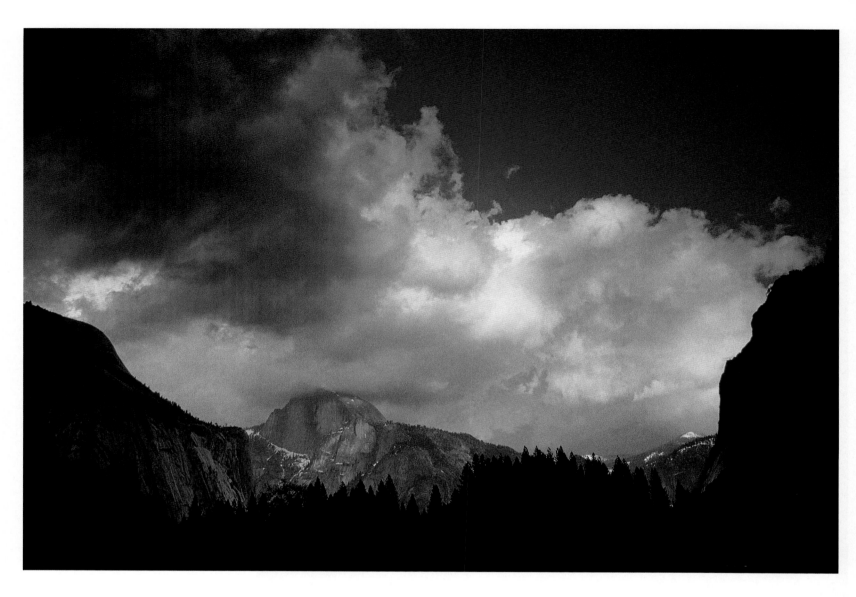

THUNDERSTORM OVER HALF
DOME, 1988.

"A richly modeled cumulous cloud
rising above the dark woods, about
11 A.M., swelling with a visible
motion straight up into the calm,
sunny sky to a height of 12,000 to
14,000 feet above the sea, its white,
pearly bosses relieved by gray and
pale purple shadows in the hollows,
and showing outlines as keenly
defined as those of the glacier-
polished domes. In less than an
hour it attains full development and
stands poised in the blazing
sunshine like some colossal
mountain, as beautiful in form and
finish as if it were to become a
permanent addition to the
landscape."

*Accompanied by seventy other
workshop photographers, I made
this image in a Yosemite meadow.
We were waiting for evening light to
beam underneath the clouds onto
Half Dome. Most people were using
telephoto lenses to single out the
Dome by itself. When fine warm
light never came, I altered my
photograph by questioning my
original assumptions. I quickly
realized that the Dome was no
longer the Valley's most prominent
feature. I switched to an ultrawide
lens to include all of the great
thunderhead that dwarfed Half
Dome and the confining walls of
the Valley below.*

Then we may safely go back of it and view the crystal shower from beneath, each drop wavering and pulsing as it makes its way through the air, and flashing off jets of colored light of ravishing beauty. But all this is invisible from the bottom of the Valley, like a thousand other interesting things. One must labor for beauty as for bread, here as elsewhere.

### THE GRANDEUR OF THE YOSEMITE FALL

During the time of the spring floods the best near view of the fall is obtained from Fern Ledge on the east side above the blinding spray at a height of about 400 feet above the base of the fall. A climb of about 1400 feet from the Valley has to be made, and there is no trail, but to any one fond of climbing this will make the ascent all the more delightful. A narrow part of the ledge extends to the side of the fall and back of it, enabling us to approach it as closely as we wish. When the afternoon sunshine is streaming through the throng of comets, ever wasting, ever renewed, the marvelous fineness, firmness and variety of their forms are beautifully revealed. At the top of the fall they seem to burst forth in irregular spurts from some grand, throbbing mountain heart. Now and then one mighty throb sends forth a mass of solid water into the free air far beyond the others, which rushes alone to the bottom of the fall with long streaming tail, like combed silk, while the others, descending in clusters, gradually mingle and lose their identity. But they all rush past us with amazing velocity and display of power, though apparently drowsy and deliberate in their movements when observed from a distance of a mile or two. The heads of these comet-like masses are composed of nearly solid water, and are dense white in color like pressed snow, from the friction they suffer in rushing through the air, the portion worn off forming the tail, between the white lustrous threads and films of which faint, grayish pencilings appear, while the outer, finer sprays of water-dust, whirling in sunny eddies, are pearly gray throughout. At the bottom of the fall there is but little distinction of form visible. It is mostly a hissing, clashing, seething, up-whirling mass of scud and spray, through which the light sifts in gray and purple tones, while at times when the sun strikes at the required angle, the whole wild and apparently lawless, stormy, striving mass is changed to brilliant rainbow hues, manifesting finest harmony. The middle portion of the fall is the most openly beautiful; lower, the various forms into which the waters are wrought are more closely and voluminously veiled, while higher, towards the head, the current is comparatively simple and undivided. But even at the bottom, in the boiling clouds of spray, there is no confusion, while the rainbow light makes all divine, adding glorious beauty and peace to glorious power. This noble fall has far the richest, as well as the most powerful, voice of all the falls of the Valley, its tones varying from the sharp hiss and rustle of the wind in the glossy leaves of the live-oaks and the soft, sifting, hushing tones of the pines, to the loudest rush and roar of storm winds and thunder among the crags of the summit peaks. The low bass, booming, reverberating tones, heard under favorable circumstances five or six miles away, are formed by the dashing and exploding of heavy masses mixed with air upon two projecting ledges on the face of the cliff, the one on which we are standing and another about 200 feet above it. The torrent of massive comets is continuous at time of high water, while the explosive, booming notes are wildly intermittent, because, unless influenced by the wind, most of the heavier masses shoot out from the face of the precipice, and pass the ledges upon which at other times they are exploded. Occasionally the

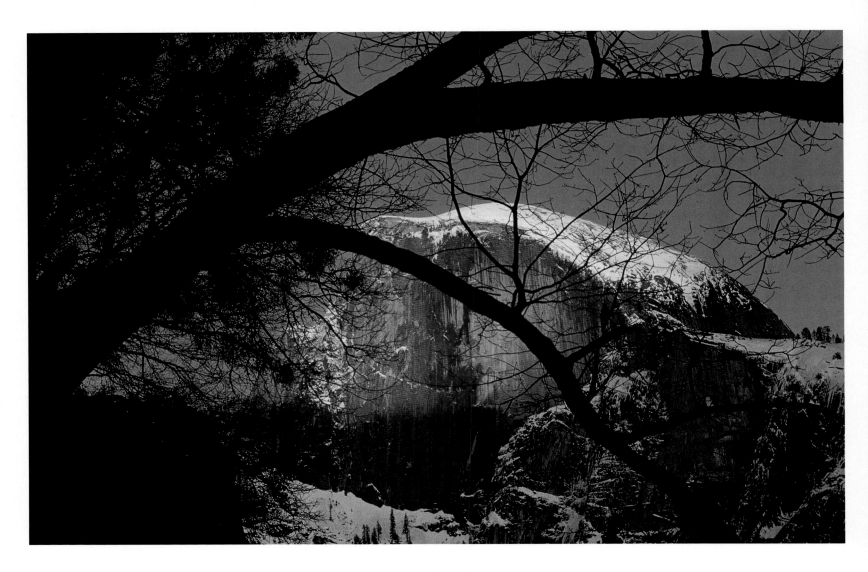

ALPENGLOW ON HALF DOME
THROUGH OAK BRANCHES, 1986.

"The Dome . . . would hardly be more 'conquered' or spoiled should man be added to her list of visitors. His louder scream and heavier scrambling would not stir a line of her countenance."

*Muir wrote those words before the National Park Service built a cabled trail to the summit of the Dome. In a literal sense he is right that the lines of the Dome have not been visually changed by the footsteps of tens of thousands of visitors. The Dome's countenance, however, depends on visual perception, which is governed by the mind as well as the eye. For me the Dome is forever changed by the climbs I have made on all four sides of her. I cannot look at or photograph the Dome without feeling a return of the emotional closeness of days and nights spent in her embrace.*

whole fall is swayed away from the front of the cliff, then suddenly dashed flat against it, or vibrated from side to side like a pendulum, giving rise to endless variety of forms and sounds.

### THE NEVADA FALL

The Nevada Fall is 600 feet high and is usually ranked next to the Yosemite in general interest among the five main falls of the Valley. Coming through the Little Yosemite in tranquil reaches, the river is first broken into rapids on a moraine boulder-bar that crosses the lower end of the Valley. Thence it pursues its way to the head of the fall in a rough, solid rock channel, dashing on side angles, heaving in heavy surging masses against elbow knobs, and swirling and swashing in pot-holes without a moment's rest. Thus, already chafed and dashed to foam, overfolded and twisted, it plunges over the brink of the precipice as if glad to escape into the open air. But before it reaches the bottom it is pulverized yet finer by impinging upon a sloping portion of the cliff about half-way down, thus making it the whitest of all the falls of the Valley, and altogether one of the most wonderful in the world.

On the north side, close to its head, a slab of granite projects over the brink, forming a fine point for a view, over its throng of streamers and wild plunging, into its intensely white bosom, and, through the broad drifts of spray, to the river far below, gathering its spent waters and rushing on again down the cañon in glad exultation into Emerald Pool, where at length it grows calm and gets rest for what still lies before it. All the features of the view correspond with the waters in grandeur and wildness. The glacier-sculptured walls of the cañon on either hand, with the sublime mass of the Glacier Point Ridge in front, form a huge triangular pit-like basin, which, filled with the roaring of the falling river, seems as if it might be the hopper of one of the mills of the gods in which the mountains were being ground.

### THE VERNAL FALL

The Vernal, about a mile below the Nevada, is 400 feet high, a staid, orderly, graceful, easy-going fall, proper and exact in every movement and gesture, with scarce a hint of the passionate enthusiasm of the Yosemite or of the impetuous Nevada, whose chafed and twisted waters hurrying over the cliff seem glad to escape into the open air, while its deep, booming, thunder-tones reverberate over the listening landscape. Nevertheless it is a favorite with most visitors, doubtless because it is more accessible than any other, more closely approached and better seen and heard. A good stairway ascends the cliff beside it and the level plateau at the head enables one to saunter safely along the edge of the river as it comes from Emerald Pool and to watch its waters, calmly bending over the brow of the precipice, in a sheet eighty feet wide, changing in color from green to purplish gray and white until dashed on a boulder talus. Thence issuing from beneath its fine broad spray-clouds we see the tremendously adventurous river still unspent, beating its way down the wildest and deepest of all its cañons in gray roaring rapids, dear to the ouzel, and below the confluence of the Illilouette, sweeping around the shoulder of the Half Dome on its approach to the head of the tranquil levels of the Valley.

### THE ILLILOUETTE FALL

The Illilouette in general appearance most resembles the Nevada. The volume of water is less than half as great, but it is about the same height (600 feet) and its

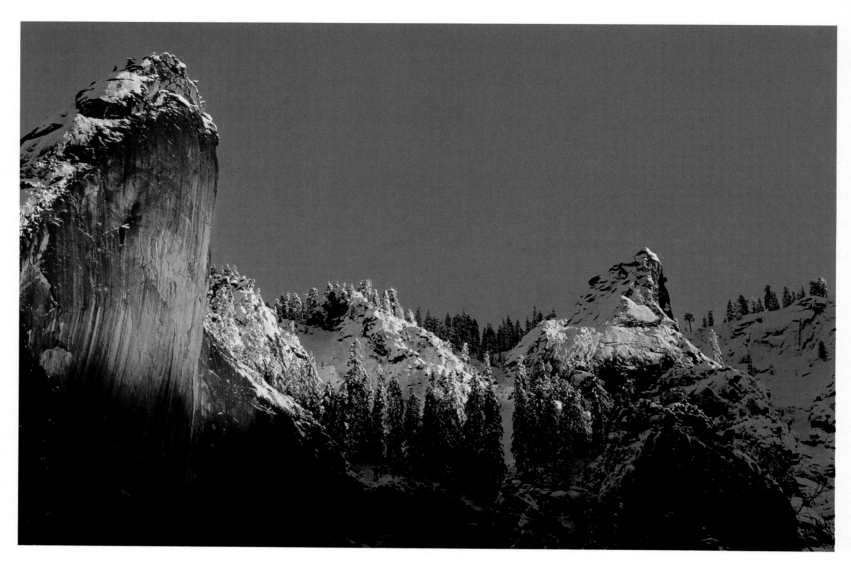

WINTER SUNSET ON LEANING
TOWER, YOSEMITE VALLEY, 1986.

"Awful in stern, immovable majesty,
how softly these rocks are adorned
. . . their brows in the sky, a
thousand flowers leaning
confidingly against their feet,
bathed in floods of water, floods of
light, while the snow and waterfalls,
the winds and avalanches and
clouds shine and sing and wreathe
about them as the years go by."

*Leaning Tower holds a special place
in my memory. In 1957 it was my
very first roped climb in Yosemite
Valley. After walking sixty miles,
most of it cross-country through the
headwaters of the San Joaquin
River, my companion and I used
ropes and pitons to ascend the
chimney to the right of the Tower.
Eight years later I returned to climb
the overhanging front face in
training for an early ascent of El
Capitan. Only in the last rays of
evening light does the Tower stand
out in bold, overhanging relief from
its companion cliffs and waterfalls.*

waters receive the same kind of preliminary tossing in a rocky, irregular channel. Therefore it is a very white and fine-grained fall. When it is in full springtime bloom it is partly divided by rocks that roughen the lip of the precipice, but this division amounts only to a kind of fluting and grooving of the column, which has a beautiful effect. It is not nearly so grand a fall as the Upper Yosemite, or so symmetrical as the Vernal, or so airily graceful and simple as the Bridal Veil, nor does it ever display so tremendous an outgush of snowy magnificence as the Nevada; but in the exquisite fineness and richness of texture of its flowing folds it surpasses them all.

One of the finest effects of sunlight on falling water I ever saw in Yosemite or elsewhere I found on the brow of this beautiful fall. It was in the Indian summer, when the leaf colors were ripe and the great cliffs and domes were transfigured in the hazy golden air. I had scrambled up its rugged talus-dammed cañon, oftentimes stopping to take breath and look back to admire the wonderful views to be had there of the great Half Dome, and to enjoy the extreme purity of the water, which in the motionless pools on this stream is almost perfectly invisible; the colored foliage of the maples, dogwoods, *Rubus* tangles, etc., and the late goldenrods and asters. The voice of the fall was now low, and the grand spring and summer floods had waned to sifting, drifting gauze and thin-broidered folds of linked and arrowy lace-work. When I reached the foot of the fall sunbeams were glinting across its head, leaving all the rest of it in shadow; and on its illumined brow a group of yellow spangles of singular form and beauty were playing, flashing up and dancing in large flame-shaped masses, wavering at times, then steadying, rising and falling in accord with the shifting forms of the water. But the color of the dancing spangles changed not at all. Nothing in clouds or flowers, on bird-wings or the lips of shells, could rival it in fineness. It was the most divinely beautiful mass of rejoicing yellow light I ever beheld—one of Nature's precious gifts that perchance may come to us but once in a lifetime.

### THE MINOR FALLS

There are many other comparatively small falls and cascades in the Valley. The most notable are the Yosemite Gorge Fall and Cascades, Tenaya Fall and Cascades, Royal Arch Falls, the two Sentinel Cascades and the falls of Cascade and Tamarack Creeks, a mile or two below the lower end of the Valley. These last are often visited. The others are seldom noticed or mentioned; although in almost any other country they would be visited and described as wonders.

The six intermediate falls in the gorge between the head of the Lower and the base of the Upper Yosemite Falls, separated by a few deep pools and strips of rapids, and three slender, tributary cascades on the west side form a series more strikingly varied and combined than any other in the Valley, yet very few of all the Valley visitors ever see them or hear of them. No available standpoint commands a view of them all. The best general view is obtained from the mouth of the gorge near the head of the Lower Fall. The two lowest of the series, together with one of the three tributary cascades, are visible from this standpoint, but in reaching it the last twenty or thirty feet of the descent is rather dangerous in time of high water, the shelving rocks being then slippery on account of spray, but if one should chance to slip when the water is low, only a bump or two and a harmless plash would be the penalty. No part of the gorge, however, is safe to any but cautious climbers.

Though the dark gorge hall of these rejoicing waters is never flushed by the purple light of morning or evening, it is warmed and cheered by the white light of noon-day, which, falling into so much foam and spray of varying degrees of fineness, makes marvelous displays of rainbow colors. So filled, indeed, is it with this pre-cious light, at favorable times it seems to take the place of common air. Laurel bushes shed fragrance into it from above and live-oaks, those fearless mountain-eers, hold fast to angular seams and lean out over it with their fringing sprays and bright mirror leaves.

One bird, the ouzel, loves this gorge and flies through it merrily, or cheerily, rather, stopping to sing on foam-washed bosses where other birds could find no rest for their feet. I have even seen a gray squirrel down in the heart of it beside the wild rejoicing water.

One of my favorite night walks was along the rim of this wild gorge in times of high water when the moon was full, to see the lunar bows in the spray.

For about a mile above Mirror Lake the Tenaya Cañon is level, and richly planted with fir, Douglas spruce and libocedrus, forming a remarkably fine grove, at the head of which is the Tenaya Fall. Though seldom seen or described, this is, I think, the most picturesque of all the small falls. A considerable distance above it, Tenaya Creek comes hurrying down, white and foamy, over a flat pavement inclined at an angle of about eighteen degrees. In time of high water this sheet of rapids is nearly seventy feet wide, and is varied in a very striking way by three parallel furrows that extend in the direction of its flow. These furrows, worn by the action of the stream upon cleavage joints, vary in width, are slightly sinuous, and have large boulders firmly wedged in them here and there in narrow places, giving rise, of course, to a complicated series of wild dashes, doublings, and upleaping arches in the swift tor-rent. Just before it reaches the head of the fall the current is divided, the left division making a vertical drop of about eighty feet in a romantic, leafy, flowery, mossy nook, while the other forms a rugged cascade.

The Royal Arch Fall in time of high water is a magnificent object, forming a broad ornamental sheet in front of the arches. The two Sentinel Cascades, 3000 feet high, are also grand spectacles when the snow is melting fast in the spring, but by the middle of summer they have diminished to mere streaks scarce noticeable amid their sublime surroundings.

### THE BEAUTY OF THE RAINBOWS

The Bridal Veil and Vernal Falls are famous for their rainbows; and special visits to them are often made when the sun shines into the spray at the most favorable angle. But amid the spray and foam and fine-ground mist ever rising from the var-ious falls and cataracts there is an affluence and variety of iris bows scarcely known to visitors who stay only a day or two. Both day and night, winter and summer, this divine light may be seen wherever water is falling, dancing, singing; telling the heart-peace of Nature amid the wildest displays of her power. In the bright spring mornings the black-walled recess at the foot of the Lower Yosemite Fall is lavishly filled with irised spray; and not simply does this span the dashing foam, but the foam itself, the whole mass of it, beheld at a certain distance, seems to be colored, and drifts and wavers from color to color, mingling with the foliage of the adjacent trees, without suggesting any relationship to the ordinary rainbow. This is perhaps the largest and most reservoir-like fountain of iris colors to be found in the Valley.

Lunar rainbows or spray-bows also abound in the glorious affluence of dashing,

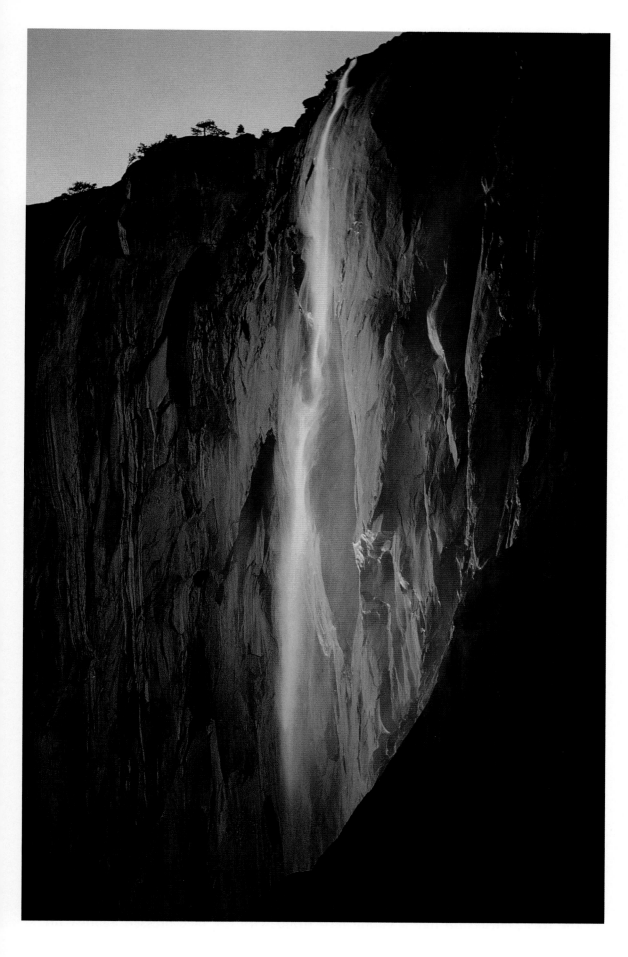

LAST LIGHT ON HORSETAIL FALL,
EL CAPITAN, 1973.

"When I reached the foot of the fall
sunbeams were glinting across its
head, leaving all the rest of it in
shadow . . . flashing up and
dancing in large flame-shaped
masses . . . rising and falling in
accord with the shifting forms of
the water. . . . It was the most
divinely beautiful mass of rejoicing
yellow light I ever beheld—one of
Nature's precious gifts that
perchance may come to us but once
in a lifetime."

*My own once-in-a-lifetime
rendezvous with last light and a
waterfall happened on an evening in
late February when the sun's last
rays hit the water of Horsetail Fall
without touching the rock of El
Capitan behind it. Thus the warm
glow on the shadowed cliff is
entirely the result of light
transmitted by a falling shaft of
sunlit water. The angle of the sun
lines up for this event only one or
two days each year. Even then the
magic fails to appear if there are
clouds on the horizon in the west,
or too little snowmelt from the rim
of the Valley to keep the
fall flowing.*

rejoicing, hurrahing, enthusiastic spring floods, their colors as distinct as those of the sun and regularly and obviously banded, though less vivid. Fine specimens may be found any night at the foot of the Upper Yosemite Fall, glowing gloriously amid the gloomy shadows and thundering waters, whenever there is plenty of moonlight and spray. Even the secondary bow is at times distinctly visible.

The best point from which to observe them is on Fern Ledge. For some time after moonrise, at time of high water, the arc has a span of about five hundred feet, and is set upright; one end planted in the boiling spray at the bottom, the other in the edge of the fall, creeping lower, of course, and becoming less upright as the moon rises higher. This grand arc of color, glowing in mild, shapely beauty in so weird and huge a chamber of night shadows, and amid the rush and roar and tumultuous dashing of this thunder-voiced fall, is one of the most impressive and most cheering of all the blessed mountain evangels.

Smaller bows may be seen in the gorge on the plateau between the Upper and Lower Falls. Once toward midnight, after spending a few hours with the wild beauty of the Upper Fall, I sauntered along the edge of the gorge, looking in here and there, wherever the footing felt safe, to see what I could learn of the night aspects of the smaller falls that dwell there. And down in an exceedingly black, pit-like portion of the gorge, at the foot of the highest of the intermediate falls, into which the moonbeams were pouring through a narrow opening, I saw a well-defined spray-bow, beautifully distinct in colors, spanning the pit from side to side, while pure white foam-waves beneath the beautiful bow were constantly springing up out of the dark into the moonlight like dancing ghosts.

### AN UNEXPECTED ADVENTURE

A wild scene, but not a safe one, is made by the moon as it appears through the edge of the Yosemite Fall when one is behind it. Once, after enjoying the night-song of the waters and watching the formation of the colored bow as the moon came round the domes and sent her beams into the wild uproar, I ventured out on the narrow bench that extends back of the fall from Fern Ledge and began to admire the dim-veiled grandeur of the view. I could see the fine gauzy threads of the fall's filmy border by having the light in front; and wishing to look at the moon through the meshes of some of the denser portions of the fall, I ventured to creep farther behind it while it was gently wind-swayed, without taking sufficient thought about the consequences of its swaying back to its natural position after the wind-pressure should be removed. The effect was enchanting: fine, savage music sounding above, beneath, around me; while the moon, apparently in the very midst of the rushing waters, seemed to be struggling to keep her place, on account of the ever-varying form and density of the water masses through which she was seen, now darkly veiled or eclipsed by a rush of thick-headed comets, now flashing out through openings between their tails. I was in fairyland between the dark wall and the wild throng of illumined waters, but suffered sudden disenchantment; for, like the witch-scene in Alloway Kirk, "in an instant all was dark." Down came a dash of spent comets, thin and harmless-looking in the distance, but they felt desperately solid and stony when they struck my shoulders, like a mixture of choking spray and gravel and big hailstones. Instinctively dropping on my knees, I gripped an angle of the rock, curled up like a young fern frond with my face pressed against my breast, and in this attitude submitted as best I could to my thundering bath. The

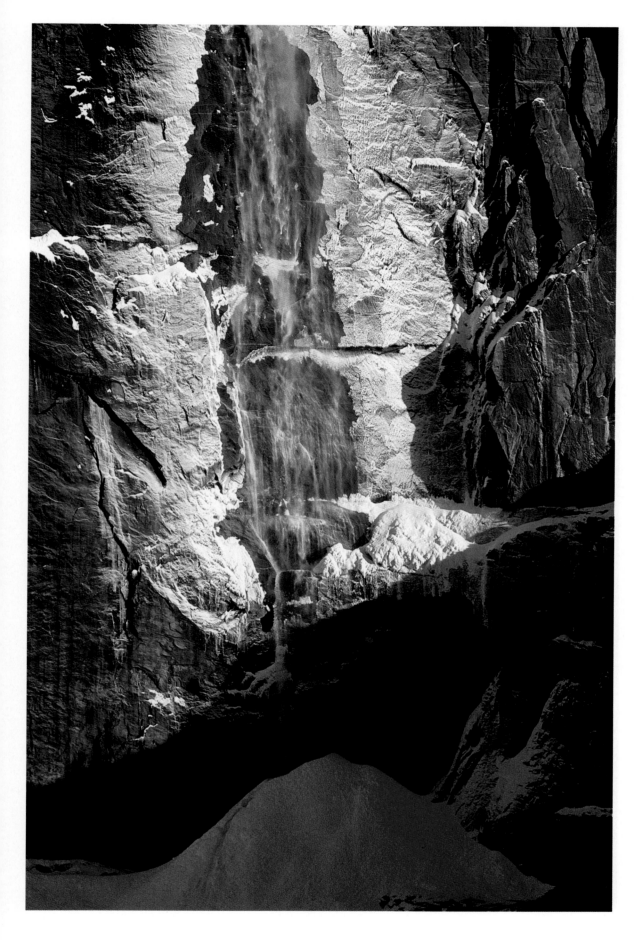

ICE CONE BELOW UPPER
YOSEMITE FALL, 1987.

"Every clear, frosty morning loud
sounds are heard booming and
reverberating from side to side of
the Valley. . . . The strange thunder
is made by the fall of sections of ice
formed of spray that is frozen on
the face of the cliff along the sides
of the Upper Yosemite Fall. . . .
This frozen spray gives rise to one
of the most interesting winter
features of the Valley—a cone of ice
at the foot of the fall, four or five
hundred feet high. . . . Anxious to
learn what I could about the
structure of this curious hill I . . .
tried to climb it . . . but a
suffocating blast, half air, half
water, followed by the fall of an
enormous mass of frozen spray
from a spot high up on the wall,
quickly discouraged me. The whole
cone was jarred by the blow. . . . I
beat a hasty retreat, chilled and
drenched, and lay down on a sunny
rock to dry."

*Modern climbers have ascended the
ice cone during periods of winter
calm, but on the day this photo was
made, nature's ice machine was
operating at full capacity, dropping
thundering tons of new ice onto the
cone every minute or two in the
early morning as the sun's heat
dislodged frozen spray from the
previous night. I made this image
during a dawn run of the Yosemite
Falls Trail carrying a 35mm camera
and telephoto lens in a special
chest pouch.*

MERCED RIVER IN WINTER,
YOSEMITE VALLEY, 1987.

"I made haste down to my Yosemite
den, not to 'hole up' and sleep the
white months away; I was out every
day, and often all night, sleeping
but little, studying the so-called
wonders and common things ever
on show, wading, climbing,
sauntering among the blessed
storms and calms, rejoicing in
almost everything alike that I could
see or hear: the glorious brightness
of frosty mornings; the sunbeams
pouring over the white domes and
crags into the groves
and waterfalls."

*Unlike summer days, winter
mornings in the Valley never seem
the same. Each one is unique in the
way that trees, meadows, cliffs, and
water's edges are frosted or covered
with snow. Especially after a major
storm, the morning is likely to bring
forth scenes that are refreshingly
new even for the most seasoned
Yosemite observers.*

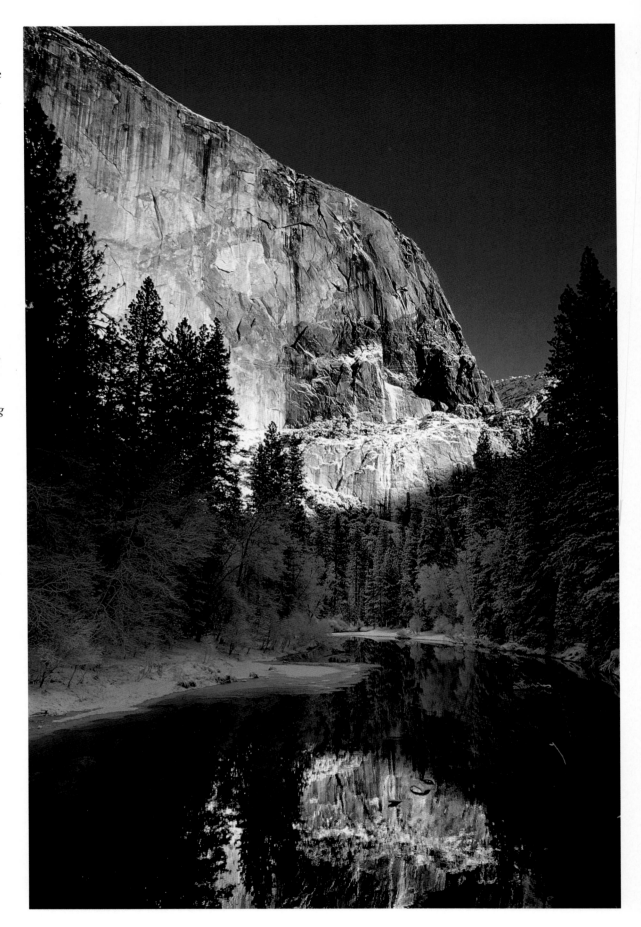

heavier masses seemed to strike like cobblestones, and there was a confused noise of many waters about my ears—hissing, gurgling, clashing sounds that were not heard as music. The situation was quickly realized. How fast one's thoughts burn in such times of stress! I was weighing chances of escape. Would the column be swayed a few inches away from the wall, or would it come yet closer? The fall was in flood and not so lightly would its ponderous mass be swayed. My fate seemed to depend on a breath of the "idle wind." It was moved gently forward, the pounding ceased, and I was once more visited by glimpses of the moon. But fearing I might be caught at a disadvantage in making too hasty a retreat, I moved only a few feet along the bench to where a block of ice lay. I wedged myself between the ice and the wall, and lay face downwards, until the steadiness of the light gave encouragement to rise and get away. Somewhat nerve-shaken, drenched, and benumbed, I made out to build a fire, warmed myself, ran home, reached my cabin before daylight, got an hour or two of sleep, and awoke sound and comfortable, better, not worse, for my hard midnight bath.

### CLIMATE AND WEATHER

Owing to the westerly trend of the Valley and its vast depth there is a great difference between the climates of the north and south sides—greater than between many countries far apart; for the south wall is in shadow during the winter months, while the north is bathed in sunshine every clear day. Thus there is mild spring weather on one side of the Valley while winter rules the other. Far up the north-side cliffs many a nook may be found closely embraced by sun-beaten rock-bosses in which flowers bloom every month of the year. Even butterflies may be seen in these high winter gardens except when snow-storms are falling and a few days after they have ceased. Near the head of the lower Yosemite Fall in January I found the ant lions lying in wait in their warm sand-cups, rock ferns being unrolled, club mosses covered with fresh-growing points, the flowers of the laurel nearly open, and the honeysuckle rosetted with bright young leaves; every plant seemed to be thinking about summer. Even on the shadow-side of the Valley the frost is never very sharp. The lowest temperature I ever observed during four winters was 7° Fahrenheit. The first twenty-four days of January had an average temperature at 9 A.M. of 32°, minimum 22°; at 3 P.M. the average was 40° 30′, the minimum 32°. Along the top of the walls, 7000 and 8000 feet high, the temperature was, of course, much lower. But the difference in temperature between the north and south sides is due not so much to the winter sunshine as to the heat of the preceding summer, stored up in the rocks, which rapidly melts the snow in contact with them. For though summer sun-heat is stored in the rocks of the south side also, the amount is much less because the rays fall obliquely on the south wall even in summer and almost vertically on the north.

The upper branches of the Yosemite streams are buried every winter beneath a heavy mantle of snow, and set free in the spring in magnificent floods. Then, all the fountains, full and overflowing, every living thing breaks forth into singing, and the glad exulting streams, shining and falling in the warm sunny weather, shake everything into music, making all the mountain-world a song.

The great annual spring thaw usually begins in May in the forest region, and in June and July on the High Sierra, varying somewhat both in time and fullness with the weather and the depth of the snow. Toward the end of summer the streams are at their lowest ebb, few even of the strongest singing much above a whisper as they slip and ripple through gravel and boulder-beds from pool to pool in the hollows of their channels, and drop in pattering showers like rain, and slip down precipices and fall in sheets of embroidery, fold over fold. But, however low their singing, it is always ineffably fine in tone, in harmony with the restful time of the year.

The first snow of the season that comes to the help of the streams usually falls in September or October, sometimes even in the latter part of August; in the midst of yellow Indian summer, when the goldenrods and gentians of the glacier meadows are in their prime. This Indian-summer snow, however, soon melts, the chilled flowers spread their petals to the sun, and the gardens as well as the streams are refreshed as if only a warm shower had fallen. The snow-storms that load the mountains to form the main fountain supply for the year seldom set in before the middle or end of November.

## WINTER BEAUTY OF THE VALLEY

When the first heavy storms stopped work on the high mountains, I made haste down to my Yosemite den, not to "hole up" and sleep the white months away; I was out every day, and often all night, sleeping but little, studying the so-called wonders and common things ever on show, wading, climbing, sauntering among the blessed storms and calms, rejoicing in almost everything alike that I could see or hear: the glorious brightness of frosty mornings; the sunbeams pouring over the white domes and crags into the groves and waterfalls, kindling marvelous iris fires in the hoarfrost and spray; the great forests and mountains in their deep noon sleep; the good-night alpenglow; the stars; the solemn gazing moon, drawing the huge domes and headlands one by one glowing white out of the shadows hushed and breathless like an audience in awful enthusiasm, while the meadows at their feet sparkle with frost-stars like the sky; the sublime darkness of storm-nights, when all the lights are out; the clouds in whose depths the frail snow-flowers grow; the behavior and many voices of the different kinds of storms, trees, birds, waterfalls, and snow-avalanches in the ever-changing weather.

Every clear, frosty morning loud sounds are heard booming and reverberating from side to side of the Valley at intervals of a few minutes, beginning soon after sunrise and continuing an hour or two like a thunder-storm. In my first winter in the Valley I could not make out the source of this noise. I thought of falling boulders, rock-blasting, etc. Not till I saw what looked like hoarfrost dropping from the side of the Fall was the problem explained. The strange thunder is made by the fall of sections of ice formed of spray that is frozen on the face of the cliff along the sides of the Upper Yosemite Fall—a sort of crystal plaster, a foot or two thick, cracked off by the sunbeams, awakening all the Valley like cock-crowing, announcing the finest weather, shouting aloud Nature's infinite industry and love of hard work in creating beauty.

## EXPLORING AN ICE CONE

This frozen spray gives rise to one of the most interesting winter features of the Valley—a cone of ice at the foot of the fall, four or five hundred feet high. From the Fern Ledge standpoint its crater-like throat is seen, down which the fall plunges with deep, gasping explosions of compressed air, and, after being well churned in the stormy interior, the water bursts forth through arched openings at its base, apparently scourged and weary and glad to escape, while belching spray, spouted up

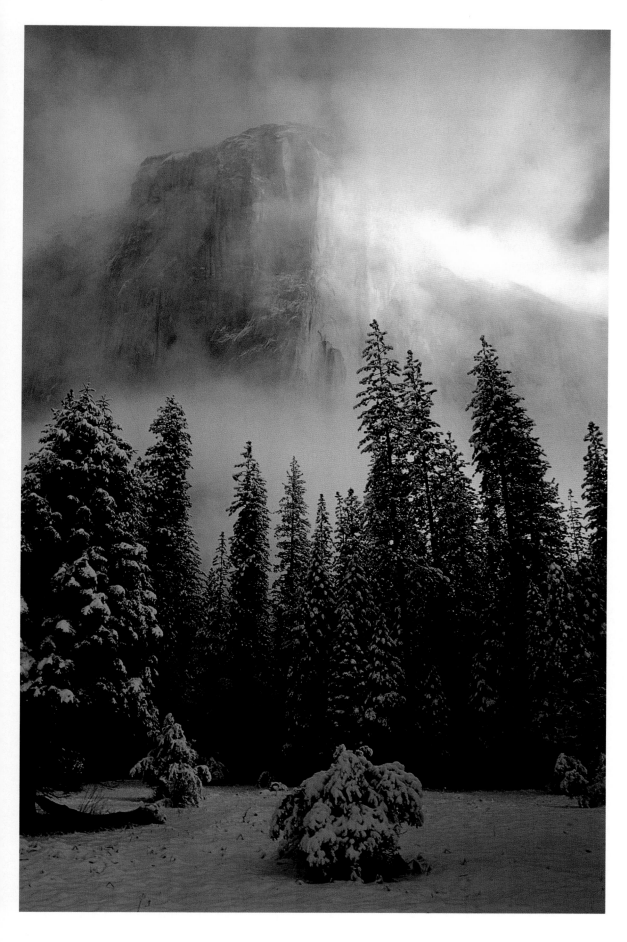

CLEARING STORM OVER EL CAPITAN, 1973.

"These beautiful days . . . do not exist as mere pictures—maps hung upon the walls of memory to brighten at times when touched by association or will. . . . They saturate themselves into every part of the body and live always."

*Muir wrote those words as a young man, only two years after coming to Yosemite. He perfectly describes the difference between "mere pictures" and visions that live forever (whether photographed or not). My most intense vision of El Capitan came in the winter of 1973, after my car became stuck in the snow shortly before El Capitan emerged from cloud at the end of a long storm. My camera was ready, but more important, my mind was already filled with what the Sierra photographer Cedric Wright called a "saturation of awareness" that comes from "the quality of emotional knowing." I had climbed the face of El Capitan several times, once barely escaping with my life during a March storm much like this one. The rock, its light, and its surroundings were already living forever within me when I had only a fleeting moment to record the parting of the mist on film. I resisted the temptation to use a telephoto to single out the cliff, or a wider lens to include the Valley floor. I simply wanted to show El Cap shrouded in golden mist with a fringe of blue-shadowed pines draped in snow.*

out of the throat past the descending current, is wafted away in irised drifts to the adjacent rocks and groves. It is built during the night and early hours of the morning; only in spells of exceptionally cold and cloudy weather is the work continued through the day. The greater part of the spray material falls in crystalline showers direct to its place, something like a small local snow-storm; but a considerable portion is first frozen on the face of the cliff along the sides of the fall and stays there until expanded and cracked off in irregular masses, some of them tons in weight, to be built into the walls of the cone; while in windy, frosty weather, when the fall is swayed from side to side, the cone is well drenched and the loose ice masses and spray-dust are all firmly welded and frozen together. Thus the finest of the downy wafts and curls of spray-dust, which in mild nights fall about as silently as dew, are held back until sunrise to make a store of heavy ice to reinforce the waterfall's thunder-tones.

While the cone is in process of formation, growing higher and wider in the frosty weather, it looks like a beautiful smooth, pure-white hill; but when it is wasting and breaking up in the spring its surface is strewn with leaves, pine branches, stones, sand, etc., that have been brought over the fall, making it look like a heap of avalanche detritus.

Anxious to learn what I could about the structure of this curious hill I often approached it in calm weather and tried to climb it, carrying an ax to cut steps. Once I nearly succeeded in gaining the summit. At the base I was met by a current of spray and wind that made seeing and breathing difficult. I pushed on backward, however, and soon gained the slope of the hill, where by creeping close to the surface most of the choking blast passed over me and I managed to crawl up with but little difficulty. Thus I made my way nearly to the summit, halting at times to peer up through the wild whirls of spray at the veiled grandeur of the fall, or to listen to the thunder beneath me; the whole hill was sounding as if it were a huge, bellowing drum. I hoped that by waiting until the fall was blown aslant I should be able to climb to the lip of the crater and get a view of the interior; but a suffocating blast, half air, half water, followed by the fall of an enormous mass of frozen spray from a spot high up on the wall, quickly discouraged me. The whole cone was jarred by the blow and some fragments of the mass sped past me dangerously near; so I beat a hasty retreat, chilled and drenched, and lay down on a sunny rock to dry.

Once during a wind-storm when I saw that the fall was frequently blown westward, leaving the cone dry, I ran up to Fern Ledge hoping to gain a clear view of the interior. I set out at noon. All the way up the storm notes were so loud about me that the voice of the fall was almost drowned by them. Notwithstanding the rocks and bushes everywhere were drenched by the wind-driven spray, I approached the brink of the precipice overlooking the mouth of the ice cone, but I was almost suffocated by the drenching, gusty spray, and was compelled to seek shelter. I searched for some hiding-place in the wall from whence I might run out at some opportune moment when the fall with its whirling spray and torn shreds of comet tails and trailing, tattered skirts was borne westward, as I had seen it carried several times before, leaving the cliffs on the east side and the ice hill bare in the sunlight. I had not long to wait, for, as if ordered so for my special accommodation, the mighty downrush of comets with their whirling drapery swung westward and remained aslant for nearly half an hour. The cone was admirably lighted and deserted by the water, which fell most of the time on the rocky western slopes mostly outside of the cone. The mouth into which the fall pours was, as near as I could guess, about one hundred feet in diameter north and south and about two hundred feet east and west, which is about the shape and size of the fall at its best in its normal condition at this season.

The crater-like opening was not a true oval, but more like a huge coarse mouth. I could see down the throat about one hundred feet or perhaps farther.

The fall precipice overhangs from a height of 400 feet above the base; therefore the water strikes some distance from the base of the cliff, allowing space for the accumulation of a considerable mass of ice between the fall and the wall.

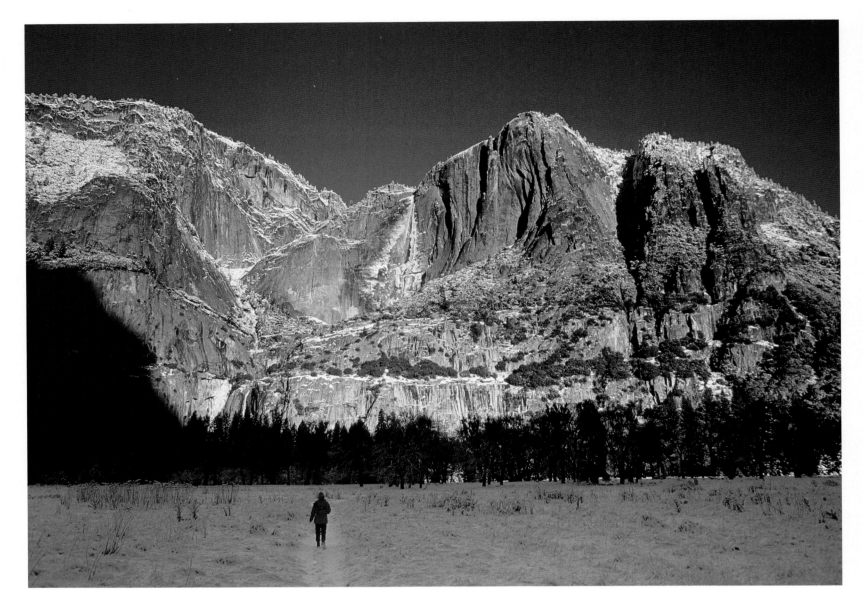

WINTER WALK ON THE VALLEY
FLOOR, 1988.

"Most delightful it is to stand in the
middle of Yosemite on still clear
mornings after snowstorms and
watch the throng of avalanches as
they come down, rejoicing, to their
places, whispering, thrilling like
birds, or booming and roaring
like thunder."

*When dawn arrives after a
snowstorm, Yosemite Valley regains
a primeval feeling. Few visitors are
about at this time, either on foot or
in vehicles. Trails and tracks
through the meadows are buried
under a uniform blanket of white
that dampens all but the
loudest sounds.*

CHAPTER II

# Winter Storms and Spring Floods

THE BRIDAL VEIL and the Upper Yosemite Falls, on account of their height and exposure, are greatly influenced by winds. The common summer winds that come up the river cañon from the plains are seldom very strong; but the north winds do some very wild work, worrying the falls and the forests, and hanging snow-banners on the comet-peaks. One wild winter morning I was awakened by a storm-wind that was playing with the falls as if they were mere wisps of mist and making the great pines bow and sing with glorious enthusiasm. The Valley had been visited a short time before by a series of fine snow-storms, and the floor and the cliffs and all the region round about were lavishly adorned with its best winter jewelry, the air was full of fine snow-dust, and pine branches, tassels and empty cones were flying in an almost continuous flock.

Soon after sunrise, when I was seeking a place safe from flying branches, I saw the Lower Yosemite Fall thrashed and pulverized from top to bottom into one glorious mass of rainbow dust; while a thousand feet above it the main Upper Fall was suspended on the face of the cliff in the form of an inverted bow, all silvery white and fringed with short wavering strips. Then, suddenly assailed by a tremendous blast, the whole mass of the fall was blown into threads and ribbons, and driven back over the brow of the cliff whence it came, as if denied admission to the Valley. This kind of storm-work was continued about ten or fifteen minutes; then another change in the play of the huge exulting swirls and billows and upheaving domes of the gale allowed the baffled fall to gather and arrange its tattered waters, and sink down again in its place. As the day advanced, the gale gave no sign of dying, excepting brief lulls, the Valley was filled with its weariless roar, and the cloudless sky grew garish-white from myriads of minute, sparkling snow-spicules. In the afternoon, while I watched the Upper Fall from the shelter of a big pine tree, it was suddenly arrested in its descent at a point about half-way down, and was neither blown upward nor driven aside, but simply held stationary in mid-air, as if gravitation below that point in the path of its descent had ceased to act. The ponderous flood, weighing hundreds of tons, was sustained, hovering, hesitating, like a bunch of thistledown, while I counted one hundred and ninety. All this time the ordinary amount of water was coming over the cliff and accumulating in the air, swedging and widening and forming an irregular cone about seven hundred feet high, tapering to the top of the wall, the whole standing still, resting on the invisible arm of the North Wind. At length, as if commanded to go on again, scores of arrowy comets shot forth from the bottom of the suspended mass as if escaping from separate outlets.

The brow of El Capitan was decked with long snow-streamers like hair, Clouds' Rest was fairly enveloped in drifting gossamer films, and the Half Dome loomed up in the garish light like a majestic, living creature clad in the same gauzy, wind-woven drapery, while upward currents meeting at times overhead made it smoke like a volcano.

CLEARING STORM IN PONDEROSA
PINE FOREST, YOSEMITE
VALLEY, 1979.

"The noble yellow pines stand
hushed and motionless as if under a
spell until the morning sunshine
begins to sift through their laden
spires; then the dense masses on the
ends of the leafy branches begin to
shift and fall, those from the upper
branches striking the lower ones in
succession, enveloping each tree in a
hollow conical avalanche of fairy
fineness; while the relieved branches
spring up and wave with startling
effect in the general stillness, as if
each tree was moving of its
own volition."

*I used to watch Valley pines unload
their snowy burdens with childlike
abandon. With a crack and a hiss,
limbs would suddenly snap
upwards, freed from a load of snow
that filled the air far more densely
than during the wildest storm. As
the flakes fell to earth, backlit by
the sun, I was reminded of the
idyllic vision I discovered as a boy
when I first turned over the snow-
scene paperweight on my father's
desk. One day, however, as I
walked through the pines after an
especially heavy snowfall, a large
tree snapped at its base from the
snow load and fell toward me.
Great beauty and great power are
never very far from one another
in nature.*

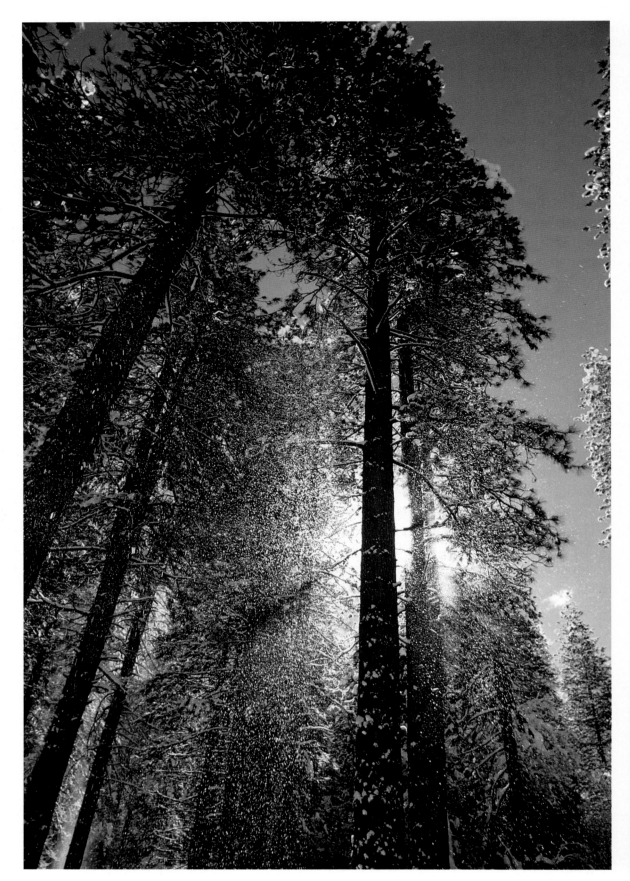

Glorious as are these rocks and waters arrayed in storm robes, or chanting rejoicing in every-day dress, they are still more glorious when rare weather conditions meet to make them sing with floods. Only once during all the years I have lived in the Valley have I seen it in full flood bloom. In 1871 the early winter weather was delightful; the days all sunshine, the nights all starry and calm, calling forth fine crops of frost-crystals on the pines and withered ferns and grasses for the morning sunbeams to sift through. In the afternoon of December 16, when I was sauntering on the meadows, I noticed a massive crimson cloud growing in solitary grandeur above the Cathedral Rocks, its form scarcely less striking than its color. It had a picturesque, bulging base like an old sequoia, a smooth, tapering stem, and a bossy, down-curling crown like a mushroom; all its parts were colored alike, making one mass of translucent crimson. Wondering what the meaning of that strange, lonely red cloud might be, I was up betimes next morning looking at the weather, but all seemed tranquil as yet. Towards noon gray clouds with a close, curly grain like bird's-eye maple began to grow, and late at night rain fell, which soon changed to snow. Next morning the snow on the meadows was about ten inches deep, and it was still falling in a fine, cordial storm. During the night of the 18th heavy rain fell on the snow, but as the temperature was 34°, the snow-line was only a few hundred feet above the bottom of the Valley, and one had only to climb a little higher than the tops of the pines to get out of the rain-storm into the snow-storm. The streams, instead of being increased in volume by the storm, were diminished, because the snow sponged up part of their waters and choked the smaller tributaries. But about midnight the temperature suddenly rose to 42°, carrying the snow-line far beyond the Valley walls, and next morning Yosemite was rejoicing in a glorious flood. The comparatively warm rain falling on the snow was at first absorbed and held back, and so also was that portion of the snow that the rain melted, and all that was melted by the warm wind, until the whole mass of snow was saturated and became sludgy, and at length slipped and rushed simultaneously from a thousand slopes in wildest extravagance, heaping and swelling flood over flood, and plunging into the Valley in stupendous avalanches.

Awakened by the roar, I looked out and at once recognized the extraordinary character of the storm. The rain was still pouring in torrent abundance and the wind at gale speed was doing all it could with the flood-making rain.

The section of the north wall visible from my cabin was fairly streaked with new falls—wild roaring singers that seemed strangely out of place. Eager to get into the midst of the show, I snatched a piece of bread for breakfast and ran out. The mountain waters, suddenly liberated, seemed to be holding a grand jubilee. The two Sentinel Cascades rivaled the great falls at ordinary stages, and across the Valley by the Three Brothers I caught glimpses of more falls than I could readily count; while the whole Valley throbbed and trembled, and was filled with an awful, massive, solemn, sea-like roar. After gazing a while enchanted with the network of new falls that were adorning and transfiguring every rock in sight, I tried to reach the upper meadows, where the Valley is widest, that I might be able to see the walls on both sides, and thus gain general views. But the river was over its banks and the meadows were flooded, forming an almost continuous lake dotted with blue sludgy islands, while innumerable streams roared like lions across my path and were sweeping forward rocks and logs with tremendous energy over ground where tiny gilias had been growing but a short time before. Climbing into the talus slopes, where these savage torrents were broken among earthquake boulders, I managed to cross them, and force my way up the Valley to Hutchings' Bridge, where I crossed the river and waded to the middle of the upper meadow. Here most of the new falls were in sight, probably the most glorious assemblage of waterfalls ever displayed from any one standpoint. On that portion of the south wall between Hutchings' and the Sentinel there were ten falls plunging and booming from a height of nearly three thousand feet, the smallest of which might have been heard miles away. In the neighborhood of Glacier Point there were six; between the Three Brothers and Yosemite Fall, nine; between Yosemite and Royal Arch Falls, ten; from Washington Column to Mount Watkins, ten; on the slopes of Half Dome and Clouds' Rest, facing Mirror Lake and Tenaya Cañon, eight; on the shoulder of Half Dome, facing the Valley, three: fifty-six new falls occupying the upper end of the Valley, besides a countless host of silvery threads gleaming everywhere. In all the Valley there must have been upwards of a hundred. As if celebrating some great event, falls and cascades in Yosemite costume were coming down everywhere from fountain basins, far and near; and, though newcomers, they behaved and sang as if they had lived here always.

All summer-visitors will remember the comet forms of the Yosemite Fall and the laces of the Bridal Veil and Nevada. In the falls of this winter jubilee the lace forms predominated, but there was no lack of thunder-toned comets. The lower portion of one of the Sentinel Cascades was composed of two main white torrents with the space between them filled in with chained and beaded gauze of intricate pattern, through the singing threads of which the purplish-gray rock could be dimly seen. The series above Glacier Point was still more complicated in structure, displaying every form that one could imagine water might be dashed and combed and woven into. Those on the north wall between Washington Column and the Royal Arch Fall were so nearly related they formed an almost continuous sheet, and these again were but slightly separated from those about Indian Cañon. The group about the Three Brothers and El Capitan, owing to the topography and cleavage of the cliffs back of them, was more broken and irregular. The Tissiack Cascades were comparatively small, yet sufficient to give that noblest of mountain rocks a glorious voice. In the midst of all this extravagant rejoicing the great Yosemite Fall was scarce heard until about three o'clock in the afternoon. Then I was startled by a sudden thundering crash as if a rock avalanche had come to the help of the roaring waters. This was the flood-wave of Yosemite Creek, which had just arrived, delayed by the distance it had to travel, and by the choking snows of its widespread fountains. Now, with volume tenfold increased beyond its springtime fullness, it took its place as leader of the glorious choir.

And the winds, too, were singing in wild accord, playing on every tree and rock, surging against the huge brows and domes and outstanding battlements, deflected hither and thither and broken into a thousand cascading, roaring currents in the cañons, and low bass, drumming swirls in the hollows. And these again, reacting on the clouds, eroded immense cavernous spaces in their gray depths and swept forward the resulting detritus in ragged trains like the moraines of glaciers. These cloud movements in turn published the work of the winds, giving them a visible body, and enabling us to trace them. As if endowed with independent motion, a detached cloud would rise hastily to the very top of the wall as if on some important

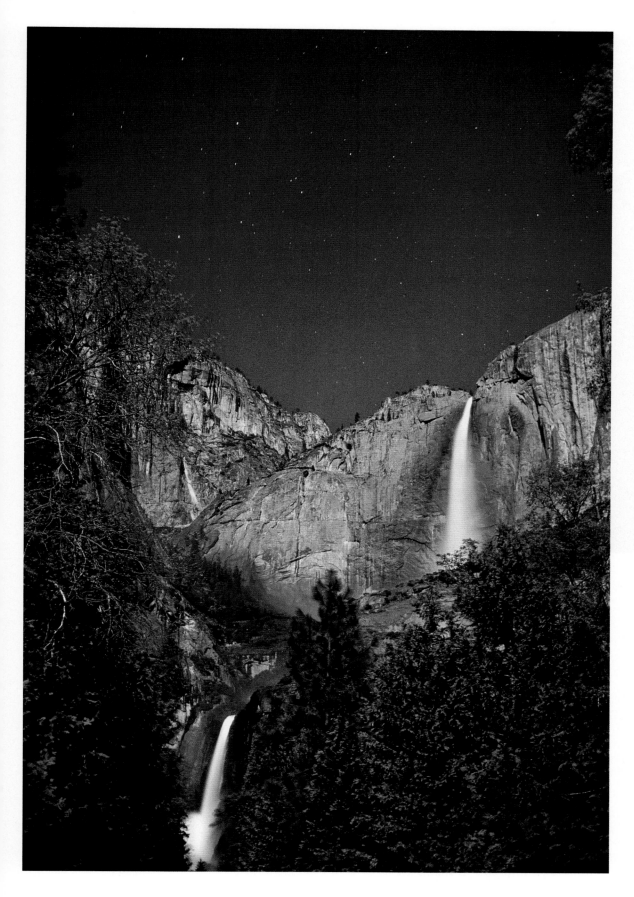

## YOSEMITE FALLS BY MOONLIGHT, 1986.

"A wild scene, but not a safe one, is made by the moon as it appears through the edge of the Yosemite Fall when one is behind it. Once, after enjoying the night-song of the waters . . . as the moon came round the domes and sent her beams into the wild uproar, I ventured out on the narrow bench that extends back of the fall from Fern Ledge. . . . Wishing to look at the moon through the meshes of some of the denser portions of the fall, I ventured to creep father behind it while it was gently wind-swayed. . . . I was in fairyland between the dark wall and the wild throng of illumined waters, but suffered sudden disenchantment. . . . Down came a dash of spent comets, thin and harmless-looking in the distance, but they felt desperately solid and stony when they struck my shoulders, like a mixture of choking spray and gravel and big hailstones. Instinctively dropping on my knees, I gripped an angle of the rock, curled up like a young fern frond with my face pressed against my breast, and in this attitude submitted as best I could to my thundering bath."

*I have never tried to repeat Muir's moonlight waterfall rendezvous. From a safer distance, however, I made this 45-second exposure by the light of the full moon. In such a situation the ways in which the film sees differently than the eye are accentuated. The waterfall becomes a soft gossamer blur, while the sky, black to my eye, records its blueness over time on film. The stars, all white points to me, record themselves on film as streaks of motion that are too slow for me to perceive, with colors I could not see, because the human eye perceives stars only in black and white with the highly light-sensitive rods instead of the color-sensitive cones that dominate daylight vision. In this case, photography allowed me to see more than met my eye.*

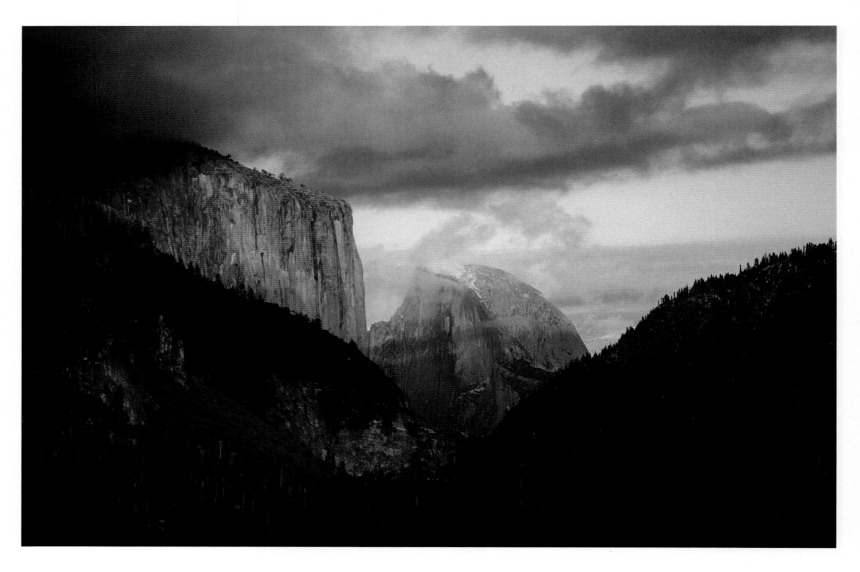

SUNSET AFTER A STORM,
YOSEMITE VALLEY, 1970.

"These canyons are not gloomy
gorges, savage and inaccessible. . . .
They are flowery pathways
conducting to the snowy, icy
fountains . . . presenting
throughout all their courses a rich
variety of novel and attractive
scenery—the most attractive that
has yet been discovered in the
mountain ranges of the world."

*From a vantage point on the road to
Crane Flat, the two major features
of Yosemite—El Capitan and Half
Dome—appear next to one
another, even though they are seven
miles apart. A strong telephoto is
required to single them out of the
scene, although for most of the year
the air is too murky to make an
acceptable photograph. One day in
1970 the National Park Service
called me to help rescue my friend
Warren Harding, who had been
holed up in one spot on the side of
El Capitan for several days during a
November storm. As I drove into
the Valley, the clouds were lifting
and the air was extremely clear. El
Capitan was bathed in sunset red,
separated in color from a bluish
Half Dome, partly under the
shadow of a cloud.*

errand, examining the faces of the cliffs, and then perhaps as suddenly descend to sweep imposingly along the meadows, trailing its draggled fringes through the pines, fondling the waving spires with infinite gentleness, or, gliding behind a grove or a single tree, bringing it into striking relief, as it bowed and waved in solemn rhythm. Sometimes, as the busy clouds drooped and condensed or dissolved to misty gauze, half of the Valley would be suddenly veiled, leaving here and there some lofty headland cut off from all visible connection with the walls, looming alone, dim, spectral, as if belonging to the sky—visitors, like the new falls, come to take part in the glorious festival. Thus for two days and nights in measureless extravagance the storm went on, and mostly without spectators, at least of a terrestrial kind. I saw nobody out—bird, bear, squirrel, or man. Tourists had vanished months before, and the hotel people and laborers were out of sight, careful about getting cold, and satisfied with views from windows. The bears, I suppose, were in their cañon-boulder dens, the squirrels in their knot-hole nests, the grouse in close fir groves, and the small singers in the Indian Cañon chaparral, trying to keep warm and dry. Strange to say, I did not see even the water-ouzels, though they must have greatly enjoyed the storm.

This was the most sublime waterfall flood I ever saw—clouds, winds, rocks, waters, throbbing together as one. And then to contemplate what was going on simultaneously with all this in other mountain temples; the Big Tuolumne Cañon—how the white waters and the winds were singing there! And in Hetch Hetchy Valley and the great King's River yosemite, and in all the other Sierra cañons and valleys from Shasta to the southernmost fountains of the Kern, thousands of rejoicing flood waterfalls chanting together in jubilee dress.

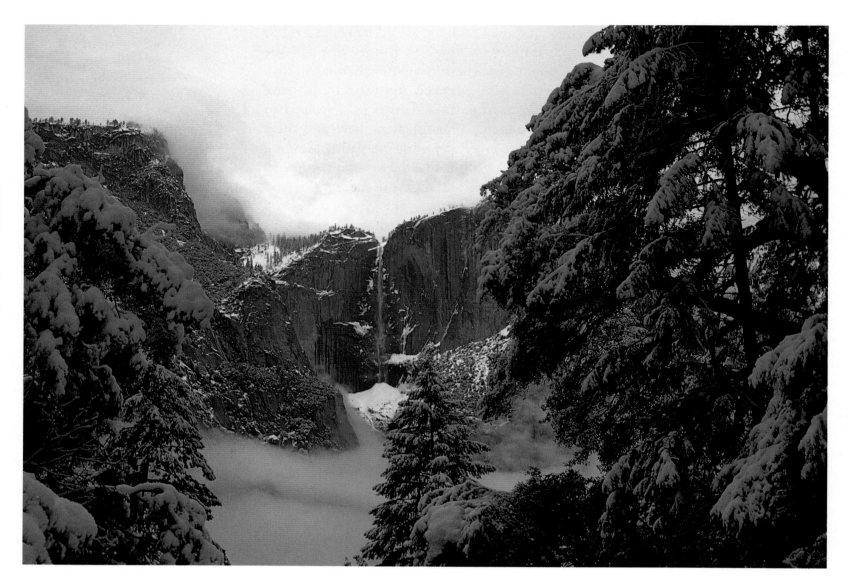

STORMY MORNING FROM THE
GLACIER POINT FOUR-MILE TRAIL,
1971.

"One fine Yosemite morning after a
heavy snowfall . . . I set out early to
climb by a side canyon to the top of
a commanding ridge . . . three
thousand feet above the Valley. . . .
Most of the way I sank waist deep,
almost out of sight in some places."

*In the sixties and early seventies I
climbed to the Valley rim several
times in deep snow. One time
afternoon avalanche danger was so
high that I opted for a cold night
alone in a tree without a sleeping
bag. On the February day when I
made this image, snow filled the
contours of the upper Four-Mile
Trail to Glacier Point so completely
that I needed an ice ax to traverse
the final half mile.*

# CHAPTER III

# Snow-Storms

As HAS BEEN already stated, the first of the great snow-storms that replenish the Yosemite fountains seldom sets in before the end of November. Then, warned by the sky, wide-awake mountaineers, together with the deer and most of the birds, make haste to the lowlands or foothills; and burrowing marmots, mountain beavers, wood-rats, and other small mountain people, go into winter quarters, some of them not again to see the light of day until the general awakening and resurrection of the spring in June or July. The fertile clouds, drooping and condensing in brooding silence, seem to be thoughtfully examining the forests and streams with reference to the work that lies before them. At length, all their plans perfected, tufted flakes and single starry crystals come in sight, solemnly swirling and glinting to their blessed appointed places; and soon the busy throng fills the sky and makes darkness like night. The first heavy fall is usually from about two to four feet in depth; then with intervals of days or weeks of bright weather storm succeeds storm, heaping snow on snow, until thirty to fifty feet has fallen. But on account of its settling and compacting, and waste from melting and evaporation, the average depth actually found at any time seldom exceeds ten feet in the forest regions, or fifteen feet along the slopes of the summit peaks. After snow-storms come avalanches, varying greatly in form, size, behavior and in the songs they sing; some on the smooth slopes of the mountains are short and broad; others long and river-like in the side cañons of yosemites and in the main cañons, flowing in regular channels and booming like waterfalls, while countless smaller ones fall everywhere from laden trees and rocks and lofty cañon walls. Most delightful it is to stand in the middle of Yosemite on still clear mornings after snow-storms and watch the throng of avalanches as they come down, rejoicing, to their places, whispering, thrilling like birds, or booming and roaring like thunder. The noble yellow pines stand hushed and motionless as if under a spell until the morning sunshine begins to sift through their laden spires; then the dense masses on the ends of the leafy branches begin to shift and fall, those from the upper branches striking the lower ones in succession, enveloping each tree in a hollow conical avalanche of fairy fineness; while the relieved branches spring up and wave with startling effect in the general stillness, as if each tree was moving of its own volition. Hundreds of broad cloud-shaped masses may also be seen, leaping over the brows of the cliffs from great heights, descending at first with regular avalanche speed until, worn into dust by friction, they float in front of the precipices like irised clouds. Those which descend from the brow of El Capitan are particularly fine; but most of the great Yosemite avalanches flow in regular channels like cascades and waterfalls. When the snow first gives way on the upper slopes of their basins, a dull rushing, rumbling sound is heard which rapidly increases and seems to draw nearer with appalling intensity of tone. Presently the white flood comes bounding into sight over bosses and sheer places, leaping from bench to bench, spreading and narrowing and throwing off clouds of whirling dust like the spray of foaming cataracts. Compared with waterfalls and cascades, avalanches are short-lived, few of them lasting more than a minute or two, and the sharp, clashing sounds so common in falling water are mostly wanting; but in their low massy thundertones and purple-tinged whiteness, and in their dress, gait, gestures and general behavior, they are much alike.

## AVALANCHES

Besides these common after-storm avalanches that are to be found not only in the Yosemite but in all the deep, sheer-walled cañons of the Range there are two other important kinds, which may be called annual and century avalanches, which still further enrich the scenery. The only place about the Valley where one may be sure to see the annual kind is on the north slope of Clouds' Rest. They are composed of heavy, compacted snow, which has been subjected to frequent alternations of freezing and thawing. They are developed on cañon and mountain-sides at an elevation of from nine to ten thousand feet, where the slopes are inclined at an angle too low to shed off the dry winter snow, and which accumulates until the spring thaws sap their foundations and make them slippery; then away in grand style go the ponderous icy masses without any fine snow-dust. Those of Clouds' Rest descend like thunderbolts for more than a mile.

The great century avalanches and the kind that mow wide swaths through the upper forests occur on mountain-sides about ten or twelve thousand feet high, where under ordinary weather conditions the snow accumulated from winter to winter lies at rest for many years, allowing trees, fifty to a hundred feet high, to grow undisturbed on the slopes beneath them. On their way down through the woods they seldom fail to make a perfectly clean sweep, stripping off the soil as well as the trees, clearing paths two or three hundred yards wide from the timber line to the glacier meadows or lakes, and piling their uprooted trees, head downward, in rows along the sides of the gaps like lateral moraines. Scars and broken branches of the trees standing on the sides of the gaps record the depth of the overwhelming flood; and when we come to count the annual wood-rings on the uprooted trees we learn that some of these immense avalanches occur only once in a century or even at still wider intervals.

## A RIDE ON AN AVALANCHE

Few Yosemite visitors ever see snow avalanches and fewer still know the exhilaration of riding on them. In all my mountaineering I have enjoyed only one avalanche ride, and the start was so sudden and the end came so soon I had but little time to think of the danger that attends this sort of travel, though at such times one thinks fast. One fine Yosemite morning after a heavy snowfall, being eager to see

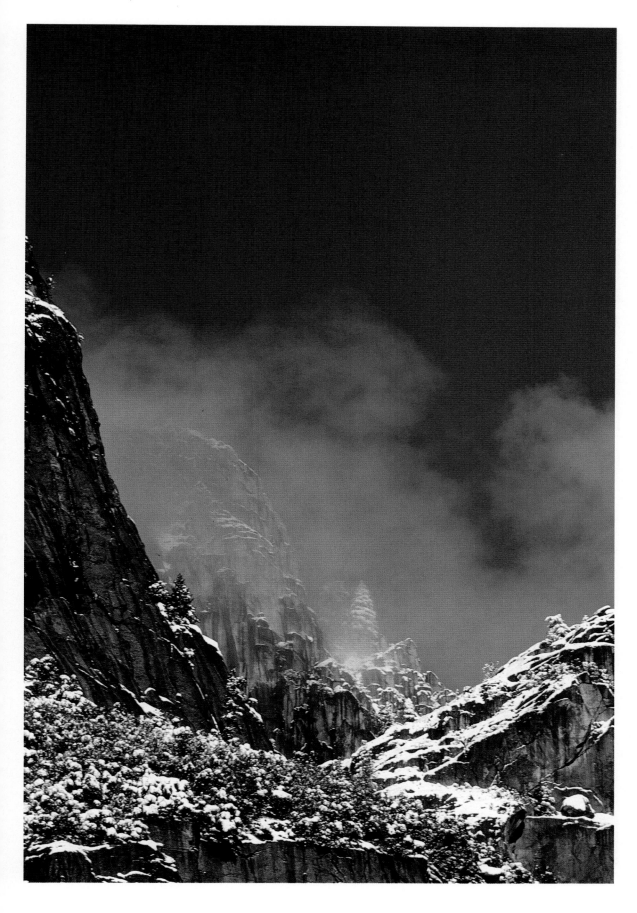

MORING LIGHT ON THE VALLEY RIM NEAR YOSEMITE FALLS, 1973.

"One wild winter morning I was awakened by a storm-wind. . . . The Valley had been visited a short time before by a series of fine snowstorms, and the floor and the cliffs and all the region round about were lavishly adorned with its best winter jewelry, the air was full of fine snow-dust, and pine branches, tassels and empty cones were flying in an almost continuous flock."

*One morning after reaching Yosemite Valley on skis from the high country, I awoke to wild winds scouring snow from the tops of the cliffs. I used a telephoto lens to bring a scene 2,500 feet above me to eye level, appearing much as it had the previous day, but with the added splendor of spindrift and morning light.*

HALF DOME AND FOREST
CLEARING, 1979.

"Then comes the snow, for the clouds are ripe, the meadows of the sky are in bloom, and shed their radiant blossoms like an orchard in the spring. Lightly, lightly they lodge in the brown grasses and in the tasseled needles of the pines, falling hour after hour, day after day, silently, lovingly—all the winds hushed—glancing and circling hither, thither, glinting against one another, rays interlocking in flakes as large as daisies; and then the dry grasses, and the trees, and the stones are all equally abloom again."

*Deep winter on the Yosemite Valley floor lasts for a few days at best. While the high country lies buried for the season, the Valley alternates between apparent winter and spring, as rising daytime temperatures quickly melt away the uniform whiteness that Muir saw more often than we do in the especially snowy decade surrounding his early visits.*

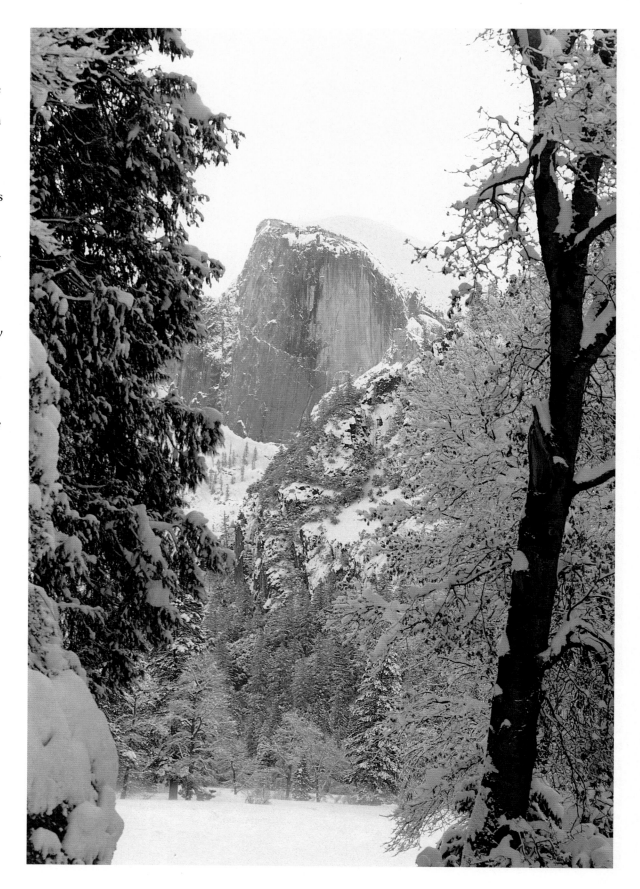

as many avalanches as possible and wide views of the forest and summit peaks in their new white robes before the sunshine had time to change them, I set out early to climb by a side cañon to the top of a commanding ridge a little over three thousand feet above the Valley. On account of the looseness of the snow that blocked the cañon I knew the climb would require a long time, some three or four hours as I estimated; but it proved far more difficult than I had anticipated. Most of the way I sank waist deep, almost out of sight in some places. After spending the whole day to within half an hour or so of sundown, I was still several hundred feet below the summit. Then my hopes were reduced to getting up in time to see the sunset. But I was not to get summit views of any sort that day, for deep trampling near the cañon head, where the snow was strained, started an avalanche, and I was swished down to the foot of the cañon as if by enchantment. The wallowing ascent had taken nearly all day, the descent only about a minute. When the avalanche started I threw myself on my back and spread my arms to try to keep from sinking. Fortunately, though the grade of the cañon is very steep, it is not interrupted by precipices large enough to cause outbounding or free plunging. On no part of the rush was I buried. I was only moderately imbedded on the surface or at times a little below it, and covered with a veil of back-streaming dust particles; and as the whole mass beneath and about me joined in the flight there was no friction, though I was tossed here and there and lurched from side to side. When the avalanche swedged and came to rest I found myself on top of the crumpled pile without a bruise or scar. This was a fine experience. Hawthorne says somewhere that steam has spiritualized travel; though unspiritual smells, smoke, etc., still attend steam travel. This flight in what might be called a milky way of snow-stars was the most spiritual and exhilarating of all the modes of motion I have ever experienced. Elijah's flight in a chariot of fire could hardly have been more gloriously exciting.

### THE STREAMS IN OTHER SEASONS

In the spring, after all the avalanches are down and the snow is melting fast, then all the Yosemite streams, from their fountains to their falls, sing their grandest songs. Countless rills make haste to the rivers, running and singing soon after sunrise, louder and louder with increasing volume until sundown; then they gradually fail through the frosty hours of the night. In this way the volume of the upper branches of the river is nearly doubled during the day, rising and falling as regularly as the tides of the sea. Then the Merced overflows its banks, flooding the meadows, sometimes almost from wall to wall in some places, beginning to rise towards sundown just when the streams on the fountains are beginning to diminish, the difference in time of the daily rise and fall being caused by the distance the upper flood streams have to travel before reaching the Valley. In the warmest weather they seem fairly to shout for joy and clash their upleaping waters together like clapping of hands; racing down the cañons with white manes flying in glorious exuberance of strength, compelling huge, sleeping boulders to wake up and join in their dance and song, to swell their exulting chorus.

In early summer, after the flood season, the Yosemite streams are in their prime, running crystal clear, deep and full but not overflowing their banks—about as deep through the night as the day, the difference in volume so marked in spring being now too slight to be noticed. Nearly all the weather is cloudless and everything is at its brightest—lake, river, garden and forest with all their life. Most of the plants are in full flower. The blessed ouzels have built their mossy huts and are now singing their best songs with the streams.

In tranquil, mellow autumn, when the year's work is about done and the fruits are ripe, birds and seeds out of their nests, and all the landscape is glowing like a benevolent countenance, then the streams are at their lowest ebb, with scarce a memory left of their wild spring floods. The small tributaries that do not reach back to the lasting snow fountains of the summit peaks shrink to whispering, tinkling currents. After the snow is gone from the basins, excepting occasional thunder-showers, they are now fed only by small springs whose waters are mostly evaporated in passing over miles of warm pavements, and in feeling their way slowly from pool to pool through the midst of boulders and sand. Even the main rivers are so low they may easily be forded, and their grand falls and cascades, now gentle and approachable, have waned to sheets of embroidery.

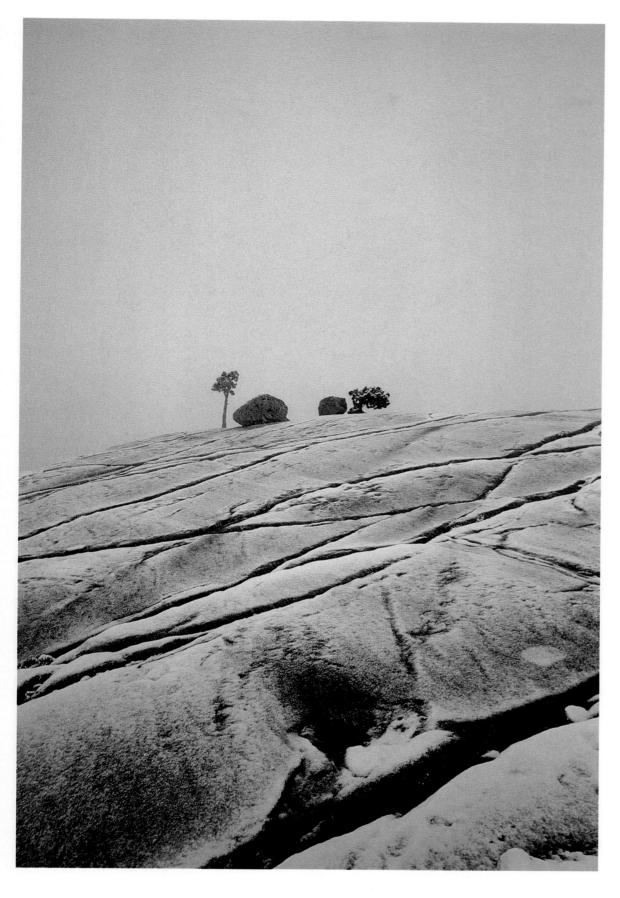

DWARF JEFFREY PINE AND
JUNIPER WITH GLACIAL ERRATICS,
OLMSTED POINT, 1973.

"The Master Builder chose for a
tool, not the earthquake nor
lightning to rend and split asunder,
not the stormy torrent nor eroding
rain, but the tender snow-flowers,
noiselessly falling through
unnumbered seasons, the offspring
of the sun and sea."

*Few glacial pathways are more
obvious to the modern eye than this
one beside a parking lot on the
Tioga Pass highway. In summer the
scene makes a mediocre photograph
because it is cluttered by a busy
jumble of trees and rocks nearby,
but during the first fall storm, snow
simplified the scene with a veil of
white in the air that gently merged
with the snow-dusted features of
dome, erratic boulders, and
dwarf trees.*

TWILIGHT MIST, MERCED RIVER, YOSEMITE VALLEY, 1986.

"Watching the circling seasons, listening to the songs of the waters and winds and birds, would be endless pleasure. And what glorious cloud-lands I would see, storms and calms, a new heaven and a new earth every day."

*One winter evening when the Valley was filled with mist, I found crowds of onlookers watching last light on Bridalveil Fall and El Capitan. The light on those features was fine, but all of one color, so I decided to continue on to find a place where warm light would be contrasted against some coolly lit element of a winter evening. I found what I was looking for along the Merced River, where boulders coated in snow reflected the blue light of the sky, while the air all around turned vivid pink. At most times, this particular spot makes a rather boring photograph, but as John Muir discovered for himself, to find a new heaven and earth every day, you need only look well about you.*

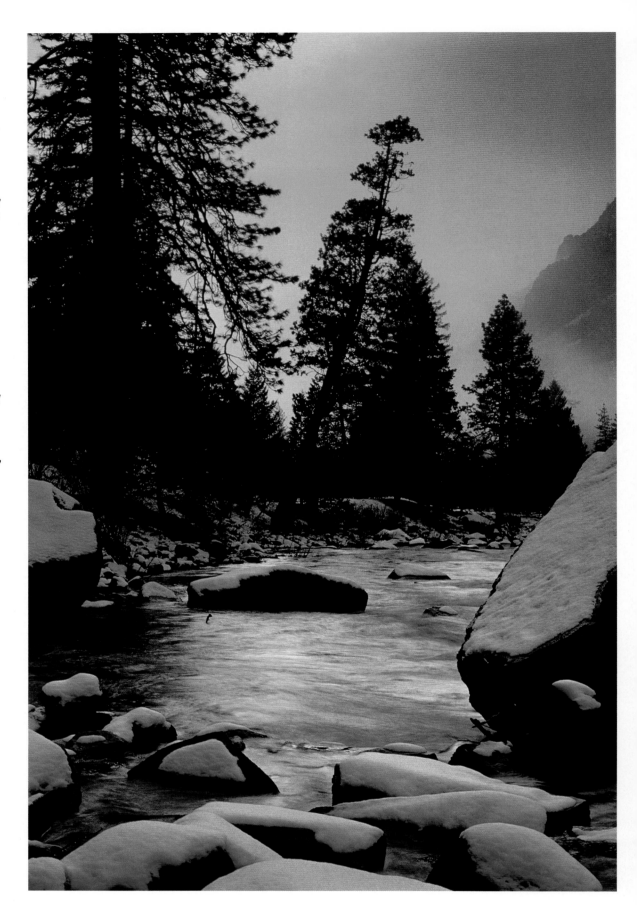

CHAPTER IV

# Snow Banners

BUT IT IS ON the mountain tops, when they are laden with loose, dry snow and swept by a gale from the north, that the most magnificent storm scenery is displayed. The peaks along the axis of the Range are then decorated with resplendent banners, some of them more than a mile long, shining, streaming, waving with solemn exuberant enthusiasm as if celebrating some surpassingly glorious event.

The snow of which these banners are made falls on the High Sierra in most extravagant abundance, sometimes to a depth of fifteen or twenty feet, coming from the fertile clouds not in large tangled flakes such as one oftentimes sees in Yosemite, seldom even in complete crystals, for many of the starry blossoms fall before they are ripe, while most of those that attain perfect development as six-petaled flowers are more or less broken by glinting and chafing against one another on the way down to their work. This dry frosty snow is prepared for the grand banner-waving celebrations by the action of the wind. Instead of at once finding rest like that which falls into the tranquil depths of the forest, it is shoved and rolled and beaten against boulders and out-jutting rocks, swirled in pits and hollows like sand in river pot-holes, and ground into sparkling dust. And when storm-winds find this snow-dust in a loose condition on the slopes above the timber-line they toss it back into the sky and sweep it onward from peak to peak in the form of smooth regular banners, or in cloudy drifts, according to the velocity and direction of the wind, and the conformation of the slopes over which it is driven. While thus flying through the air a small portion escapes from the mountains to the sky as vapor; but far the greater part is at length locked fast in bossy overcurling cornices along the ridges, or in stratified sheets in the glacier cirques, some of it to replenish the small residual glaciers and remain silent and rigid for centuries before it is finally melted and sent singing down home to the sea.

But, though snow-dust and storm-winds abound on the mountains, regular shapely banners are, for causes we shall presently see, seldom produced. During the five winters that I spent in Yosemite I made many excursions to high points above the walls in all kinds of weather to see what was going on outside; from all my lofty outlooks I saw only one banner-storm that seemed in every way perfect. This was in the winter of 1873, when the snow-laden peaks were swept by a powerful norther. I was awakened early in the morning by a wild storm-wind and of course I had to make haste to the middle of the Valley to enjoy it. Rugged torrents and avalanches from the main wind-flood overhead were roaring down the side cañons and over the cliffs, arousing the rocks and the trees and the streams alike into glorious hurrahing enthusiasm, shaking the whole Valley into one huge song. Yet inconceivable as it must seem even to those who love all Nature's wildness, the storm was telling its story on the mountains in still grander characters.

### A WONDERFUL WINTER SCENE

I had long been anxious to study some points in the structure of the ice-hill at the foot of the Upper Yosemite Fall, but, as I have already explained, blinding spray had hitherto prevented me from getting sufficiently near it. This morning the entire body of the Fall was oftentimes torn into gauzy strips and blown horizontally along the face of the cliff, leaving the ice-hill dry; and while making my way to the top of Fern Ledge to seize so favorable an opportunity to look down its throat, the peaks of the Merced group came in sight over the shoulder of the South Dome, each waving a white glowing banner against the dark blue sky, as regular in form and firm and fine in texture as if it were made of silk. So rare and splendid a picture, of course, smothered everything else and I at once began to scramble and wallow up the snow-choked Indian Cañon to a ridge about 8000 feet high, commanding a general view of the main summits along the axis of the Range, feeling assured I should find them bannered still more gloriously; nor was I in the least disappointed. I reached the top of the ridge in four or five hours, and through an opening in the woods the most imposing wind-storm effect I ever beheld came full in sight; unnumbered mountains rising sharply into the cloudless sky, their bases solid white, their sides plashed with snow, like ocean rocks with foam, and on every summit a magnificent silvery banner, from two thousand to six thousand feet in length, slender at the point of attachment, and widening gradually until about a thousand or fifteen hundred feet in breadth, and as shapely and as substantial looking in texture as the banners of the finest silk, all streaming and waving free and clear in the sun-glow with nothing to blur the sublime picture they made.

Fancy yourself standing beside me on this Yosemite Ridge. There is a strange garish glitter in the air and the gale drives wildly overhead, but you feel nothing of its violence, for you are looking out through a sheltered opening in the woods, as through a window. In the immediate foreground there is a forest of silver firs, their foliage warm yellow-green, and the snow beneath them is strewn with their plumes, plucked off by the storm; and beyond a broad, ridgy, cañon-furrowed, dome-dotted middle ground, darkened here and there with belts of pines, you behold the lofty snow-laden mountains in glorious array, waving their banners with jubilant enthusiasm as if shouting aloud for joy. They are twenty miles away, but you would not wish them nearer, for every feature is distinct, and the whole wonderful show is seen in its right proportions, like a painting on the sky.

And now after this general view, mark how sharply the ribs and buttresses and summits of the mountains are defined, excepting the portions veiled by the banners; how gracefully and nobly the banners are waving in accord with the throbbing of the wind-flood; how trimly each is attached to the very summit of its peak like a streamer at a mast-head; how bright and glowing white they are, and how finely their fading fringes are penciled on the sky! See how solid white and opaque they are at the point of attachment and how filmy and translucent toward the end, so that the parts of the peaks past which they are streaming look dim as if seen through

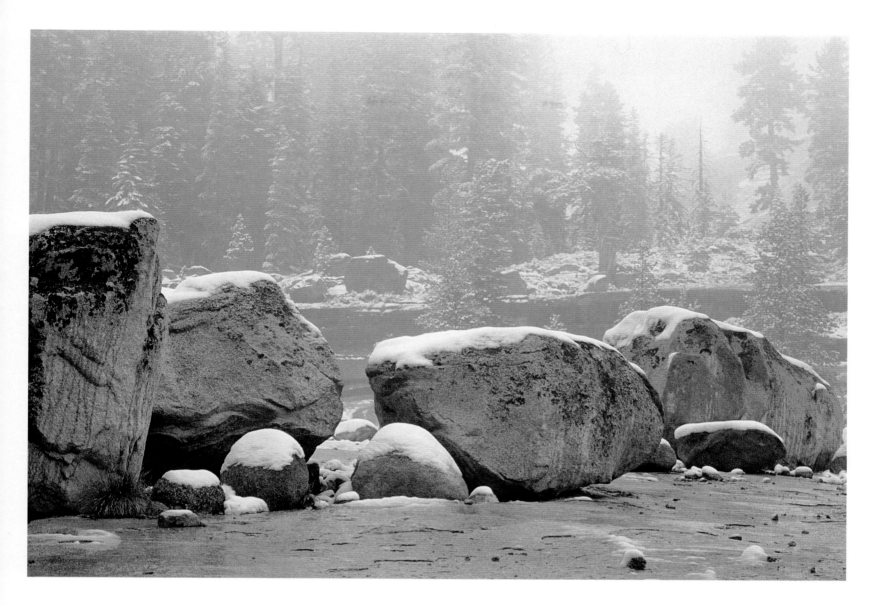

GLACIAL ERRATICS ABOVE SNOW
CREEK, 1986.

"Reading these grand mountain
manuscripts displayed through
every vicissitude of heat and cold,
calm and storm, upheaving
volcanoes and down-grinding
glaciers, we see that everything in
Nature called destruction must be
creation—a change from beauty
to beauty."

*Ice once traveled much of the route
of the present Tioga Pass highway.
Although that past landscape no
longer exists, it can hardly be called
destroyed. These boulders, so
carefully poised on a pathway of
smooth granite, were gently
dropped by the retreating ice at a
time so recent that human beings
may already have been in the
American West. Blanketed in snow,
these glacial erratics stand apart
from the landscape, but in summer
tens of thousands of visitors drive
to within a few feet of them without
a second glance.*

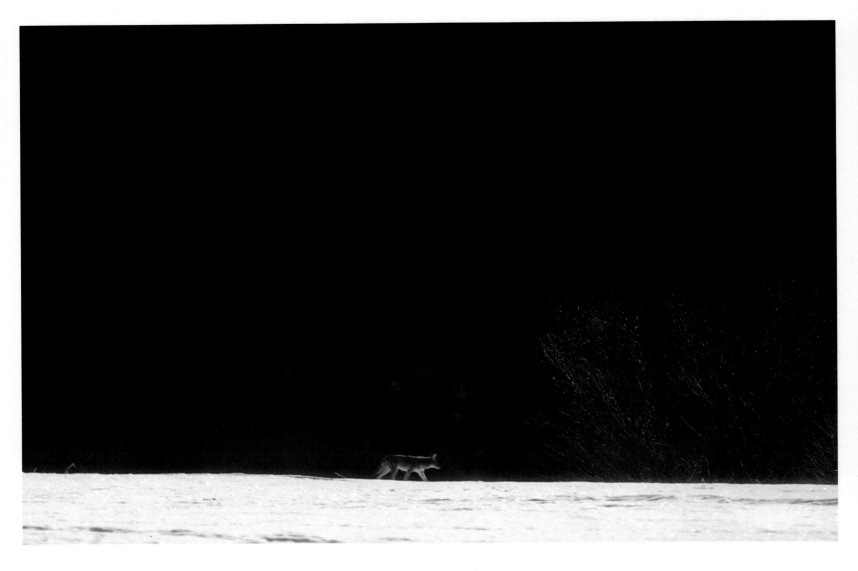

COYOTE ON A WINTER MORNING,
VALLEY FLOOR, 1969.

"Most wild animals get into the
world and out of it without
being noticed."

*During the three warmer seasons of
the year, Yosemite's coyotes are
seldom seen. In the winter, however,
they brazenly walk the Valley floor
in full view of park visitors. With
each passing year they seem ever
more approachable, and even
though I've made some stunning
close portraits of "wild" coyotes
staring right at my camera, my
favorite vision is this one of twenty
years ago, in which a coyote walked
the border between sun and shadow,
unaware of my presence as I caught
his profile with a long telephoto
lens. When he heard the click of my
shutter, he quickly sidestepped to
the right, merging into the
blackness of the shadows, becoming
virtually invisible.*

a veil of ground glass. And see how some of the longest of the banners on the highest peaks are streaming perfectly free from peak to peak across intervening notches or passes, while others overlap and partly hide one another.

As to their formation, we find that the main causes of the wondrous beauty and perfection of those we are looking at are the favorable direction and force of the wind, the abundance of snow-dust, and the form of the north sides of the peaks. In general, the north sides are concave in both their horizontal and vertical sections, having been sculptured into this shape by the residual glaciers that lingered in the protecting northern shadows, while the sun-beaten south sides, having never been subjected to this kind of glaciation, are convex or irregular. It is essential, therefore, not only that the wind should move with great velocity and steadiness to supply a sufficiently copious and continuous stream of snow-dust, but that it should come from the north. No perfect banner is ever hung on the Sierra peaks by the south wind. Had the gale to-day blown from the south, leaving the other conditions unchanged, only swirling, interfering, cloudy drifts would have been produced; for the snow, instead of being spouted straight up and over the tops of the peaks in condensed currents to be drawn out as streamers, would have been driven over the convex southern slopes from peak to peak like white pearly fog.

It appears, therefore, that shadows in great part determine not only the forms of lofty ice mountains, but also those of the snow banners that the wild winds hang upon them.

### EARTHQUAKE STORMS

The avalanche taluses, leaning against the walls at intervals of a mile or two, are among the most striking and interesting of the secondary features of the Valley. They are from about three to five hundred feet high, made up of huge, angular, well-preserved, unshifting boulders, and instead of being slowly weathered from the cliffs like ordinary taluses, they were all formed suddenly and simultaneously by a great earthquake that occurred at least three centuries ago. And though thus hurled into existence in a few seconds or minutes, they are the least changeable of all the Sierra soil-beds. Excepting those which were launched directly into the channels of swift rivers, scarcely one of their wedged and interlacing boulders has moved since the day of their creation; and though mostly made up of huge blocks of granite, many of them from ten to fifty feet cube, weighing thousands of tons with only a few small chips, trees and shrubs make out to live and thrive on them and even delicate herbaceous plants—draperia, collomia, zauschneria, etc., soothing and coloring their wild rugged slopes with gardens and groves.

I was long in doubt on some points concerning the origin of these taluses. Plainly enough they were derived from the cliffs above them, because they are of the size of scars on the wall, the rough angular surface of which contrasts with the rounded, glaciated, unfractured parts. It was plain, too, that instead of being made up of material slowly and gradually weathered from the cliffs like ordinary taluses, almost every one of them had been formed suddenly in a single avalanche, and had not been increased in size during the last three or four centuries, for trees three or four hundred years old are growing on them, some standing at the top close to the wall without a bruise or broken branch, showing that scarcely a single boulder had ever fallen among them. Furthermore, all these taluses throughout the Range seemed by the trees and lichens growing on them to be of the same age. All the phenomena thus pointed straight to a grand ancient earthquake. But for years I left the question open, and went on from cañon to cañon, observing again and again; measuring the heights of taluses throughout the Range on both flanks, and the variations in the angles of their surface slopes; studying the way their boulders had been assorted and related and brought to rest, and their correspondence in size with the cleavage joints of the cliffs from whence they were derived, cautious about making up my mind. But at last all doubt as to their formation vanished.

At half-past two o'clock of a moonlit morning in March, I was awakened by a tremendous earthquake, and though I had never before enjoyed a storm of this sort, the strange thrilling motion could not be mistaken, and I ran out of my cabin, both glad and frightened, shouting, "A noble earthquake! A noble earthquake!" feeling sure I was going to learn something. The shocks were so violent and varied, and succeeded one another so closely, that I had to balance myself carefully in walking as if on the deck of a ship among waves, and it seemed impossible that the high cliffs of the Valley could escape being shattered. In particular, I feared that the sheer-fronted Sentinel Rock, towering above my cabin, would be shaken down, and I took shelter back of a large yellow pine, hoping that it might protect me from at least the smaller outbounding boulders. For a minute or two the shocks became more and more violent—flashing horizontal thrusts mixed with a few twists and battering, explosive, upheaving jolts—as if Nature were wrecking her Yosemite temple, and getting ready to build a still better one.

I was now convinced before a single boulder had fallen that earthquakes were the talus-makers and positive proof soon came. It was a calm moonlight night, and no sound was heard for the first minute or so, save low, muffled, underground, bubbling rumblings, and the whispering and rustling of the agitated trees, as if Nature were holding her breath. Then, suddenly, out of the strange silence and strange motion there came a tremendous roar. The Eagle Rock on the south wall, about a half a mile up the Valley, gave way and I saw it falling in thousands of the great boulders I had so long been studying, pouring to the Valley floor in a free curve luminous from friction, making a terribly sublime spectacle—an arc of glowing, passionate fire, fifteen hundred feet span, as true in form and as serene in beauty as a rainbow in the midst of the stupendous, roaring rock-storm. The sound was so tremendously deep and broad and earnest, the whole earth like a living creature seemed to have at last found a voice and to be calling to her sister planets. In trying to tell something of the size of this awful sound it seems to me that if all the thunder of all the storms I had ever heard were condensed into one roar it would not equal this rock-roar at the birth of a mountain talus. Think, then, of the roar that arose to heaven at the simultaneous birth of all the thousands of ancient cañon-taluses throughout the length and breadth of the Range!

The first severe shocks were soon over, and eager to examine the new-born talus I ran up the Valley in the moonlight and climbed upon it before the huge blocks, after their fiery flight, had come to complete rest. They were slowly settling into their places, chafing, grating against one another, groaning, and whispering; but no motion was visible except in a stream of small fragments pattering down the face of the cliff. A cloud of dust particles, lighted by the moon, floated out across the whole breadth of the Valley, forming a ceiling that lasted until after sunrise, and the air was filled with the odor of crushed Douglas spruces from a grove that had been mowed down and mashed like weeds.

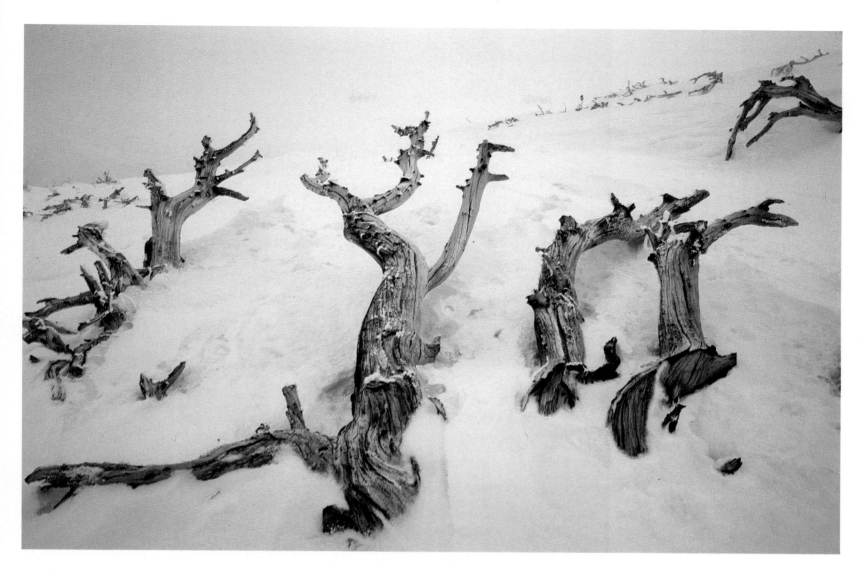

WHITEBARK PINE SNAGS NEAR
DONOHUE PASS, 1973.

"Again and again, as I lingered over
these charming plants, I said, How
came you here? How do you live
through the winter? Our roots, they
explained, reach far down the joints
of the summer warmed rocks, and
beneath our fine snow mantle
killing frosts cannot reach us, while
we sleep away the dark half of the
year dreaming of spring."

*Trees, like people, have distinct
personalities. Some, like the oaks
and the cedars, maintain dignity at
all costs, refusing to go where they
might be compromised by deep
snows and high winds. Others, such
as the Sierra juniper, face the
elements boldly and alone with
their heavy trunks powerfully
attached to cracks and fissures. The
whitebark pines, however, seem
most aligned with Muir's vision of
life-forms—including man—
adapting themselves to new
surroundings. At nine thousand
feet, beside a stream, a whitebark is
an ordinary pine, not much
different in appearance from a
lodgepole. Fifteen hundred feet
higher, whitebark clusters hug the
ground, flagged to the east by the
prevailing winds, delicate forms
that survive by flowing with the air
and the snow.*

MOONSET OVER MOUNT RITTER
AND BANNER PEAK, 1988.

"After gaining a point about
halfway to the top, I was suddenly
brought to a dead stop, with arms
outspread, clinging close to the face
of the rock, unable to move hand or
foot either up or down. My doom
appeared fixed. I *must* fall. . . .
Then my trembling muscles became
firm again, every rift and flaw in the
rock was seen as through a
microscope, and my limbs moved
with a positiveness and precision
with which I seemed to have
nothing at all to do. Had I been
borne aloft upon wings, my
deliverance could not have been
more complete."

*After John Muir made his
harrowing ascent of Mount Ritter
in 1873, he strongly urged that it be
included in Yosemite National Park,
as indeed it was in the original
1890 Act of Congress. In 1905,
however, the entire Minaret region
south of Donohue Pass was
withdrawn from the park so it
could be opened for mining, an
event that disturbed Muir almost as
much as the 1913 decision to build
Hetch Hetchy Dam. I include this
image because it is part of the
heritage of Muir and Yosemite. The
creation of the Ansel Adams
Wilderness in 1982 preserved
Mount Ritter and its surroundings,
including a corridor to the south
where a trans-Sierra highway from
Fresno to Mammoth had been
proposed.*

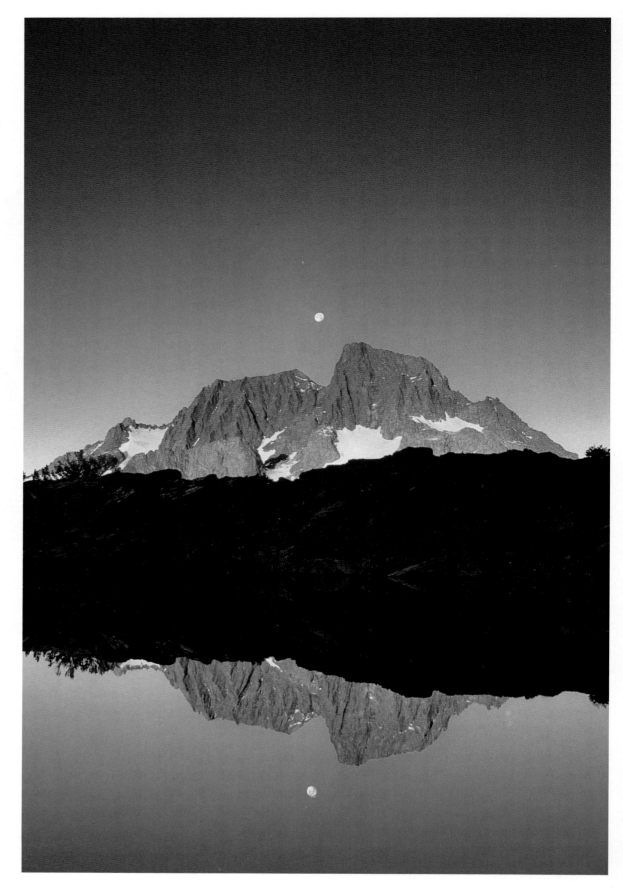

After the ground began to calm I ran across the meadow to the river to see in what direction it was flowing and was glad to find that *down* the Valley was still down. Its waters were muddy from portions of its banks having given way, but it was flowing around its curves and over its ripples and shallows with ordinary tones and gestures. The mud would soon be cleared away and the raw slips on the banks would be the only visible record of the shaking it suffered.

The Upper Yosemite Fall, glowing white in the moonlight, seemed to know nothing of the earthquake, manifesting no change in form or voice, as far as I could see or hear.

After a second startling shock, about half-past three o'clock, the ground continued to tremble gently, and smooth, hollow rumbling sounds, not always distinguishable from the rounded, bumping, explosive tones of the falls, came from deep in the mountains in a northern direction.

The few Indians fled from their huts to the middle of the Valley, fearing that angry spirits were trying to kill them; and, as I afterward learned, most of the Yosemite tribe, who were spending the winter at their village on Bull Creek forty miles away, were so terrified that they ran into the river and washed themselves—getting themselves clean enough to say their prayers, I suppose, or to die. I asked Dick, one of the Indians with whom I was acquainted, "What made the ground shake and jump so much?" He only shook his head and said, "No good. No good," and looked appealingly to me to give him hope that his life was to be spared.

In the morning I found the few white settlers assembled in front of the old Hutchings Hotel comparing notes and meditating flight to the lowlands, seemingly as sorely frightened as the Indians. Shortly after sunrise a low, blunt, muffled rumbling, like distant thunder, was followed by another series of shocks, which, though not nearly so severe as the first, made the cliffs and domes tremble like jelly, and the big pines and oaks thrill and swish and wave their branches with startling effect. Then the talkers were suddenly hushed, and the solemnity on their faces was sublime. One in particular of these winter neighbors, a somewhat speculative thinker with whom I had often conversed, was a firm believer in the cataclysmic origin of the Valley; and I now jokingly remarked that his wild tumble-down-and-engulfment hypothesis might soon be proved, since these underground rumblings and shakings might be the forerunners of another Yosemite-making cataclysm, which would perhaps double the depth of the Valley by swallowing the floor, leaving the ends of the roads and trails dangling three or four thousand feet in the air. Just then came the third series of shocks, and it was fine to see how awfully silent and solemn he became. His belief in the existence of a mysterious abyss, into which the suspended floor of the Valley and all the domes and battlements of the walls might at any moment go roaring down, mightily troubled him. To diminish his fears and laugh him into something like reasonable faith, I said, "Come, cheer up; smile a little and clap your hands, now that kind Mother Earth is trotting us on her knee to amuse us and make us good." But the well-meant joke seemed irreverent and utterly failed, as if only prayerful terror could rightly belong to the wild beauty-making business. Even after all the heavier shocks were over I could do nothing to reassure him. On the contrary, he handed me the keys of his little store to keep, saying that with a companion of like mind he was going to the lowlands to stay until the fate of poor, trembling Yosemite was settled. In vain I rallied them on their fears, calling attention to the strength of the granite walls of our Valley home, the very best and solidest masonry in the world, and less likely to collapse and sink than the sedimentary lowlands to which they were looking for safety; and saying that in any case they sometime would have to die, and so grand a burial was not to be slighted. But they were too seriously panic-stricken to get comfort from anything I could say.

During the third severe shock the trees were so violently shaken that the birds flew out with frightened cries. In particular, I noticed two robins flying in terror from a leafless oak, the branches of which swished and quivered as if struck by a heavy battering-ram. Exceedingly interesting were the flashing and quivering of the elastic needles of the pines in the sunlight and the waving up and down of the branches while the trunks stood rigid. There was no swaying, waving or swirling as in wind-storms, but quick, quivering jerks, and at times the heavy tasseled branches moved as if they had all been pressed down against the trunk and suddenly let go, to spring up and vibrate until they came to rest again. Only the owls seemed to be undisturbed. Before the rumbling echoes had died away a hollow-voiced owl began to hoot in philosophical tranquillity from near the edge of the new talus as if nothing extraordinary had occurred, although, perhaps, he was curious to know what all the noise was about. His "hoot-too-hoot-too-whoo" might have meant, "what's a' the steer, kimmer?"

It was long before the Valley found perfect rest. The rocks trembled more or less every day for over two months, and I kept a bucket of water on my table to learn what I could of the movements. The blunt thunder in the depths of the mountains was usually followed by sudden jarring, horizontal thrusts from the northward, often succeeded by twisting, upjolting movements. More than a month after the first great shock, when I was standing on a fallen tree up the Valley near Lamon's winter cabin, I heard a distinct bubbling thunder from the direction of Tenaya Cañon. Carlo, a large intelligent St. Bernard dog standing beside me seemed greatly astonished, and looked intently in that direction with mouth open and uttered a low *Wouf!* as if saying, "What's that?" He must have known that it was not thunder, though like it. The air was perfectly still, not the faintest breath of wind perceptible, and a fine, mellow, sunny hush pervaded everything, in the midst of which came that subterranean thunder. Then, while we gazed and listened, came the corresponding shocks, distinct as if some mighty hand had shaken the ground. After the sharp horizontal jars died away, they were followed by a gentle rocking and undulating of the ground so distinct that Carlo looked at the log on which he was standing to see who was shaking it. It was the season of flooded meadows and the pools about me, calm as sheets of glass, were suddenly thrown into low ruffling waves.

Judging by its effects, this Yosemite, or Inyo earthquake, as it is sometimes called, was gentle as compared with the one that gave rise to the grand talus system of the Range and did so much for the cañon scenery. Nature, usually so deliberate in her operations, then created, as we have seen, a new set of features, simply by giving the mountains a shake—changing not only the high peaks and cliffs, but the streams. As soon as these rock avalanches fell, the streams began to sing new songs; for in many places thousands of boulders were hurled into their channels, roughening and half-damming them, compelling the waters to surge and roar in rapids where before they glided smoothly. Some of the streams were completely dammed; driftwood, leaves, etc., gradually filling the interstices between the boulders, thus

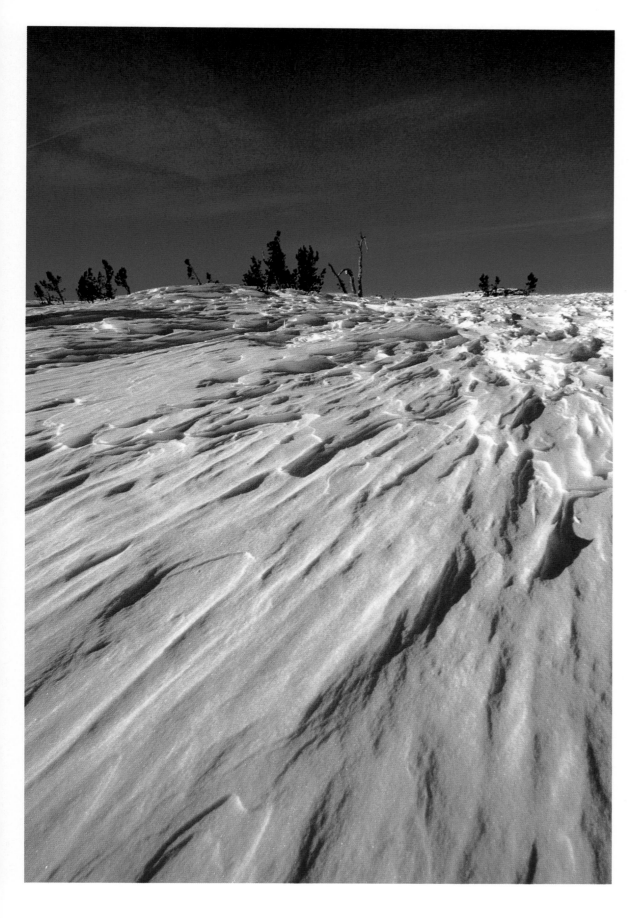

WIND-ETCHED SNOW AT
CATHEDRAL PASS, 1988.

"Only in the roar of storms do these mighty solitudes find voice at all commensurate with their grandeur."

*On Cathedral Pass in February, I found a landscape dominated by a fierce east wind that not only howled in my ears from every rock and tree, but also left its mark on the snow around me. The patterns fascinated me because the flutings of snow appeared to converge in the distance; in reality they maintained a constant width, like a pair of railroad tracks. The illusion enhanced the impression that I would never reach the pass because I seemed to be getting no closer to that point in the distance where the flutings appeared to merge at the pass.*

giving rise to lakes and level reaches; and these again, after being gradually filled in, were changed to meadows, through which the streams are now silently meandering; while at the same time some of the taluses took the places of old meadows and groves. Thus rough places were made smooth, and smooth places rough. But, on the whole, by what at first sight seemed pure confounded confusion and ruin, the landscapes were enriched; for gradually every talus was covered with groves and gardens, and made a finely proportioned and ornamental base for the cliffs. In this work of beauty, every boulder is prepared and measured and put in its place more thoughtfully than are the stones of temples. If for a moment you are inclined to regard these taluses as mere draggled, chaotic dumps, climb to the top of one of them, and run down without any haggling, puttering hesitation, boldly jumping from boulder to boulder with even speed. You will then find your feet playing a tune, and quickly discover the music and poetry of these magnificent rock piles—a fine lesson; and all Nature's wildness tells the same story—the shocks and outbursts of earthquakes, volcanoes, geysers, roaring, thundering waves and floods, the silent uprush of sap in plants, storms of every sort—each and all are the orderly beauty-making love-beats of Nature's heart.

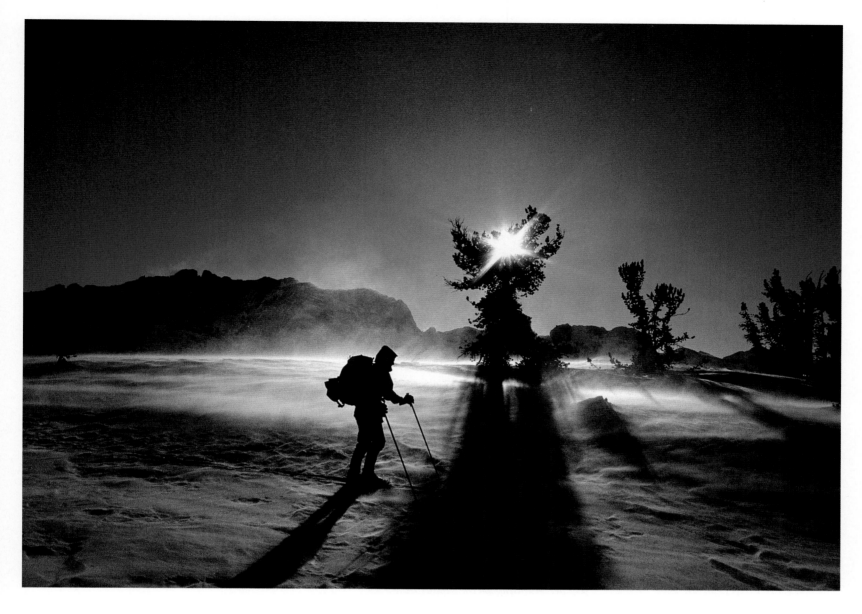

**GROUND BLIZZARD IN THE TUOLUMNE HIGH COUNTRY, 1988.**

"Hawthorne says that steam has spiritualized travel, notwithstanding the smoke, friction, smells, and clatter of boat and rail riding. This flight in a milky way of snow flowers was the most spiritual of all my travels."

*When I skied through this ground blizzard, I lost touch with the firm boundaries of my physical world. The sky was clear and blue at eye level, while wind-churned snow veiled the ground and my feet from view. Sometimes I was moving when I thought I was standing still; other times I waited to see objects draw closer, convinced that I was still gliding downhill, when in fact my skis had stopped on some unseen obstruction beneath the moving current of snowflakes.*

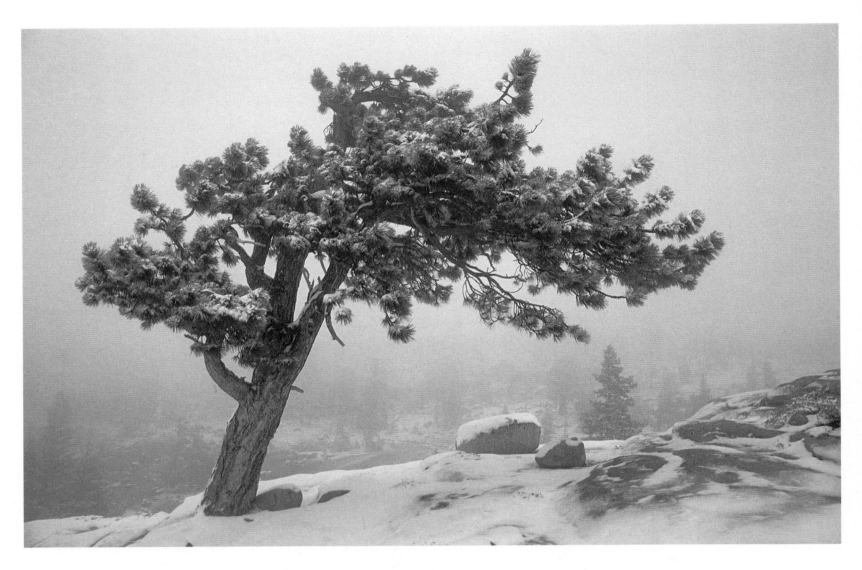

WIND-FLAGGED JEFFREY PINE,
OLMSTED POINT, 1986.

"God has cared for these trees,
saved them from drought, disease,
avalanches, and a thousand
straining, leveling tempests and
floods; but he cannot save them
from fools—only Uncle Sam can
do that."

*In my mother's notes from a 1923
crossing of the Yosemite high
country, I came across a poignant
question: "Why do we carry in our
minds the picture of the knotted,
twisted tree or dead tree hit by
lightning and forget the sedate,
proper trees that have grown
according to pattern?"*

*The answer is not obvious when
you are standing in the center of a
forest of regular trees. One day,
however, I looked back at a forest
from above timberline and saw it as
a metaphor for all societies of living
things. In the distance was a sea of
healthy, well-formed trees, crowded
together under a single canopy of
green branches. In the foreground
were rugged individuals, pushing
the absolute limits of timberline
existence, each with its own unique
configuration. Some were living,
some were dead, but each of these
trees held my interest longer than
the "regular guys" in the middle of
the crowd. The forms of these old
warriors reflected the forces of the
natural world around them, while
the forms in the center of the pack
reflected more genetic inheritance
and less individual life experience.*

## CHAPTER V

# The Trees of the Valley

THE MOST INFLUENTIAL of the Valley trees is the yellow pine (*Pinus ponderosa*). It attains its noblest dimensions on beds of water-washed, coarsely-stratified moraine material, between the talus slopes and meadows, dry on the surface, well-watered below and where not too closely assembled in groves the branches reach nearly to the ground, forming grand spires 200 to 220 feet in height. The largest that I have measured is standing alone almost opposite the Sentinel Rock, or a little to the westward of it. It is a little over eight feet in diameter and about 220 feet high. Climbing these grand trees, especially when they are waving and singing in worship in wind-storms, is a glorious experience. Ascending from the lowest branch to the topmost is like stepping up stairs through a blaze of white light, every needle thrilling and shining as if with religious ecstasy.

Unfortunately there are but few sugar pines in the Valley, though in the King's yosemite they are in glorious abundance. The incense cedar (*Libocedrus decurrens*) with cinnamon-colored bark and yellow-green foliage is one of the most interesting of the Yosemite trees. Some of them are 150 feet high, from six to ten feet in diameter, and they are never out of sight as you saunter among the yellow pines. Their bright brown shafts and towers of flat, frond-like branches make a striking feature of the landscapes throughout all the seasons. In midwinter, when most of the other trees are asleep, this cedar puts forth its flowers in millions—the pistillate pale green and inconspicuous, but the staminate bright yellow, tingeing all the branches and making the trees as they stand in the snow look like gigantic goldenrods. The branches, outspread in flat plumes and, beautifully fronded, sweep gracefully downward and outward, except those near the top, which aspire; the lowest, especially in youth and middle age, droop to the ground, overlapping one another, shedding off rain and snow like shingles, and making fine tents for birds and campers. This tree frequently lives more than a thousand years and is well worthy its place beside the great pines and the Douglas spruce.

The two largest specimens I know of the Douglas spruce, about eight feet in diameter, are growing at the foot of the Liberty Cap near the Nevada Fall, and on the terminal moraine of the small residual glacier that lingered in the shady Illilouette Cañon.

After the conifers, the most important of the Yosemite trees are the oaks, two species; the California live-oak (*Quercus agrifolia*), with black trunks, reaching a thickness of from four to nearly seven feet, wide spreading branches and bright deeply-scalloped leaves. It occupies the greater part of the broad sandy flats of the upper end of the Valley, and is the species that yields the acorns so highly prized by the Indians and woodpeckers.

The other species is the mountain live-oak, or golden-cup oak (*Quercus chrysole-*

*pis*), a sturdy mountaineer of a tree, growing mostly on the earthquake taluses and benches of the sunny north wall of the Valley. In tough, unwedgeable, knotty strength, it is the oak of oaks, a magnificent tree.

The largest and most picturesque specimen in the Valley is near the foot of the Tenaya Fall, a romantic spot seldom seen on account of the rough trouble of getting to it. It is planted on three huge boulders and yet manages to draw sufficient moisture and food from this craggy soil to maintain itself in good health. It is twenty feet in circumference, measured above a large branch between three and four feet in diameter that has been broken off. The main knotty trunk seems to be made up of craggy granite boulders like those on which it stands, being about the same color as the mossy, lichened boulders and about as rough. Two moss-lined caves near the ground open back into the trunk, one on the north side, the other on the west, forming picturesque, romantic seats. The largest of the main branches is eighteen feet and nine inches in circumference, and some of the long pendulous branchlets droop over the stream at the foot of the fall where it is gray with spray. The leaves are glossy yellow-green, ever in motion from the wind from the fall. It is a fine place to dream in, with falls, cascades, cool rocks lined with hypnum three inches thick; shaded with maple, dogwood, alder, willow; grand clumps of lady-ferns where no hand may touch them; light filtering through translucent leaves; oaks fifty feet high; lilies eight feet high in a filled lake basin near by, and the finest libocedrus groves and tallest ferns and goldenrods.

In the main river cañon below the Vernal Fall and on the shady south side of the Valley there are a few groves of the silver fir (*Abies concolor*), and superb forests of the magnificent species around the rim of the Valley.

On the tops of the domes is found the sturdy, storm-enduring red cedar (*Juniperus occidentalis*). It never makes anything like a forest here, but stands out separate and independent in the wind, clinging by slight joints to the rock, with scarce a handful of soil in sight of it, seeming to depend chiefly on snow and air for nourishment, and yet it has maintained tough health on this diet for two thousand years or more. The largest hereabouts are from five to six feet in diameter and fifty feet in height.

The principal river-side trees are poplar, alder, willow, broad-leaved maple, and Nuttall's flowering dogwood. The poplar (*Populus trichocarpa*), often called balm-of-Gilead from the gum on its buds, is a tall tree, towering above its companions and gracefully embowering the banks of the river. Its abundant foliage turns bright yellow in the fall, and the Indian-summer sunshine sifts through it in delightful tones over the slow-gliding waters when they are at their lowest ebb.

Some of the involucres of the flowering dogwood measure six to eight inches in diameter, and the whole tree when in flower looks as if covered with snow. In the spring when the streams are in flood it is the whitest of trees. In Indian summer the leaves become bright crimson, making a still grander show than the flowers.

The broad-leaved maple and mountain maple are found mostly in the cool cañons at the head of the Valley, spreading their branches in beautiful arches over the foaming streams.

Scattered here and there are a few other trees, mostly small—the mountain mahogany, cherry, chestnut-oak, and laurel. The California nutmeg (*Torreya californica*), a handsome evergreen, belonging to the yew family, forms small groves near the cascades a mile or two below the foot of the Valley.

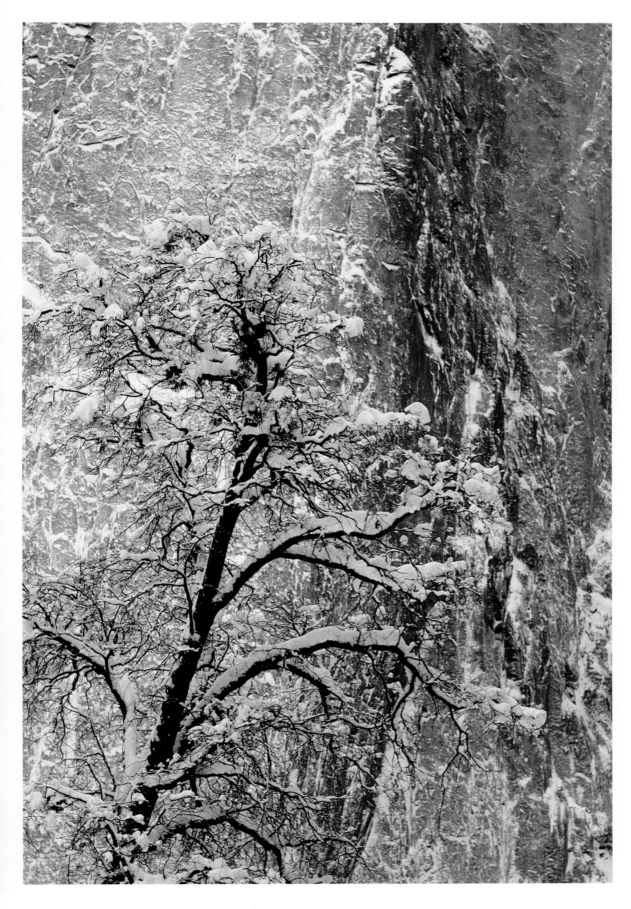

OAK TREE AND MIDDLE
CATHEDRAL ROCK, 1979.

"The rocks where the exposure to
storms is greatest are all the more
lavishly clothed upon with beauty—
beauty growing with and depending
upon the violence of the gale."

*I originally made this image as part
of a pair of the same scene, in
summer and winter. When there was
no snow, I had been drawn by the
contrast of textures of oak bark,
granite, and green leaves. With the
addition of snow, however, a hidden
sameness came out, a sense of
similar contours and textures in tree
and cliff alike. The winter scene
stands on its own as an example of
how beauty in nature increases not
with the addition of extra colors or
complexity, but with elements that
reduce a scene to the most
basic simplicities.*

WINTER IN THE MERCED GROVE
OF GIANT SEQUOIAS, 1979.

"No doubt these trees would make
good lumber after passing through
a sawmill, as George Washington
after passing through the hands of a
French cook would have made
good food."

*Of what use are giant sequoias if
not for lumber? All trees strictly fit
the timber industry's adage of being
a "renewable resource," but by the
same definition, so do all human
beings, with a lifespan far shorter
than the three thousand years of a
sequoia. Intact groves have a
collective wisdom to impart to us.
John Muir discovered that they are
not relics of some lost era when
they blanketed the Sierra, but rather
are complete little ecosystems that
have not grown much larger or
smaller over the last few thousand
years. When some scientists recently
tried to interpret isolated data to
support a theory that central
California underwent a long, dry
period with rainfall only a third of
the present, the old trees spoke,
saying, "We're here, and we've been
here in the same places requiring a
constant and delicate balance of
moisture and shade for thousands
of years, right through the period
that you, who were not alive at the
time, suspect was so dry."*

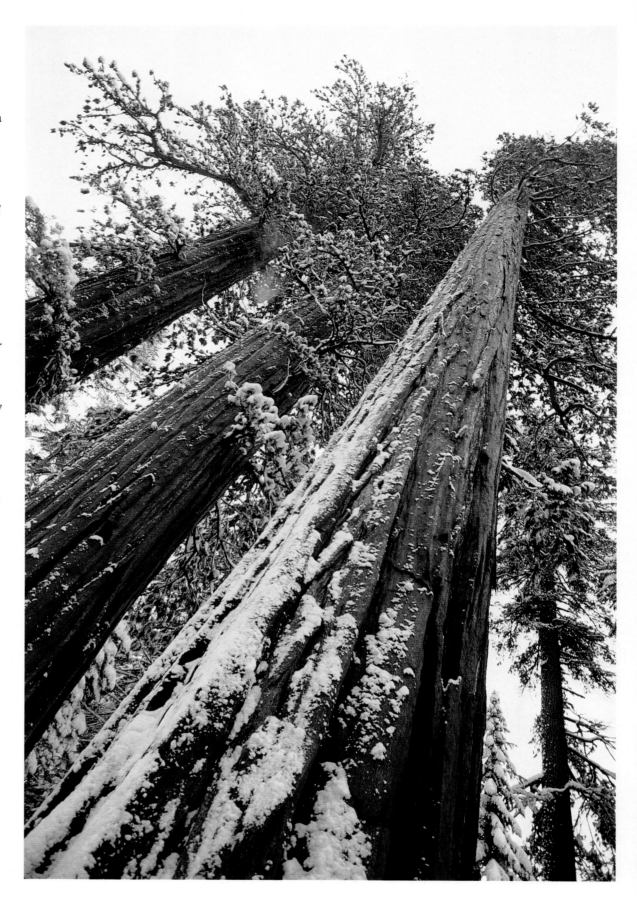

CHAPTER VI

# The Forest Trees in General

FOR THE USE of the ever-increasing number of Yosemite visitors who make extensive excursions into the mountains beyond the Valley, a sketch of the forest trees in general will probably be found useful. The different species are arranged in zones and sections, which brings the forest as a whole within the comprehension of every observer. These species are always found as controlled by the climates of different elevations, by soil and by the comparative strength of each species in taking and holding possession of the ground; and so appreciable are these relations the traveler need never be at a loss in determining within a few hundred feet his elevation above sea level by the trees alone; for, notwithstanding some of the species range upward for several thousand feet and all pass one another more or less, yet even those species possessing the greatest vertical range are available in measuring the elevation; inasmuch as they take on new forms corresponding with variations in altitude. Entering the lower fringe of the forest composed of Douglas oaks and Sabine pines, the trees grow so far apart that not one-twentieth of the surface of the ground is in shade at noon. After advancing fifteen or twenty miles towards Yosemite and making an ascent of from two to three thousand feet you reach the lower margin of the main pine belt, composed of great sugar pine, yellow pine, incense cedar and sequoia. Next you come to the magnificent silver-fir belt and lastly to the upper pine belt, which sweeps up to the feet of the summit peaks in a dwarfed fringe, to a height of from ten to twelve thousand feet. That this general order of distribution depends on climate as affected by height above the sea, is seen at once, but there are other harmonies that become manifest only after observation and study. One of the most interesting of these is the arrangement of the forest in long curving bands, braided together into lace-like patterns in some places and outspread in charming variety. The key to these striking arrangements is the system of ancient glaciers; where they flowed the trees followed, tracing their courses along the sides of cañons, over ridges, and high plateaus. The cedar of Lebanon, said Sir Joseph Hooker, occurs upon one of the moraines of an ancient glacier. All the forests of the Sierra are growing upon moraines, but moraines vanish like the glaciers that make them. Every storm that falls upon them wastes them, carrying away their decaying, disintegrating material into new formations, until they are no longer recognizable without tracing their transitional forms down the Range from those still in process of formation in some places through those that are more and more ancient and more obscured by vegetation and all kinds of postglacial weathering. It appears, therefore, that the Sierra forests indicate the extent and positions of ancient moraines as well as they do belts of climate.

One will have no difficulty in knowing the Nut Pine (*Pinus Sabiniana*), for it is the first conifer met in ascending the Range from the west, springing up here and there among Douglas oaks and thickets of ceanothus and manzanita; its extreme upper limit being about 4000 feet above the sea, its lower about from 500 to 800 feet. It is remarkable for its loose, airy, wide-branching habit, and thin gray foliage. Full-grown specimens are from forty to fifty feet in height and from two to three feet in diameter. The trunk usually divides into three or four main branches about fifteen or twenty feet from the ground that, after bearing away from one another, shoot straight up and form separate summits. Their slender, grayish needles are from eight to twelve inches long, and inclined to droop, contrasting with the rigid, dark-colored trunk and branches. No other tree of my acquaintance so substantial in its body has foliage so thin and pervious to the light. The cones are from five to eight inches long and about as large in thickness; rich chocolate-brown in color and protected by strong, down-curving hooks which terminate the scales. Nevertheless the little Douglas squirrel can open them. Indians climb the trees like bears and beat off the cones or recklessly cut off the more fruitful branches with hatchets, while the squaws gather and roast them until the scales open sufficiently to allow the hard-shell seeds to be beaten out. The curious little *Pinus attenuata* is found at an elevation of from 1500 to 3000 feet, growing in close groves and belts. It is exceedingly slender and graceful, although trees that chance to stand alone send out very long, curved branches, making a striking contrast to the ordinary grove form. The foliage is of the same peculiar gray-green color as that of the nut pine, and is worn about as loosely, so that the body of the tree is scarcely obscured by it. At the age of seven or eight years it begins to bear cones in whorls on the main axis, and as they never fall off, the trunk is soon picturesquely dotted with them. Branches also soon become fruitful. The average size of the tree is about thirty or forty feet in height and twelve to fourteen inches in diameter. The cones are about four inches long, and covered with a sort of varnish and gum, rendering them impervious to moisture.

No observer can fail to notice the admirable adaptation of this curious pine to the fire-swept regions where alone it is found. After a running fire has scorched and killed it the cones open and the ground beneath it is then sown broadcast with all the seeds ripened during its whole life. Then up spring a crowd of bright, hopeful seedlings, giving beauty for ashes in lavish abundance.

### THE SUGAR PINE, KING OF PINE TREES

Of all the world's eighty or ninety species of pine trees, the Sugar Pine (*Pinus Lambertiana*) is king, surpassing all others, not merely in size but in lordly beauty and majesty. In the Yosemite region it grows at an elevation of from 3000 to 7000 feet above the sea and attains most perfect development at a height of about 5000 feet. The largest specimens are commonly about 220 feet high and from six to eight feet in diameter four feet from the ground, though some grand old patriarch may be met here and there that has enjoyed six or eight centuries of storms and attained a thickness of ten or even twelve feet, still sweet and fresh in every fiber. The trunk is a remarkably smooth, round, delicately-tapered shaft, straight and regular as if turned in a lathe, mostly without limbs, purplish brown in color and usually enlivened with tufts of a yellow lichen. Toward the head of this magnificent column long branches sweep gracefully outward and downward, sometimes forming a palm-like crown, but far more impressive than any palm crown I ever beheld. The needles are about three inches long in fascicles of five, and arranged in rather close tassels at

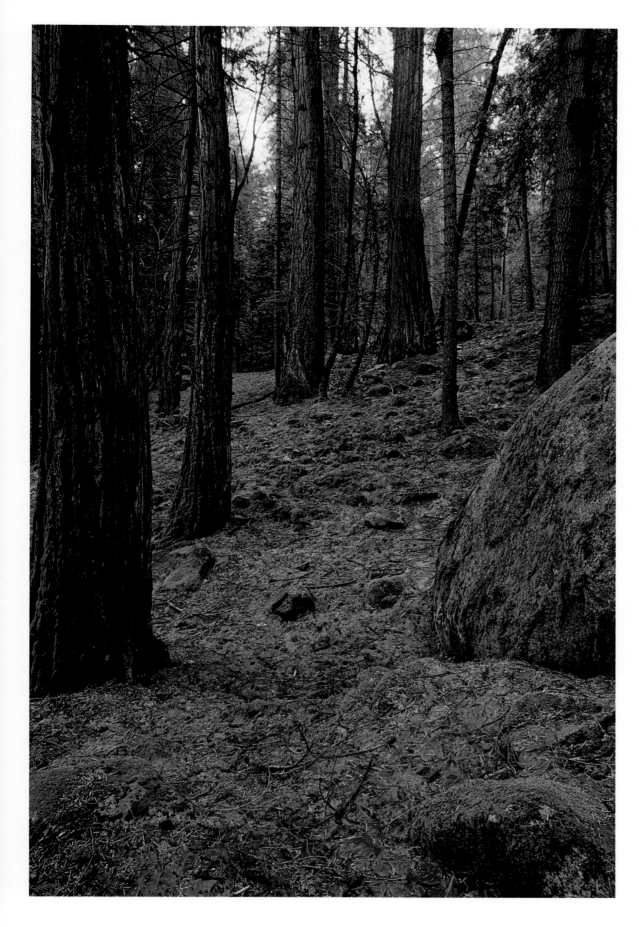

INCENSE CEDAR FOREST,
YOSEMITE VALLEY, 1987.

"I never saw a discontented tree.
They grip the ground as though
they liked it, and though fast
rooted, they travel . . . with us
around the sun two million miles a
day, and through space heaven
knows how fast and far!"

*My fascination with forest floors
began in 1957 when my aunt
Marion Avery took me on a twenty-
fifth reunion of the Yosemite Field
School, which had spent several
summers picking out square plots a
hundred feet on a side and mapping
every rock, every tree, every flower
within. A teenager, I expected to be
bored helping a bunch of old fogeys
re-create a map after twenty-five
years, but each increment of change
begged a question and led me
toward viewing the natural world as
a participant rather than as a
classroom observer. I wondered
why some trees were only inches
bigger than before, while some were
much larger, and others seemed
almost unchanged. Flowers moved,
but pebbles were often in exactly
the same place. Mosses clung to the
same side of the same rocks. Thus
in 1987 when I saw the colors and
patterns beneath this cedar trunk
after thirty more years had passed, I
got down on my knees, and as I
homed in with a wide-angle lens, I
remembered similar times, mapping
a forest floor with an aunt who,
unlike the cedars before me, was no
longer on this earth.*

the ends of slender branchlets that clothe the long outsweeping limbs. How well they sing in the wind, and how strikingly harmonious an effect is made by the long cylindrical cones, depending loosely from the ends of the long branches! The cones are about fifteen to eighteen inches long, and three in diameter; green, shaded with dark purple on their sunward sides. They are ripe in September and October of the second year from the flower. Then the flat, thin scales open and the seeds take wing, but the empty cones become still more beautiful and effective as decorations, for their diameter is nearly doubled by the spreading of the scales, and their color changes to yellowish brown while they remain, swinging on the tree all the following winter and summer, and continue effectively beautiful even on the ground many years after they fall. The wood is deliciously fragrant, fine in grain and texture and creamy yellow, as if formed of condensed sunbeams. The sugar from which the common name is derived is, I think, the best of sweets. It exudes from the heartwood where wounds have been made by forest fires or the ax, and forms irregular, crisp, candy-like kernels of considerable size, something like clusters of resin beads. When fresh it is white, but because most of the wounds on which it is found have been made by fire the sap is stained and the hardened sugar becomes brown. Indians are fond of it, but on account of its laxative properties only small quantities may be eaten. No tree lover will ever forget his first meeting with the sugar pine. In most pine trees there is the sameness of expression which to most people is apt to become monotonous, for the typical spiral form of conifers, however beautiful, affords little scope for appreciable individual character. The sugar pine is as free from conventionalities as the most picturesque oaks. No two are alike, and though they toss out their immense arms in what might seem extravagant gestures they never lose their expression of serene majesty. They are the priests of pines and seem ever to be addressing the surrounding forest. The yellow pine is found growing with them on warm hillsides, and the silver fir on cool northern slopes; but, noble as these are, the sugar pine is easily king, and spreads his arms above them in blessing while they rock and wave in sign of recognition. The main branches are sometimes forty feet long, yet persistently simple, seldom dividing at all, excepting near the end; but anything like a bare cable appearance is prevented by the small, tasseled branchlets that extend all around them; and when these superb limbs sweep out symmetrically on all sides, a crown sixty or seventy feet wide is formed, which, gracefully poised on the summit of the noble shaft, is a glorious object. Commonly, however, there is a preponderance of limbs toward the east, away from the direction of the prevailing winds.

Although so unconventional when full-grown, the sugar pine is a remarkably proper tree in youth—a strict follower of coniferous fashions—slim, erect, with leafy branches kept exactly in place, each tapering in outline and terminating in a spiry point. The successive forms between the cautious neatness of youth and the bold freedom of maturity offer a delightful study. At the age of fifty or sixty years, the shy, fashionable form begins to be broken up. Specialized branches push out and bend with the great cones, giving individual character, that becomes more marked from year to year. Its most constant companion is the yellow pine. The Douglas spruce, libocedrus, sequoia, and the silver fir are also more or less associated with it; but on many deep-soiled mountain-sides, at an elevation of about 5000 feet above the sea, it forms the bulk of the forest, filling every swell and hollow and down-plunging ravine. The majestic crowns, approaching each other in bold curves, make a glorious canopy through which the tempered sunbeams pour, silvering the needles, and gilding the massive boles and the flowery, park-like ground into a scene of enchantment.

On the most sunny slopes the white-flowered, fragrant chamaebatia is spread like a carpet, brightened during early summer with the crimson sarcodes, the wild rose, and innumerable violets and gilias. Not even in the shadiest nooks will you find any rank, untidy weeds or unwholesome darkness. In the north sides of ridges the boles are more slender, and the ground is mostly occupied by an underbrush of hazel, ceanothus, and flowering dogwood, but not so densely as to prevent the traveler from sauntering where he will; while the crowning branches are never impenetrable to the rays of the sun, and never so interblended as to lose their individuality.

### THE YELLOW OR SILVER PINE

The Silver Pine (*Pinus ponderosa*), or Yellow Pine, as it is commonly called, ranks second among the pines of the Sierra as a lumber tree, and almost rivals the sugar pine in stature and nobleness of port. Because of its superior powers of enduring variations of climate and soil, it has a more extensive range than any other conifer growing on the Sierra. On the western slope it is first met at an elevation of about 2000 feet, and extends nearly to the upper limit of the timber-line. Thence, crossing the range by the lowest passes, it descends to the eastern base, and pushes out for a considerable distance into the hot, volcanic plains, growing bravely upon well-watered moraines, gravelly lake basins, climbing old volcanoes and dropping ripe cones among ashes and cinders.

The average size of full-grown trees on the western slope, where it is associated with the sugar pine, is a little less than 200 feet in height and from five to six feet in diameter, though specimens considerably larger may easily be found. Where there is plenty of free sunshine and other conditions are favorable, it presents a striking contrast in form to the sugar pine, being a symmetrical spire, formed of a straight round trunk, clad with innumerable branches that are divided over and over again. Unlike the Yosemite form, about one-half of the trunk is commonly branchless, but where it grows at all close three-fourths or more is naked, presenting then a more slender and elegant shaft than any other tree in the woods. The bark is mostly arranged in massive plates, some of them measuring four or five feet in length by eighteen inches in width, with a thickness of three or four inches, forming a quite marked and distinguishing feature. The needles are of a fine, warm, yellow-green color, six to eight inches long, firm and elastic, and crowded in handsome, radiant tassels on the upturning ends of the branches. The cones are about three or four inches long, and two and a half wide, growing in close, sessile clusters among the leaves.

The species attains its noblest form in filled-up lake basins, especially in those of the older yosemites, and as we have seen, so prominent a part does it form of their groves that it may well be called the Yosemite Pine.

The Jeffrey variety attains its finest development in the northern portion of the Range, in the wide basins of the McCloud and Pitt Rivers, where it forms magnificent forests scarcely invaded by any other tree. It differs from the ordinary form in size, being only about half as tall, in its redder and more closely-furrowed bark, grayish-green foliage, less divided branches, and much larger cones; but intermediate forms come in which make a clear separation impossible, although some bot-

YOUNG LODGEPOLE PINES, CRANE
FLAT MEADOW, 1983.

"When one comes out of the woods
everything is novel . . . even our
fellow beings are regarded with
something of the same keenness and
freshness of perception that is
brought to a new species of
wild animal."

*These young lodgepoles are not
growing in a forest. They have
chosen the edge of a meadow,
which at some time in the not-so-
distant past was a mountain lake.
Soon the forest will creep inward,
surrounding the young trees before
they reach maturity. For the
moment, they stand apart, singled
out by the morning dew and
sunlight as forerunners of a
future forest.*

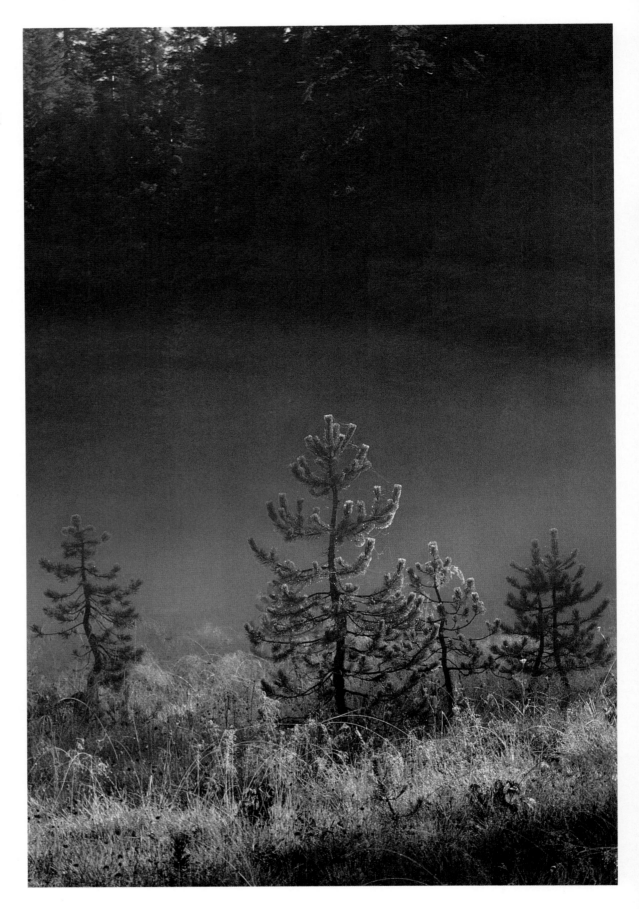

anists regard it as a distinct species. It is this variety of ponderosa that climbs storm-swept ridges alone, and wanders out among the volcanoes of the Great Basin. Whether exposed to extremes of heat or cold, it is dwarfed like many other trees, and becomes all knots and angles, wholly unlike the majestic forms we have been sketching. Old specimens, bearing cones about as big as pineapples, may sometimes be found clinging to rifted rocks at an elevation of 7000 or 8000 feet, whose highest branches scarce reach above one's shoulders.

I have often feasted on the beauty of these noble trees when they were towering in all their winter grandeur, laden with snow—one mass of bloom; in summer, too, when the brown, staminate clusters hang thick among the shimmering needles, and the big purple burrs are ripening in the mellow light; but it is during cloudless wind-storms that these colossal pines are most impressively beautiful. Then they bow like willows, their leaves streaming forward all in one direction, and, when the sun shines upon them at the required angle, entire groves glow as if every leaf were burnished silver. The fall of tropic light on the crown of a palm is a truly glorious spectacle, the fervid sun-flood breaking upon the glossy leaves in long lance-rays, like mountain water among boulders at the foot of an enthusiastic cataract. But to me there is something more impressive in the fall of light upon these noble, silver pine pillars: it is beaten to the finest dust and shed off in myriads of minute sparkles that seem to radiate from the very heart of the tree, as if like rain, falling upon fertile soil, it had been absorbed to reappear in flowers of light. This species also gives forth the finest wind music. After listening to it in all kinds of winds, night and day, season after season, I think I could approximate to my position on the mountain by this pine music alone. If you would catch the tone of separate needles climb a tree in breezy weather. Every needle is carefully tempered and gives forth no un-certain sound, each standing out with no interference excepting during heavy gales; then you may detect the click of one needle upon another, readily distinguishable from the free wind-like hum.

When a sugar pine and one of this species equal in size are observed together, the latter is seen to be more simple in manners, more lively and graceful, and its beauty is of a kind more easily appreciated; on the other hand it is less dignified and orig-inal in demeanor. The yellow pine seems ever eager to shoot aloft, higher and higher. Even while it is drowsing in autumn sun-gold you may still detect a skyward aspiration, but the sugar pine seems too unconsciously noble and too complete in every way to leave room for even a heavenward care.

### THE DOUGLAS SPRUCE

The Douglas Spruce (*Pseudotsuga Douglasii*) is one of the largest and longest-lived of the giants that flourish throughout the main pine belt, often attaining a height of nearly 200 feet, and a diameter of six or seven feet. Where the growth is not too close, the stout, spreading branches, covering more than half of the trunk, are hung with innumerable slender, drooping sprays, handsomely feathered with the short leaves which radiate at right angles all around them. This vigorous tree is ever beau-tiful, welcoming the mountain winds and the snow as well as the mellow summer light; and it maintains its youthful freshness undiminished from century to century through a thousand storms. It makes its finest appearance during the months of June and July, when the brown buds at the ends of the sprays swell and open, re-vealing the young leaves, which at first are bright yellow, making the tree appear as if covered with gay blossoms; while the pendulous bracted cones, three or four inches long, with their shell-like scales, are a constant adornment.

The young trees usually are assembled in family groups, each sapling exquisitely symmetrical. The primary branches are whorled regularly around the axis, generally in fives, while each is draped with long, feathery sprays that descend in lines as free and as finely drawn as those of falling water.

In Oregon and Washington it forms immense forests, growing tall and mast-like to a height of 300 feet, and is greatly prized as a lumber tree. Here it is scattered among other trees, or forms small groves, seldom ascending higher than 5500 feet, and never making what would be called a forest. It is not particular in its choice of soil: wet or dry, smooth or rocky, it makes out to live well on them all. Two of the largest specimens, as we have seen, are in Yosemite; one of these, more than eight feet in diameter, is growing on a moraine; the other, nearly as large, on angular blocks of granite. No other tree in the Sierra seems so much at home on earthquake taluses and many of these huge boulder-slopes are almost exclusively occupied by it.

## THE INCENSE CEDAR

Incense Cedar (*Libocedrus decurrens*), already noticed among the Yosemite trees, is quite generally distributed throughout the pine belt without exclusively occupying any considerable area, or even making extensive groves. On the warmer mountain slopes it ascends to about 5000 feet, and reaches the climate most congenial to it at a height of about 4000 feet, growing vigorously at this elevation in all kinds of soil and, in particular, it is capable of enduring more moisture about its roots than any of its companions excepting only the sequoia.

Casting your eye over the general forest from some ridge-top you can identify it by the color alone of its spiry summits, a warm yellow-green. In its youth up to the age of seventy or eighty years, none of its companions forms so strictly tapered a cone from top to bottom. As it becomes older it oftentimes grows strikingly irregular and picturesque. Large branches push out at right angles to the trunk, forming stubborn elbows and shoot up parallel with the axis. Very old trees are usually dead at the top. The flat fragrant plumes are exceedingly beautiful: no waving fern-frond is finer in form and texture. In its prime the whole tree is thatched with them, but if you would see the libocedrus in all its glory you must go to the woods in midwinter when it is laden with myriads of yellow flowers about the size of wheat grains, forming a noble illustration of Nature's immortal virility and vigor. The mature cones, about three-fourths of an inch long, borne on the ends of the plumy branchlets, serve to enrich still more the surpassing beauty of this winter-blooming tree-goldenrod.

## THE SILVER FIRS

We come now to the most regularly planted and most clearly defined of the main forest belts, composed almost exclusively of two Silver Firs—*Abies concolor* and *Abies magnifica*—extending with but little interruption 450 miles at an elevation of from 5000 to 9000 feet above the sea. In its youth *A. concolor* is a charmingly symmetrical tree with its flat plumy branches arranged in regular whorls around the whitish-gray axis which terminates in a stout, hopeful shoot, pointing straight to the zenith, like an admonishing finger. The leaves are arranged in two horizontal

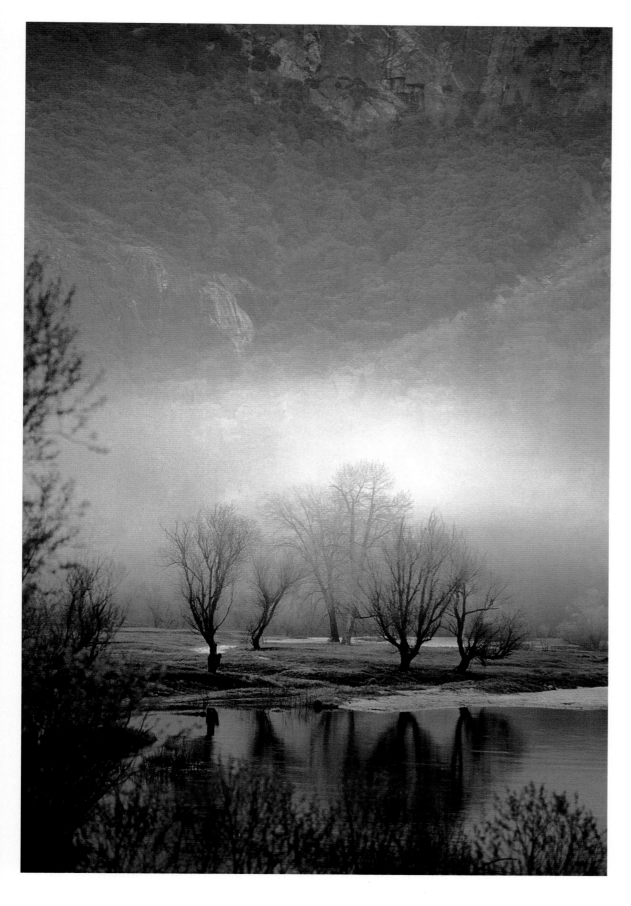

MIST OVER THE MERCED RIVER, YOSEMITE VALLEY, 1976.

"How wondrous fine are the particles in showers of dew, thousands required for a single drop, growing in the dark as silently as the grass! What pains are taken to keep this wilderness in health— showers of snow, showers of rain, showers of dew, floods of light, floods of invisible vapor, clouds, winds, all sorts of weather."

*For years I came to Yosemite because of its extraordinary cliffs and waterfalls, but scenes like this one have taught me not to overlook the more mundane features, especially when the interplay of light and moisture brings them out of their relative obscurity.*

rows along branchlets that commonly are less than eight years old, forming handsome plumes, pinnated like the fronds of ferns. The cones are grayish-green when ripe, cylindrical, from three to four inches long, and one and a half to two inches wide, and stand upright on the upper horizontal branches. Full-grown trees in favorable situations are usually about 200 feet high and five or six feet in diameter. As old age creeps on, the rough bark becomes rougher and grayer, the branches lose their exact regularity of form, many that are snow-bent are broken off and the axis often becomes double or otherwise irregular from accidents to the terminal bud or shoot. Nevertheless, throughout all the vicissitudes of its three or four centuries of life, come what may, the noble grandeur of this species, however obscured, is never lost.

The magnificent Silver Fir, or California Red Fir (*Abies magnifica*), is the most symmetrical of all the Sierra giants, far surpassing its companion species in this respect and easily distinguished from it by the purplish-red bark, which is also more closely furrowed than that of the white, and by its larger cones, its more regularly whorled and fronded branches, and its shorter leaves, which grow all around the branches and point upward instead of being arranged in two horizontal rows. The branches are mostly whorled in fives, and stand out from the straight, red-purple bole in level, or in old trees in drooping collars, every branch regularly pinnated like fern-fronds, making broad plumes, singularly rich and sumptuous-looking. The flowers are in their prime about the middle of June; the male red, growing on the underside of the branches in crowded profusion, giving a very rich color to all the trees; the female greenish-yellow, tinged with pink, standing erect on the upper side of the topmost branches, while the tufts of young leaves, about as brightly colored as those of the Douglas spruce, make another grand show. The cones mature in a single season from the flowers. When mature they are about six to eight inches long, three or four in diameter, covered with a fine gray down and streaked and beaded with transparent balsam, very rich and precious-looking, and stand erect like casks on the topmost branches. The inside of the cone is, if possible, still more beautiful. The scales and bracts are tinged with red and the seed-wings are purple with bright iridescence. Both of the silver firs live between two and three centuries when the conditions about them are at all favorable. Some venerable patriarch may be seen heavily storm-marked, towering in severe majesty above the rising generation, with a protecting grove of hopeful saplings pressing close around his feet, each dressed with such loving care that not a leaf seems wanting. Other groups are made up of trees near the prime of life, nicely arranged as if Nature had culled them with discrimination from all the rest of the woods. It is from this tree, called Red Fir by the lumbermen, that mountaineers cut boughs to sleep on when they are so fortunate as to be within its limit. Two or three rows of the sumptuous plushy-fronded branches, overlapping along the middle, and a crescent of smaller plumes mixed to one's taste with ferns and flowers for a pillow, form the very best bed imaginable. The essence of the pressed leaves seems to fill every pore of one's body. Falling water makes a soothing hush, while the spaces between the grand spires afford noble openings through which to gaze dreamily into the starry sky. The fir woods are fine sauntering-grounds at almost any time of the year, but finest in autumn when the noble trees are hushed in the hazy light and drip with balsam; and the flying, whirling seeds, escaping from the ripe cones, mottle the air like flocks of butterflies. Even in the richest part of these unrivaled forests where so many noble trees challenge

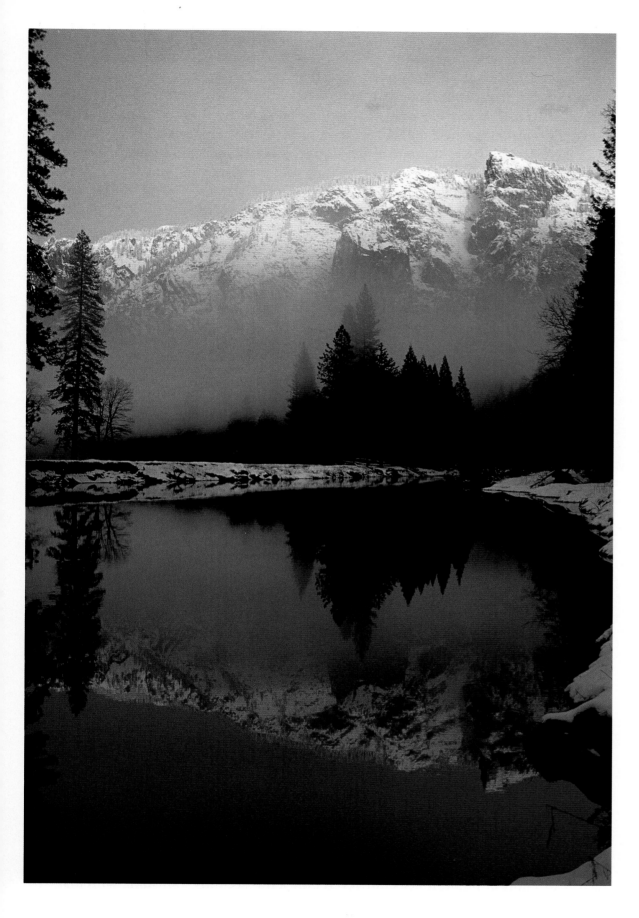

WINTER SUNSET ON TAFT POINT
FROM THE MERCED RIVER, 1986.

"When we try to pick out anything
by itself, we find it hitched to
everything else in the universe."

*Moments after I made the image of
"Twilight Mist" on page 82, I
turned around to see an equally
splendorous drama of light above
me as winter storm clouds lifted
over Taft Point. A vision of the
sunlit ridge by itself was not
complete for me. I wanted the
feeling of just how I had discovered
it, from down in the Valley beside
the river. The jumbled rocks and
rapids that had provided a fine
foreground for "Twilight Mist"
seemed too complex to match with
the ridge, so I headed upstream,
searching for just the right place to
compose a vision, as my film would
see it, of trees as silhouettes, water
as a mirror, and warm light on the
misty ridge, holding as closely as
possible to what I was seeing with
my own eyes.*

admiration we linger fondly among the colossal firs and extol their beauty again and again, as if no other tree in the world could henceforth claim our love. It is in these woods the great granite domes arise that are so striking and characteristic a feature of the Sierra. Here, too, we find the best of the garden-meadows full of lilies. A dry spot a little way back from the margin of a silver fir lily-garden makes a glorious camp-ground, especially where the slope is toward the east with a view of the distant peaks along the summit of the Range. The tall lilies are brought forward most impressively like visitors by the light of your camp-fire and the nearest of the trees with their whorled branches tower above you like larger lilies and the sky seen through the garden-opening seems one vast meadow of white lily stars.

### THE TWO-LEAVED PINE

The Two-Leaved Pine (*Pinus contorta*, var. *Murrayana*), above the Silver Fir zone, forms the bulk of the alpine forests up to a height of from 8000 to 9500 feet above the sea, growing in beautiful order on moraines scarcely changed as yet by postglacial weathering. Compared with the giants of the lower regions this is a small tree, seldom exceeding a height of eighty or ninety feet. The largest I ever measured was ninety feet high and a little over six feet in diameter. The average height of mature trees throughout the entire belt is probably not far from fifty or sixty feet with a diameter of two feet. It is a well-proportioned, rather handsome tree with grayish-brown bark and crooked, much-divided branches which cover the greater part of the trunk, but not so densely as to prevent it being seen. The lower limbs, like those of most other conifers that grow in snowy regions, curve downward, gradually take a horizontal position about half-way up the trunk, then aspire more and more toward the summit. The short, rigid needles in fascicles of two are arranged in comparatively long cylindrical tassels at the ends of the tough up-curving branches. The cones are about two inches long, growing in clusters among the needles without any striking effect except while very young, when the flowers are of a vivid crimson color and the whole tree appears to be dotted with brilliant flowers. The staminate flowers are still more showy on account of their great abundance, often giving a reddish-yellow tinge to the whole mass of foliage and filling the air with pollen. No other pine on the Range is so regularly planted as this one, covering moraines that extend along the sides of the high rocky valleys for miles without interruption. The thin bark is streaked and sprinkled with resin as though it had been showered upon the forest like rain.

Therefore this tree more than any other is subject to destruction by fire. During strong winds extensive forests are destroyed, the flames leaping from tree to tree in continuous belts that go surging and racing onward above the bending wood like prairie-grass fires. During the calm season of Indian summer the fire creeps quietly along the ground, feeding on the needles and cones; arriving at the foot of a tree, the resiny bark is ignited and the heated air ascends in a swift current, increasing in velocity and dragging the flames upward. Then the leaves catch, forming an immense column of fire, beautifully spired on the edges and tinted a rose-purple hue. It rushes aloft thirty or forty feet above the top of the tree, forming a grand spectacle, especially at night. It lasts, however, only a few seconds, vanishing with magical rapidity, to be succeeded by others along the fire-line at irregular intervals, tree after tree, upflashing and darting, leaving the trunks and branches scarcely scarred. The heat, however, is sufficient to kill the tree and in a few years the bark shrivels and falls off. Forests miles in extent are thus killed and left standing, with the branches on, but peeled and rigid, appearing gray in the distance like misty clouds. Later the branches drop off, leaving a forest of bleached spars. At length the roots decay and the forlorn gray trunks are blown down during some storm and piled one upon another, encumbering the ground until, dry and seasoned, they are consumed by another fire and leave the ground ready for a fresh crop.

In sheltered lake-hollows, on beds of alluvium, this pine varies so far from the common form that frequently it could be taken for a distinct species, growing in damp sods like grasses from forty to eighty feet high, bending all together to the breeze and whirling in eddying gusts more lively than any other tree in the woods. I frequently found specimens fifty feet high less than five inches in diameter. Being so slender and at the same time clad with leafy boughs, it is often bent and weighed down to the ground when laden with soft snow; thus forming fine ornamental arches, many of them to last until the melting of the snow in the spring.

### THE MOUNTAIN PINE

The Mountain Pine (*Pinus monticola*) is the noblest tree of the alpine zone—hardy and long-lived, towering grandly above its companions and becoming stronger and more imposing just where other species begin to crouch and disappear. At its best it is usually about ninety feet high and five or six feet in diameter, though you may find specimens here and there considerably larger than this. It is as massive and suggestive of enduring strength as an oak. About two-thirds of the trunk is commonly free of limbs, but close, fringy tufts of spray occur nearly all the way down to the ground. On trees that occupy exposed situations near its upper limit the bark is deep reddish-brown and rather deeply furrowed, the main furrows running nearly parallel to each other and connected on the old trees by conspicuous cross-furrows. The cones are from four to eight inches long, smooth, slender, cylindrical and somewhat curved. They grow in clusters of from three to six or seven and become pendulous as they increase in weight. This species is nearly related to the sugar pine and, though not half so tall, it suggests its noble relative in the way that it extends its long branches in general habit. It is first met on the upper margin of the silver fir zone, singly, in what appears as chance situations without making much impression on the general forest. Continuing up through the forests of the two-leaved pine it begins to show its distinguishing characteristic in the most marked way at an elevation of about 10,000 feet, extending its tough, rather slender arms in the frosty air, welcoming the storms and feeding on them and reaching sometimes to the grand old age of 1000 years.

### THE WESTERN JUNIPER

The Juniper, or Red Cedar (*Juniperus occidentalis*), is preëminently a rock tree, occupying the baldest domes and pavements in the upper silver fir and alpine zones, at a height of from 7000 to 9500 feet. In such situations, rooted in narrow cracks or fissures, where there is scarcely a handful of soil, it is frequently over eight feet in diameter and not much more in height. The tops of old trees are almost always dead, and large stubborn-looking limbs push out horizontally, most of them broken and dead at the end, but densely covered, and imbedded here and there with tufts or mounds of gray-green scale-like foliage. Some trees are mere storm-beaten stumps about as broad as long, decorated with a few leafy sprays, reminding one of the crumbling towers of old castles scantily draped with ivy. Its homes on bare, barren dome and ridge-top seem to have been chosen for safety against fire, for, on isolated mounds of sand and gravel free from grass and bushes on which fire could feed, it is often found growing tall and unscathed to a height of forty to sixty feet, with scarce a trace of the rocky angularity and broken limbs so characteristic a feature throughout the greater part of its range. It never makes anything like a forest; seldom even a grove. Usually it stands out separate and independent, clinging by slight joints to the rocks, living chiefly on snow and thin air and maintaining sound health on this diet for 2000 years or more. Every feature or every gesture it makes expresses steadfast, dogged endurance. The bark is of a bright cinnamon color and is handsomely braided and reticulated on thrifty trees, flaking off in thin, shining ribbons that are sometimes used by the Indians for tent matting. Its fine color and picturesqueness are appreciated by artists, but to me the juniper seems a singularly strange and taciturn tree. I have spent many a day and night in its company and always have found it silent and rigid. It seems to be a survivor of some ancient race, wholly unacquainted with its neighbors. Its broad stumpiness, of course, makes wind-waving or even shaking out of the question, but it is not this rocky rigidity that constitutes its silence. In calm, sun-days the sugar pine preaches like an enthusiastic apostle without moving a leaf. On level rocks the juniper dies standing and wastes insensibly out of existence like granite, the wind exerting about as little control over it, alive or dead, as it does over a glacier boulder.

I have spent a good deal of time trying to determine the age of these wonderful trees, but as all of the very old ones are honeycombed with dry rot I never was able to get a complete count of the largest. Some are undoubtedly more than 2000 years old, for though on deep moraine soil they grow about as fast as some of the pines, on bare pavements and smoothly glaciated, overswept ridges in the dome region they grow very slowly. One on the Starr King Ridge only two feet eleven inches in diameter was 1140 years old forty years ago. Another on the same ridge, only one foot seven and a half inches in diameter, had reached the age of 834 years. The first fifteen inches from the bark of a medium-size tree six feet in diameter, on the north Tenaya pavement, had 859 layers of wood. Beyond this the count was stopped by dry rot and scars. The largest I examined was thirty-three feet in girth, or nearly ten feet in diameter and, although I have failed to get anything like a complete count, I learned enough from this and many other specimens to convince me that most of the trees eight or ten feet thick, standing on pavements, are more than twenty centuries old rather than less. Barring accidents, for all I can see they would live forever; even when overthrown by avalanches, they refuse to lie at rest, lean stubbornly on their big branches as if anxious to rise, and while a single root holds to the rock, put forth fresh leaves with a grim, never-say-die expression.

### THE MOUNTAIN HEMLOCK

As the juniper is the most stubborn and unshakeable of trees in the Yosemite region, the Mountain Hemlock (*Tsuga Mertensiana*) is the most graceful and pliant and sensitive. Until it reaches a height of fifty or sixty feet it is sumptuously clothed down to the ground with drooping branches, which are divided again and again into delicate waving sprays, grouped and arranged in ways that are indescribably beautiful, and profusely adorned with small brown cones. The flowers also are peculiarly beautiful and effective; the female dark rich purple, the male blue, of so

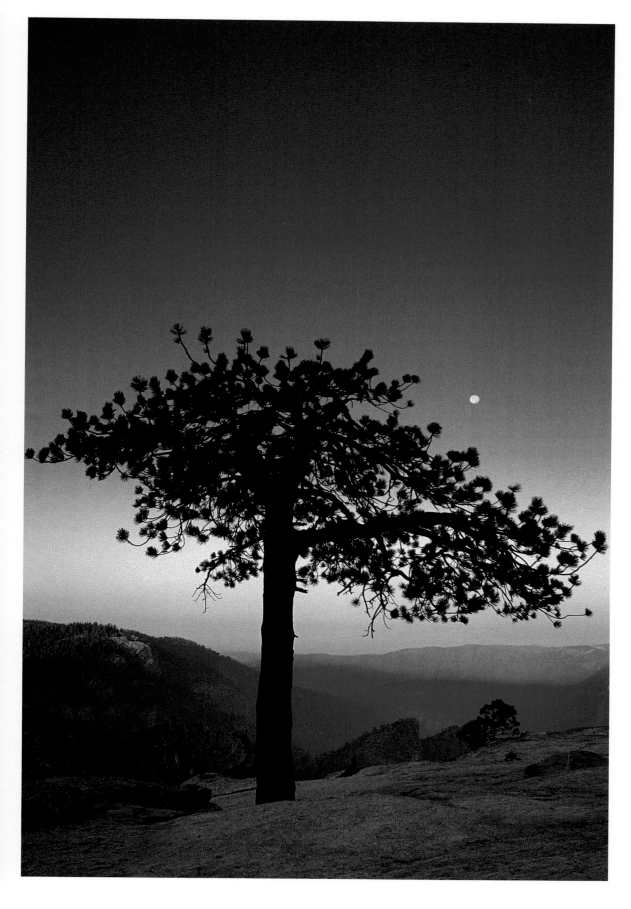

JEFFREY PINE ON TAFT POINT
OVERLOOKING YOSEMITE
VALLEY, 1987.

"Few are altogether deaf to the
preaching of pine trees. Their
sermons on the mountains go to our
hearts; and if people in general
could be got into the woods, even
for once, to hear the trees speak for
themselves, all difficulties in the way
of forest preservation
would vanish."

*In the predawn twilight, as I
readied my camera to photograph
first light on El Capitan, I noticed
the sudden congruity of the setting
moon, a lone pine, and the colored
bands of the earth shadow
descending in the sky. My intended
image of El Capitan was not nearly
as successful, partly because it was
a distant scene made from the
Valley rim rather than an intimate
scene using the rim itself as subject
matter. A few minutes after this
image was made, the rising sun
obliterated the soft, muted tones
that closely matched my feeling of
being there.*

fine and pure a tone that the best azure of the mountain sky seems to be condensed in them. Though apparently the most delicate and feminine of all the mountain trees, it grows best where the snow lies deepest, at a height of from 9000 to 9500 feet, in hollows on the northern slopes of mountains and ridges. But under all circumstances, sheltered from heavy winds or in bleak exposure to them, well fed or starved, even at its highest limit, 10,500 feet above the sea, on exposed ridge-tops where it has to crouch and huddle close in low thickets, it still contrives to put forth its sprays and branches in forms of invincible beauty, while on moist, well-drained moraines it displays a perfectly tropical luxuriance of foliage, flowers and fruit. The snow of the first winter storm is frequently soft, and lodges in the dense leafy branches, weighing them down against the trunk, and the slender, drooping axis, bending lower and lower as the load increases, at length reaches the ground, forming an ornamental arch. Then, as storm succeeds storm and snow is heaped on snow, the whole tree is at last buried, not again to see the light of day or move leaf or limb until set free by the spring thaws in June or July. Not only the young saplings are thus carefully covered and put to sleep in the whitest of white beds for five or six months of the year, but trees thirty feet high or more. From April to May, when the snow by repeated thawing and freezing is firmly compacted, you may ride over the prostrate groves without seeing a single branch or leaf of them. No other of our alpine conifers so finely veils its strength; poised in thin, white sunshine, clad with branches from head to foot, it towers in unassuming majesty, drooping as if unaffected with the aspiring tendencies of its race, loving the ground, conscious of heaven and joyously receptive of its blessings, reaching out its branches like sensitive tentacles, feeling the light and reveling in it. The largest specimen I ever found was nineteen feet seven inches in circumference. It was growing on the edge of Lake Hollow, north of Mount Hoffman, at an elevation of 9250 feet above the level of the sea, and was probably about a hundred feet in height. Fine groves of mature trees, ninety to a hundred feet in height, are growing near the base of Mount Conness. It is widely distributed from near the south extremity of the High Sierra northward along the Cascade Mountains of Oregon and Washington and the coast ranges of British Columbia to Alaska, where it was first discovered in 1827. Its northernmost limit, so far as I have observed, is in the icy fiords of Prince William Sound in latitude 61°, where it forms pure forests at the level of the sea, growing tall and majestic on the banks of glaciers. There, as in the Yosemite region, it is ineffably beautiful, the very loveliest of all the American conifers.

### THE WHITE-BARK PINE

The Dwarf Pine, or White-Bark Pine (*Pinus albicaulis*), forms the extreme edge of the timber-line throughout nearly the whole extent of the Range on both flanks. It is first met growing with the two-leaved pine on the upper margin of the alpine belt, as an erect tree from fifteen to thirty feet high and from one to two feet in diameter; thence it goes straggling up the flanks of the summit peaks, upon moraines or crumbling ledges, wherever it can get a foothold, to an elevation of from 10,000 to 12,000 feet, where it dwarfs to a mass of crumpled branches, covered with slender shoots, each tipped with a short, close-packed, leaf tassel. The bark is smooth and purplish, in some places almost white. The flowers are bright scarlet and rose-purple, giving a very flowery appearance little looked for in such a tree. The cones are about three inches long, an inch and a half in diameter, grow in rigid clusters,

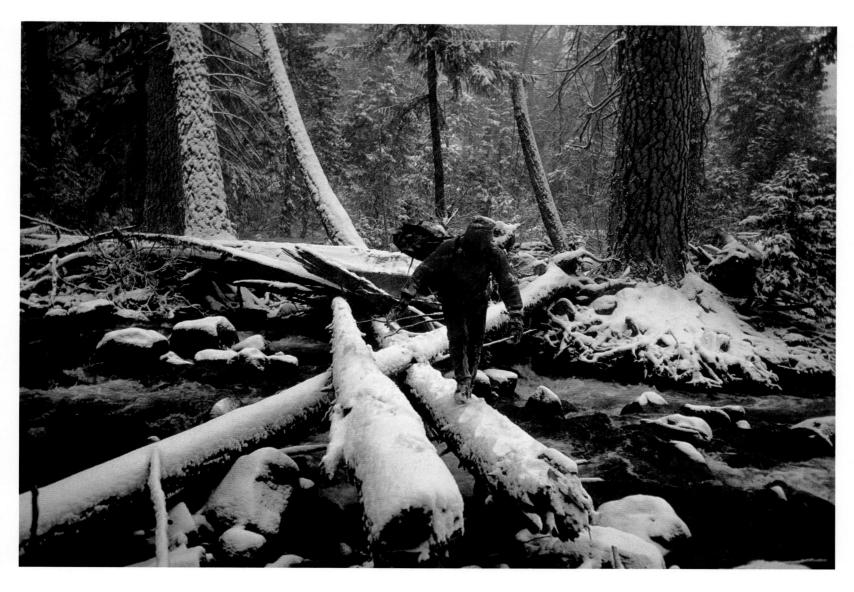

CROSSING FALLS CREEK IN
WINTER, HETCH HETCHY, 1970.

"Only by going alone in silence,
without baggage, can one truly get
into the heart of the wilderness. All
other travel is mere dust and hotels
and baggage and chatter."

*Crossing a raging stream on a
slippery log, Joe Faint and I gain an
inkling about what Muir must have
experienced countless times in his
ramblings where there were no
trails. As we retreated from a climb
in a storm, crashing through
deadfall for hours, we kept trying to
convince ourselves that although we
had no idea where we were at the
moment, we definitely were
not lost.*

and are dark chocolate in color while young, and bear beautiful pearly-white seeds about the size of peas, most of which are eaten by chipmunks and the Clarke's crows. Pines are commonly regarded as sky-loving trees that must necessarily aspire or die. This species forms a marked exception, crouching and creeping in compliance with the most rigorous demands of climate; yet enduring bravely to a more advanced age than many of its lofty relatives in the sun-lands far below it. Seen from a distance it would never be taken for a tree of any kind. For example, on Cathedral Peak there is a scattered growth of this pine, creeping like mosses over the roof, nowhere giving hint of an ascending axis. While, approached quite near, it still appears matty and heathy, and one experiences no difficulty in walking over the top of it, yet it is seldom absolutely prostrate, usually attaining a height of three or four feet with a main trunk, and with branches outspread above it, as if in ascending they had been checked by a ceiling against which they had been compelled to spread horizontally. The winter snow *is* a sort of ceiling, lasting half the year; while the pressed surface is made yet smoother by violent winds armed with cutting sand-grains that bear down any shoot which offers to rise much above the general level, and that carve the dead trunks and branches in beautiful patterns.

During stormy nights I have often camped snugly beneath the interlacing arches of this little pine. The needles, which have accumulated for centuries, make fine beds, a fact well known to other mountaineers, such as deer and wild sheep, who paw out oval hollows and lie beneath the larger trees in safe and comfortable concealment. This lowly dwarf reaches a far greater age than would be guessed. A specimen that I examined, growing at an elevation of 10,700 feet, yet looked as though it might be plucked up by the roots, for it was only three and a half inches in diameter and its topmost tassel reached hardly three feet above the ground. Cutting it half through and counting the annual rings with the aid of a lens, I found its age to be no less than 255 years. Another specimen about the same height, with a trunk six inches in diameter, I found to be 426 years old, forty years ago; and one of its supple branchlets hardly an eighth of an inch in diameter inside the bark, was seventy-five years old, and so filled with oily balsam and seasoned by storms that I tied it in knots like a whip-cord.

### THE NUT PINE

In going across the Range from the Tuolumne River Soda Springs to Mono Lake one makes the acquaintance of the curious little Nut Pine (*Pinus monophylla*). It dots the eastern flank of the Sierra to which it is mostly restricted in grayish bush-like patches, from the margin of the sage-plains to an elevation of from 7000 to 8000 feet. A more contented, fruitful and unaspiring conifer could not be conceived. All the species we have been sketching make departures more or less distant from the typical spire form, but none goes so far as this. Without any apparent cause it keeps near the ground, throwing out crooked, divergent branches like an orchard apple-tree, and seldom pushes a single shoot higher than fifteen or twenty feet above the ground.

The average thickness of the trunk is, perhaps, about ten or twelve inches. The leaves are mostly undivided, like round awls, instead of being separated, like those of other pines, into twos and threes and fives. The cones are green while growing, and are usually found over all the tree, forming quite a marked feature as seen against the bluish-gray foliage. They are quite small, only about two inches in length, and seem to have but little space for seeds; but when we come to open them, we find that about half the entire bulk of the cone is made up of sweet, nutritious nuts, nearly as large as hazel-nuts. This is undoubtedly the most important food-tree on the Sierra, and furnishes the Mona, Carson, and Walker River Indians with more and better nuts than all the other species taken together. It is the Indian's own tree, and many a white man have they killed for cutting it down. Being so low, the cones are readily beaten off with poles, and the nuts procured by roasting them until the scales open. In bountiful seasons a single Indian may gather thirty or forty bushels.

ALPENGLOW ON STORM CLOUDS,
YOSEMITE VALLEY, 1986.

"Sauntering on the meadows, I
noticed a massive crimson cloud
growing in solitary grandeur above
the Cathedral Rocks, its form
scarcely less striking than its
color. . . . All its parts were colored
like, making one mass of
translucent crimson. . . . Next
morning the snow on the meadows
was about ten inches deep."

*For years I tried to photograph
alpenglow on clouds over the Valley
without much success, both because
the glow reaches its height when the
Valley is in especially deep shadow
and because the eye sees a far
greater range of brightness than
color film does. One late winter
morning, however, I found the ideal
situation to make this image
succeed. Snow added detail to the
black-shadowed north wall of
Sentinel Rock and its surrounding
cliffs, and a pool in a meadow filled
the foreground with reflected light
and color. I used a graduated
neutral-density filter to hold the
exposure on the rich, red sky while
opening up the shadow values in the
lower regions.*

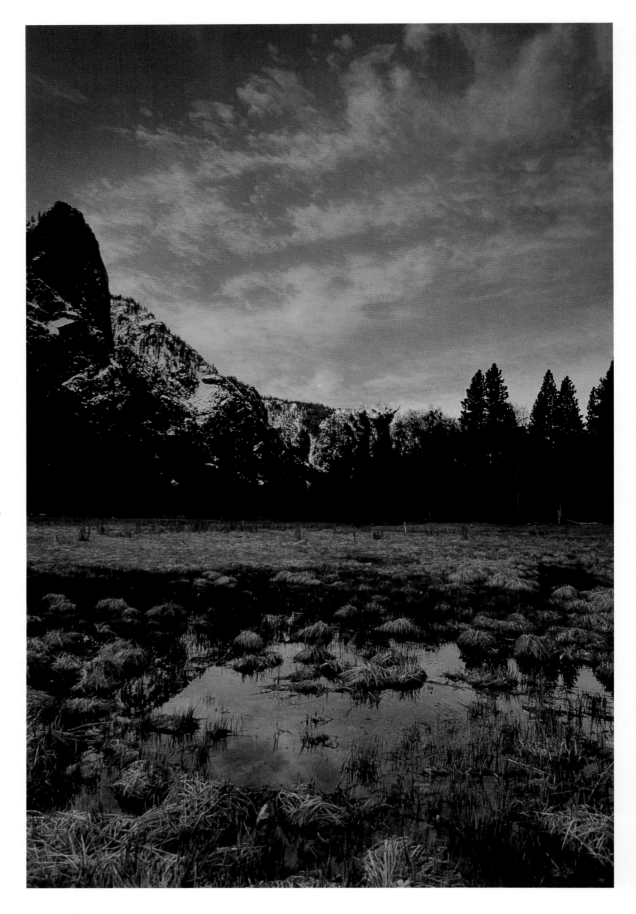

CHAPTER VII

# The Big Trees

BETWEEN THE HEAVY PINE and silver fir zones towers the Big Tree (*Sequoia gigantea*), the king of all the conifers in the world, "the noblest of the noble race." The groves nearest Yosemite Valley are about twenty miles to the westward and southward and are called the Tuolumne, Merced and Mariposa groves. It extends, a widely interrupted belt, from a very small grove on the middle fork of the American River to the head of Deer Creek, a distance of about 260 miles, its northern limit being near the thirty-ninth parallel, the southern a little below the thirty-sixth. The elevation of the belt above the sea varies from about 5000 to 8000 feet. From the American River to Kings River the species occurs only in small isolated groups so sparsely distributed along the belt that three of the gaps in it are from forty to sixty miles wide. But from Kings River southward the sequoia is not restricted to mere groves but extends across the wide rugged basins of the Kaweah and Tule Rivers in noble forests, a distance of nearly seventy miles, the continuity of this part of the belt being broken only by the main cañons. The Fresno, the largest of the northern groves, has an area of three or four square miles, a short distance to the southward of the famous Mariposa grove. Along the south rim of the cañon of the south fork of Kings River there is a majestic sequoia forest about six miles long by two wide. This is the northernmost group that may fairly be called a forest. Descending the divide between the Kings and Kaweah Rivers you come to the grand forests that form the main continuous portion of the belt. Southward the giants become more and more irrepressibly exuberant, heaving their massive crowns into the sky from every ridge and slope, waving onward in graceful compliance with the complicated topography of the region. The finest of the Kaweah section of the belt is on the broad ridge between Marble Creek and the middle fork, and is called the Giant Forest. It extends from the granite headlands, overlooking the hot San Joaquin plains, to within a few miles of the cool glacial fountains of the summit peaks. The extreme upper limit of the belt is reached between the middle and south forks of the Kaweah at a height of 8400 feet, but the finest block of big tree forests in the entire belt is on the north fork of Tule River, and is included in the Sequoia National Park.

In the northern groves there are comparatively few young trees or saplings. But here for every old storm-beaten giant there are many in their prime and for each of these a crowd of hopeful young trees and saplings, growing vigorously on moraines, rocky ledges, along water courses and meadows. But though the area occupied by the big tree increases so greatly from north to south, there is no marked increase in the size of the trees. The height of 275 feet or thereabouts and a diameter of about twenty feet, four feet from the ground is, perhaps, about the average size of what may be called full-grown trees, where they are favorably located. The specimens

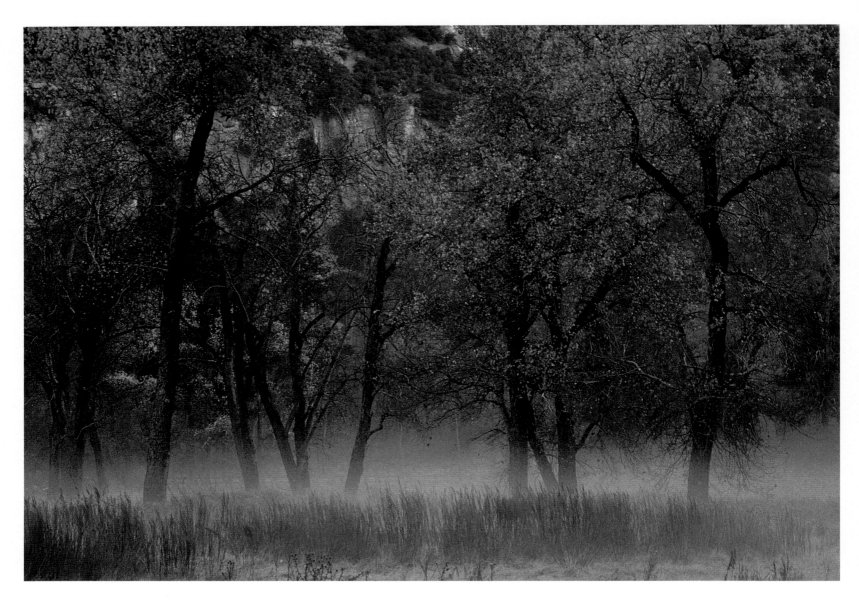

FALL COLORS IN MORNING MIST,
YOSEMITE VALLEY, 1986.

"It was one of those brooding,
changeful days that come between
the Indian summer and winter,
when . . . the clouds come and go
among the cliffs like living creatures
looking for work."

*Soon after the first fall frosts in the
Valley, morning mists begin as
evanescent streamers of soft
whiteness linked to the lowest,
coolest air that has sunk from the
heights overnight. A few minutes of
light or a breeze will clear the air,
and thus a photographer must be
ready to pursue these natural light
banks well before dawn. When I
first arrived at this scene, not only
the trees, but also my camera
position, were locked in a pea-soup
fog. Gradually the veil pulled back
to expose the trees, perfectly fringed
with soft light, minutes before the
sun's rays made the mist vanish.*

THE BIG TREES 123

twenty-five feet in diameter are not very rare and a few are nearly three hundred feet high. In the Calaveras grove there are four trees over 300 feet in height, the tallest of which as measured by the Geological Survey is 325 feet. The very largest that I have yet met in the course of my explorations is a majestic old fire-scarred monument in the Kings River forest. It is thirty-five feet and eight inches in diameter inside the bark, four feet above the ground. It is burned half through, and I spent a day in clearing away the charred surface with a sharp ax and counting the annual wood-rings with the aid of a pocket lens. I succeeded in laying bare a section all the way from the outside to the heart and counted a little over four thousand rings, showing that this tree was in its prime about twenty-seven feet in diameter at the beginning of the Christian era. No other tree in the world, as far as I know, has looked down on so many centuries as the sequoia or opens so many impressive and suggestive views into history. Under the most favorable conditions these giants probably live 5000 years or more, though few of even the larger trees are half as old. The age of one that was felled in Calaveras grove, for the sake of having its stump for a dancing-floor, was about 1300 years, and its diameter measured across the stump twenty-four feet inside the bark. Another that was felled in the Kings River forest was about the same size but nearly a thousand years older (2200 years), though not a very old-looking tree.

So harmonious and finely balanced are even the mightiest of these monarchs in all their proportions that there is never anything overgrown or monstrous about them. Seeing them for the first time you are more impressed with their beauty than their size, their grandeur being in great part invisible; but sooner or later it becomes manifest to the loving eye, stealing slowly on the senses like the grandeur of Niagara or of the Yosemite Domes. When you approach them and walk around them you begin to wonder at their colossal size and try to measure them. They bulge considerably at the base, but not more than is required for beauty and safety and the only reason that this bulging seems in some cases excessive is that only a comparatively small section is seen in near views. One that I measured in the Kings River forest was twenty-five feet in diameter at the ground and ten feet in diameter 220 feet above the ground, showing the fineness of the taper of the trunk as a whole. No description can give anything like an adequate idea of their singular majesty, much less of their beauty. Except the sugar pine, most of their neighbors with pointed tops seem ever trying to go higher, while the big tree, soaring above them all, seems satisfied. Its grand domed head seems to be poised about as lightly as a cloud, giving no impression of seeking to rise higher. Only when it is young does it show like other conifers a heavenward yearning, sharply aspiring with a long quick-growing top. Indeed, the whole tree for the first century or two, or until it is a hundred or one hundred and fifty feet high, is arrowhead in form, and, compared with the solemn rigidity of age, seems as sensitive to the wind as a squirrel's tail. As it grows older, the lower branches are gradually dropped and the upper ones thinned out until comparatively few are left. These, however, are developed to a great size, divide again and again and terminate in bossy, rounded masses of leafy branchlets, while the head becomes dome-shaped, and is the first to feel the touch of the rosy beams of the morning, the last to bid the sun good night. Perfect specimens, unhurt by running fires or lightning, are singularly regular and symmetrical in general form, though not in the least conventionalized, for they show extraordinary variety in the unity and harmony of their general outline. The immensely strong, stately shafts are free of limbs for one hundred and fifty feet or so. The large limbs reach out with equal boldness in every direction, showing no weather side, and no other tree has foliage so densely massed, so finely molded in outline and so perfectly subordinate to an ideal type. A particularly knotty, angular, ungovernable-looking branch, from five to seven or eight feet in diameter and perhaps a thousand years old, may occasionally be seen pushing out from the trunk as if determined to break across the bounds of the regular curve, but like all the others it dissolves in bosses of branchlets and sprays as soon as the general outline is approached. Except in picturesque old age, after being struck by lightning or broken by thousands of snow-storms, the regularity of forms is one of their most distinguishing characteristics. Another is the simple beauty of the trunk and its great thickness as compared with its height and the width of the branches, which makes them look more like finely modeled and sculptured architectural columns than the stems of trees, while the great limbs look like rafters, supporting the magnificent dome-head. But though so consummately beautiful, the big tree always seems unfamiliar, with peculiar physiognomy, awfully solemn and earnest; yet with all its strangeness it impresses us as being more at home than any of its neighbors, holding the best right to the ground as the oldest, strongest inhabitant. One soon becomes acquainted with new species of pine and fir and spruce as with friendly people, shaking their outstretched branches like shaking hands and fondling their little ones, while the venerable aboriginal sequoia, ancient of other days, keeps you at a distance, looking as strange in aspect and behavior among its neighbor trees as would the mastodon among the homely bears and deer. Only the Sierra juniper is at all like it, standing rigid and unconquerable on glacier pavements for thousands of years, grim and silent, with an air of antiquity about as pronounced as that of the sequoia.

The bark of the largest trees is from one to two feet thick, rich cinnamon brown, purplish on young trees, forming magnificent masses of color with the underbrush. Toward the end of winter the trees are in bloom, while the snow is still eight or ten feet deep. The female flowers are about three-eighths of an inch long, pale green, and grow in countless thousands on the ends of sprays. The male are still more abundant, pale yellow, a fourth of an inch long and when the pollen is ripe they color the whole tree and dust the air and the ground. The cones are bright grass-green in color, about two and a half inches long, one and a half wide, made up of thirty or forty strong, closely-packed, rhomboidal scales, with four to eight seeds at the base of each. The seeds are wonderfully small and light, being only from an eighth to a fourth of an inch long and wide, including a filmy surrounding wing, which causes them to glint and waver in falling and enables the wind to carry them considerable distances. Unless harvested by the squirrels, the cones discharge their seed and remain on the tree for many years. In fruitful seasons the trees are fairly laden. On two small branches one and a half and two inches in diameter I counted 480 cones. No other California conifer produces nearly so many seeds, except, perhaps, the other sequoia, the Redwood of the Coast Mountains. Millions are ripened annually by a single tree, and in a fruitful year the product of one of the northern groves would be enough to plant all the mountain ranges in the world.

As soon as any accident happens to the crown, such as being smashed off by lightning, the branches beneath the wound, no matter how situated, seem to be excited, like a colony of bees that have lost their queen, and become anxious to repair the damage. Limbs that have grown outward for centuries at right angles to

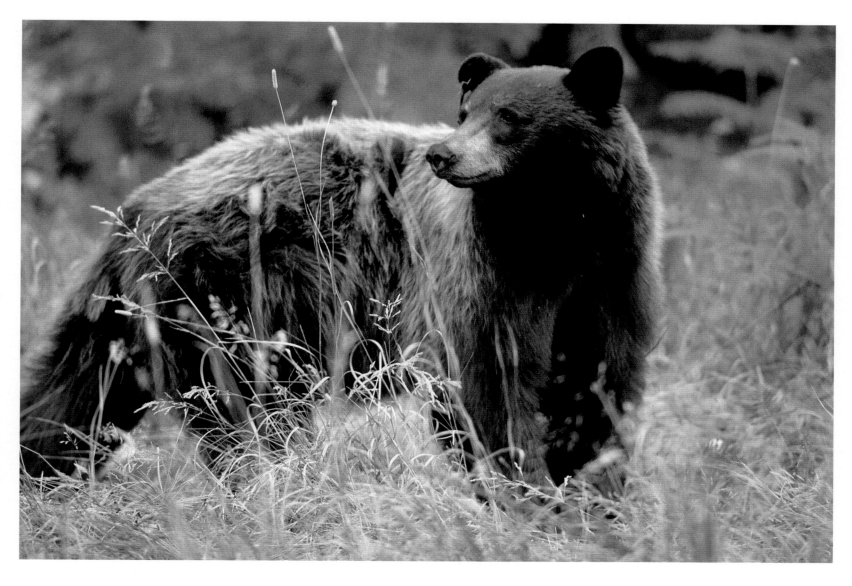

BLACK BEAR, YOSEMITE
VALLEY, 1987.

"Bears are made of the same dust as we, and breathe the same winds and drink of the same waters. . . . [A bear's] life not long, not short, knows no beginning, no ending. To him life unstinted, unplanned, is above the accidents of time, and his years, markless and boundless, equal Eternity. God bless Yosemite bears!"

*Late one evening I was walking beside the Merced River when I surprised a bear just ten feet from me. Instead of running away, the bear ran in front of me and dived into the river with a loud splash. Intrigued, I chased after him, crossing the river on a log. He headed into the old orchard near*

*Camp Curry in search of apples. As I focused my telephoto lens, I saw that the bear looked exceptionally lean and hungry. The year had been dry, and the berry crop was poor. Without extra body fat, the bear's resemblance to a dog was striking. I felt a sense of closeness beyond physical distance, and was reminded that here was a being whose evolutionary development had many parallels to my own. The ancestors of modern bears split from the dog family during the same era that my progenitors separated from the ancestors of modern apes. During the ice ages, a wave of giantism swept through almost all mammals living in northern climates. Bears emerged with enlarged bodies, yet with the same sort of wild nature as their*

*canine cousins: curious, impulsive, unpredictable, and imaginatively destructive. Humans emerged from the same era with relatively small bodies and enlarged brains. Or, as one park biologist aptly put it, "At the root of the bear problem is a considerable overlap between the intelligence of the smartest bear and the dumbest visitor."*

the trunk begin to turn upward to assist in making a new crown, each speedily assuming the special form of true summits. Even in the case of mere stumps, burned half through, some mere ornamental tuft will try to go aloft and do its best as a leader in forming a new head. Groups of two or three are often found standing close together, the seeds from which they sprang having probably grown on ground cleared for their reception by the fall of a large tree of a former generation. They are called "loving couples," "three graces," etc. When these trees are young they are seen to stand twenty or thirty feet apart, by the time they are full-grown their trunks will touch and crowd against each other and in some cases even appear as one.

It is generally believed that the sequoia was once far more widely distributed over the Sierra; but after long and careful study I have come to the conclusion that it never was, at least since the close of the glacial period, because a diligent search along the margins of the groves, and in the gaps between fails to reveal a single trace of its previous existence beyond its present bounds. Notwithstanding, I feel confident that if every sequoia in the Range were to die to-day, numerous monuments of their existence would remain, of so imperishable a nature as to be available for the student more than ten thousand years hence.

In the first place, no species of coniferous tree in the Range keeps its members so well together as the sequoia; a mile is, perhaps, the greatest distance of any straggler from the main body, and all of those stragglers that have come under my observation are young, instead of old monumental trees, relics of a more extended growth.

Again, the great trunks of the sequoia last for centuries after they fall. I have a specimen block of sequoia wood, cut from a fallen tree, which is hardly distinguishable from a similar section cut from a living tree, although the one cut from the fallen trunk has certainly lain on the damp forest floor more than 380 years, probably thrice as long. The time-measure in the case is simply this: When the ponderous trunk to which the old vestige belonged fell, it sunk itself into the ground, thus making a long, straight ditch, and in the middle of this ditch a silver fir four feet in diameter and 380 years old was growing, as I determined by cutting it half through and counting the rings, thus demonstrating that the remnant of the trunk that made the ditch has lain on the ground *more* than 380 years. For it is evident that, to find the whole time, we must add to the 380 years the time that the vanished portion of the trunk lay in the ditch before being burned out of the way, plus the time that passed before the seed from which the monumental fir sprang fell into the prepared soil and took root. Now, because sequoia trunks are never wholly consumed in one forest fire, and those fires recur only at considerable intervals, and because sequoia ditches after being cleared are often left unplanted for centuries, it becomes evident that the trunk-remnant in question may probably have lain a thousand years or more. And this instance is by no means a rare one.

Again, admitting that upon those areas supposed to have been once covered with sequoia forests, every tree may have fallen, and every trunk may have been burned or buried, leaving not a remnant, many of the ditches made by the fall of the ponderous trunks, and the bowls made by their upturning roots, would remain patent for thousands of years after the last vestige of the trunks that made them had vanished. Much of this ditch-writing would no doubt be quickly effaced by the flood-action of overflowing streams and rain-washing; but no inconsiderable portion would remain enduringly engraved on ridge-tops beyond such destructive action; for, where all the conditions are favorable, it is almost imperishable. Now these

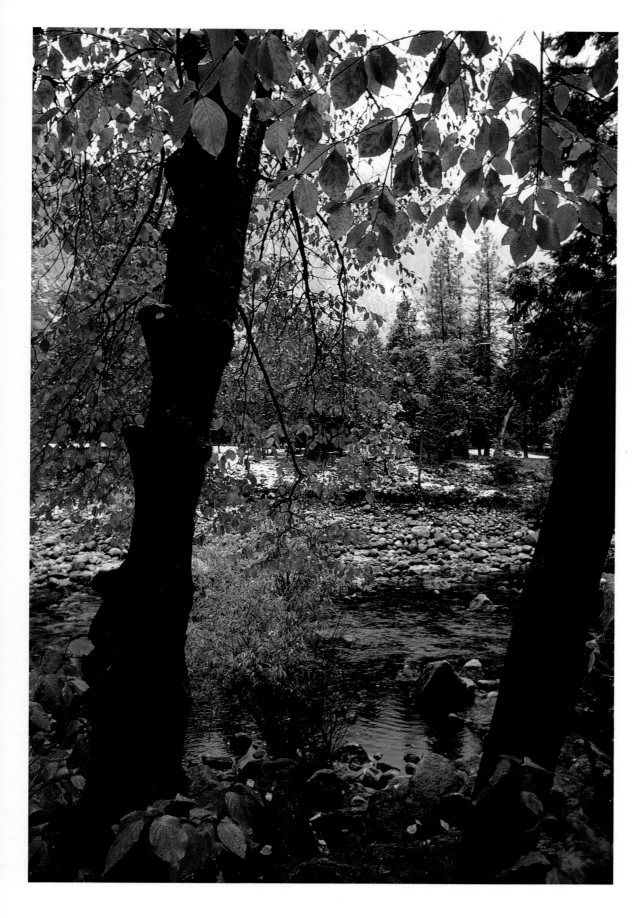

FALL COLORS BELOW BRIDALVEIL FALL, 1978.

"The world needs the woods, and is beginning to come to them; but it is not yet ready for the fine banks and braes of the lower Sierra, any more than for storms. Tourists make their way through the foot-hill landscapes as if blind to all their best beauty, and like children seek the emphasized mountains."

*I stopped to photograph this scene because I saw the trees and leaves as a nice frame for an image of Bridalveil Fall and Leaning Tower. While looking through the lens, I decided that the foreground was plenty interesting in its own right. I purposely hid my intended subjects behind the foliage, made this image, and then shot another, more typical one of the fall. When I later compared the two, there was no question in my mind that the low Sierra river's edge scene was more evocative without grandiose cliffs and waterfalls to draw away the eye.*

historic ditches and root-bowls occur in all the present sequoia groves and forests, but, as far as I have observed, not the faintest vestige of one presents itself outside of them.

We therefore conclude that the area covered by sequoia has not been diminished during the last eight or ten thousand years, and probably not at all in post-glacial time. Nevertheless, the questions may be asked: Is the species verging toward extinction? What are its relations to climate, soil, and associated trees?

All the phenomena bearing on these questions also throw light, as we shall endeavor to show, upon the peculiar distribution of the species, and sustain the conclusion already arrived at as to the question of former extension. In the northern groups, as we have seen, there are few young trees or saplings growing up around the old ones to perpetuate the race, and inasmuch as those aged sequoias, so nearly childless, are the only ones commonly known, the species, to most observers, seems doomed to speedy extinction, as being nothing more than an expiring remnant, vanquished in the so-called struggle for life by pines and firs that have driven it into its last strongholds in moist glens where the climate is supposed to be exceptionally favorable. But the story told by the majestic continuous forests of the south creates a very different impression. No tree in the forest is more enduringly established in concordance with both climate and soil. It grows heartily everywhere—on moraines, rocky ledges, along watercourses, and in the deep, moist alluvium of meadows with, as we have seen, a multitude of seedlings and saplings crowding up around the aged, abundantly able to maintain the forest in prime vigor. So that if all the trees of any section of the main sequoia forest were ranged together according to age, a very promising curve would be presented, all the way up from last year's seedlings to giants, and with the young and middle-aged portion of the curve many times longer than the old portion. Even as far north as the Fresno, I counted 536 saplings and seedlings, growing promisingly upon a landslip not exceeding two acres in area. This soil-bed was about seven years old, and had been seeded almost simultaneously by pines, firs, libocedrus, and sequoia, presenting a simple and instructive illustration of the struggle for life among the rival species; and it was interesting to note that the conditions thus far affecting them have enabled the young sequoias to gain a marked advantage. Toward the south where the sequoia becomes most exuberant and numerous, the rival trees become less so; and where they mix with sequoias they grow up beneath them like slender grasses among stalks of Indian corn. Upon a bed of sandy flood-soil I counted ninety-four sequoias, from one to twelve feet high, on a patch of ground once occupied by four large sugar pines which lay crumbling beneath them—an instance of conditions which have enabled sequoias to crowd out the pines. I also noted eighty-six vigorous saplings upon a piece of fresh ground prepared for their reception by fire. Thus fire, the great destroyer of the sequoia, also furnishes the bare ground required for its growth from the seed. Fresh ground is, however, furnished in sufficient quantities for the renewal of the forests without the aid of fire—by the fall of old trees. The soil is thus upturned and mellowed, and many trees are planted for every one that falls.

It is constantly asserted in a vague way that the Sierra was vastly wetter than now, and that the increasing drought will of itself extinguish the sequoia, leaving its ground to other trees supposed capable of flourishing in a drier climate. But that the sequoia can and does grow on as dry ground as any of its present rivals is manifest in a thousand places. "Why, then," it will be asked, "are sequoias always found only in well-watered places?" Simply because a growth of sequoias creates those streams. The thirsty mountaineer knows well that in every sequoia grove he will find running water, but it is a mistake to suppose that the water is the cause of the grove being there; on the contrary, the grove is the cause of the water being there. Drain off the water and the trees will remain, but cut off the trees, and the streams will vanish. Never was cause more completely mistaken for effect than in the case of these related phenomena of sequoia woods and perennial streams.

When attention is called to the method of sequoia stream-making, it will be apprehended at once. The roots of this immense tree fill the ground, forming a thick sponge that absorbs and holds back the rain and melting snow, only allowing it to ooze and flow gently. Indeed, every fallen leaf and rootlet, as well as long clasping root, and prostrate trunk, may be regarded as a dam hoarding the bounty of storm-clouds, and dispensing it as blessings all through the summer, instead of allowing it to go headlong in short-lived floods.

Since, then, it is a fact that thousands of sequoias are growing thriftily on what is termed dry ground, and even clinging like mountain pines to rifts in granite precipices, and since it has also been shown that the extra moisture found in connection with the denser growths is an effect of their presence, instead of a cause of their presence, then the notions as to the former extension of the species and its near approach to extinction, based upon its supposed dependence on greater moisture, are seen to be erroneous.

The decrease in rain and snowfall since the close of the glacial period in the Sierra is much less than is commonly guessed. The highest post-glacial water-marks are well preserved in all the upper river channels, and they are not greatly higher than the spring flood-marks of the present; showing conclusively that no extraordinary decrease has taken place in the volume of the upper tributaries of post-glacial Sierra streams since they came into existence. But, in the meantime, eliminating all this complicated question of climatic change, the plain fact remains that the present rain and snowfall is abundantly sufficient for the luxuriant growth of sequoia forests. Indeed, all my observations tend to show that in a prolonged drought the sugar pines and firs would perish before the sequoia, not alone because of the greater longevity of individual trees, but because the species can endure more drought, and make the most of whatever moisture falls.

Again, if the restriction and irregular distribution of the species be interpreted as a result of the desiccation of the Range, then instead of increasing as it does in individuals toward the south where the rainfall is less, it should diminish. If, then, the peculiar distribution of sequoia has not been governed by superior conditions of soil as to fertility or moisture, by what has it been governed?

In the course of my studies I observed that the northern groves, the only ones I was at first acquainted with, were located on just those portions of the general forest soil-belt that were first laid bare toward the close of the glacial period when the ice-sheet began to break up into individual glaciers. And while searching the wide basin of the San Joaquin, and trying to account for the absence of sequoia where every condition seemed favorable for its growth, it occurred to me that this remarkable gap in the sequoia belt fifty miles wide is located exactly in the basin of the vast, ancient *mer de glace* of the San Joaquin and Kings River basins which poured its frozen floods to the plain through this gap as its channel. I then perceived that the next great gap in the belt to the northward, forty miles wide, extending

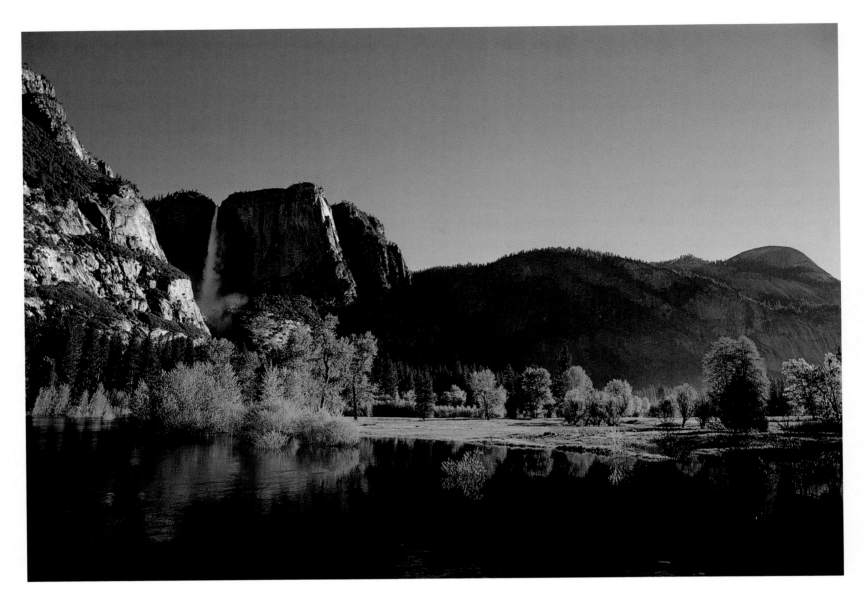

MERCED RIVER IN FLOOD BELOW
YOSEMITE FALLS, 1974.

"Down through the middle of the
Valley flows the crystal Merced,
River of Mercy, peacefully quiet,
reflecting lilies and trees and the
onlooking rocks. . . . In the spring,
after all the avalanches are down
and the snow is melting fast . . . the
Merced overflows its banks,
flooding the meadows, sometimes
almost from wall to wall in
some places."

*The raw power and simplicity of
Yosemite Falls in spring pouring
into the verdant Valley are not easy
to capture on film. Haze, smoke,
harsh light, and a lack of clear*
*patterns on the Valley floor all
combine to challenge the
photographer who wishes
something more than a tight close-
up of the falls without the Valley. I
imagined the image I wanted to see,
then set out to create it. In another
location I had discovered a way to
make spring oaks stand out in vivid
relief. On an especially clear spring
morning I sought out a viewpoint
where the flooding river simplified
my foreground, where black
shadows dropped out much of the
middle ground, and use of a
polarizer darkened the sky and
enriched the green of the oaks as
the first rays of morning sun
singled them out from the
surrounding darkness.*

between the Calaveras and Tuolumne groves, occurs in the basin of the great ancient mer de glace of the Tuolumne and Stanislaus basins; and that the smaller gap between the Merced and Mariposa groves occurs in the basin of the smaller glacier of the Merced. The wider the ancient glacier, the wider the corresponding gap in the sequoia belt.

Finally, pursuing my investigations across the basins of the Kaweah and Tule, I discovered that the sequoia belt attained its greatest development just where, owing to the topographical peculiarities of the region, the ground had been best protected from the main ice-rivers that continued to pour past from the summit fountains long after the smaller local glaciers had been melted.

Taking now a general view of the belt, beginning at the south, we see that the majestic ancient glaciers were shed off right and left down the valleys of Kern and Kings Rivers by the lofty protective spurs outspread embracingly above the warm sequoia-filled basins of the Kaweah and Tule. Then, next northward, occurs the wide sequoia-less channel, or basin of the ancient San Joaquin and Kings River mer de glace; then the warm, protected spots of Fresno and Mariposa groves; then the sequoia-less channel of the ancient Merced glacier; next the warm, sheltered ground of the Merced and Tuolumne groves; then the sequoia-less channel of the grand ancient mer de glace of the Tuolumne and Stanislaus; then the warm old ground of the Calaveras and Stanislaus groves. It appears, therefore, that just where, at a certain period in the history of the Sierra, the glaciers were not, there the sequoia is, and just where the glaciers were, there the sequoia is not.

But although all the observed phenomena bearing on the post-glacial history of this colossal tree point to the conclusion that it never was more widely distributed on the Sierra since the close of the glacial epoch; that its present forests are scarcely past prime, if, indeed, they have reached prime; that the post-glacial day of the species is probably not half done; yet, when from a wider outlook the vast antiquity of the genus is considered, and its ancient richness in species and individuals—comparing our Sierra Giant and *Sequoia sempervirens* of the Coast Range, the only other living species of sequoia, with the twelve fossil species already discovered and described by Heer and Lesquereux, some of which flourished over vast areas in the Arctic regions and in Europe and our own territories, during tertiary and cretaceous times—then, indeed, it becomes plain that our two surviving species, restricted to narrow belts within the limits of California, are mere remnants of the genus, both as to species and individuals, and that they may be verging to extinction. But the verge of a period beginning in cretaceous times may have a breadth of tens of thousands of years, not to mention the possible existence of conditions calculated to multiply and re-extend both species and individuals.

There is no absolute limit to the existence of any tree. Death is due to accidents, not, as that of animals, to the wearing out of organs. Only the leaves die of old age. Their fall is foretold in their structure; but the leaves are renewed every year, and so also are the essential organs—wood, roots, bark, buds. Most of the Sierra trees die of disease, insects, fungi, etc., but nothing hurts the big tree. I never saw one that was sick or showed the slightest sign of decay. Barring accidents, it seems to be immortal. It is a curious fact that all the very old sequoias had lost their heads by lightning strokes. "All things come to him who waits." But of all living things, sequoia is perhaps the only one able to wait long enough to make sure of being struck by lightning.

So far as I am able to see at present only fire and the ax threaten the existence of these noblest of God's trees. In Nature's keeping they are safe, but through the agency of man destruction is making rapid progress, while in the work of protection only a good beginning has been made. The Fresno grove, the Tuolumne, Merced and Mariposa groves are under the protection of the Federal Government in the Yosemite National Park. So are the General Grant and Sequoia National Parks; the latter, established twenty-one years ago, has an area of 240 square miles and is efficiently guarded by a troop of cavalry under the direction of the Secretary of the Interior; so also are the small General Grant National Park, established at the same time with an area of four square miles, and the Mariposa grove, about the same size and the small Merced and Tuolumne group. Perhaps more than half of all the big trees have been thoughtlessly sold and are now in the hands of speculators and mill men. It appears, therefore, that far the largest and important section of protected big trees is in the great Sequoia National Park, now easily accessible by rail to Lemon Cove and thence by a good stage road into the giant forest of the Kaweah and thence by trail to other parts of the park; but large as it is it should be made much larger. Its natural eastern boundary is the High Sierra and the northern and southern boundaries are the Kings and Kern Rivers. Thus could be included the sublime scenery on the headwaters of these rivers and perhaps nine-tenths of all the big trees in existence. All private claims within these bounds should be gradually extinguished by purchase by the Government. The big tree, leaving all its higher uses out of the count, is a tree of life to the dwellers of the plain dependent on irrigation, a never-failing spring, sending living waters to the lowland. For every grove cut down a stream is dried up. Therefore all California is crying, "Save the trees of the fountains." Nor, judging by the signs of the times, is it likely that the cry will cease until the salvation of all that is left of *Sequoia gigantea* is made sure.

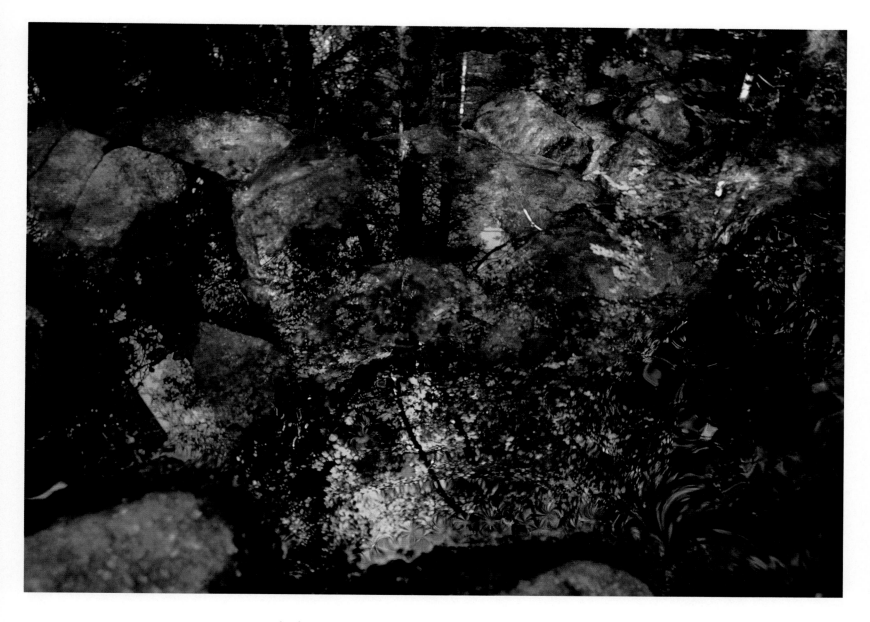

REFLECTIONS IN FERN SPRING, YOSEMITE VALLEY, 1969.

"There is in some minds a tendency toward a wrong love of the marvelous and mysterious, which leads to the belief that whatever is remote must be better than what is near."

*This is one of the earliest Yosemite images that really satisfied me. I had just purchased a 24mm lens, an extreme wide-angle for the time. I went around the Valley experimenting to see how things I liked would appear on film through my new lens. Remembering a reflection I had seen in Fern Spring as I bent over to drink after a climb, I returned there with no preconceptions of light or proper time of day. The result is more abstract than my later work, and I've never been able to improve on it, even with many more years of photographic experience. I've gone back time after time, never getting anything close to that first kaleidoscopic vision. A different, more ordered Fern Spring image appears in the opening pages.*

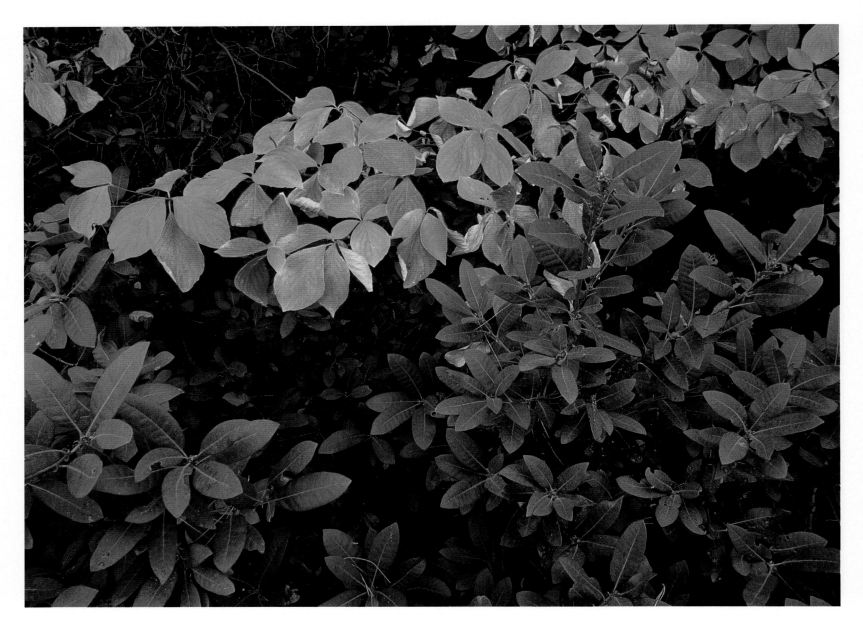

DOGWOOD AND BAY LEAVES,
1987.

"The flowering dogwood . . . when
in flower looks as if covered with
snow. In the spring when the
streams are in flood it is the whitest
of trees. In Indian summer the
leaves become bright crimson,
making a still grander show than
the flowers."

*Visitors familiar with New
England's fall colors are usually
disappointed with Yosemite's
yellows and tans, but dogwood
provides a unique exception. With
its propensity for holding some
green leaves after others have
turned fully red, it erupts out of
deep shadows as if lit from within.*

## CHAPTER VIII

# The Flowers

YOSEMITE was all one glorious flower garden before plows and scythes and trampling, biting horses came to make its wide open spaces look like farmers' pasture fields. Nevertheless, countless flowers still bloom every year in glorious profusion on the grand talus slopes, wall benches and tablets, and in all the fine, cool side-cañons up to the rim of the Valley, and beyond, higher and higher, to the summits of the peaks. Even on the open floor and in easily-reached side-nooks many common flowering plants have survived and still make a brave show in the spring and early summer. Among these we may mention tall œnotheras, *Pentstemon lutea*, and *P. Douglasii* with fine blue and red flowers; spraguea, scarlet zauschneria, with its curious radiant rosettes characteristic of the sandy flats; mimulus, eunanus, blue and white violets, geranium, columbine, erythraea, larkspur, collomia, draperia, gilias, heleniums, bahia, goldenrods, daisies, honeysuckle; heuchera, bolandra, saxifrages, gentians; in cool cañon nooks and on Clouds' Rest and the base of Starr King Dome you may find *Primula suffrutescens*, the only wild primrose discovered in California, and the only known shrubby species in the genus. And there are several fine orchids, habenaria, and cypripedium, the latter very rare, once common in the Valley near the foot of Glacier Point, and in a bog on the rim of the Valley near a place called Gentry's Station, now abandoned. It is a very beautiful species, the large oval lip white, delicately veined with purple; the other petals and the sepals purple, strap-shaped, and elegantly curled and twisted.

Of the lily family, fritillaria, smilacina, chlorogalum and several fine species of brodiæa, Ithuriel's spear, and others less prized are common, and the favorite calochortus, or Mariposa lily, a unique genus of many species, something like the tulips of Europe but far finer. Most of them grow on the warm foothills below the Valley, but two charming species, *C. cœruleus* and *C. nudus*, dwell in springy places on the Wawona road a few miles beyond the brink of the walls.

The snow plant (*Sarcodes sanguinea*) is more admired by tourists than any other in California. It is red, fleshy and watery and looks like a gigantic asparagus shoot. Soon after the snow is off the ground it rises through the dead needles and humus in the pine and fir woods like a bright glowing pillar of fire. In a week or so it grows to a height of eight or twelve inches with a diameter of an inch and a half or two inches; then its long fringed bracts curl aside, allowing the twenty- or thirty-five-lobed, bell-shaped flowers to open and look straight out from the axis. It is said to grow up through the snow; on the contrary, it always waits until the ground is warm, though with other early flowers it is occasionally buried or half-buried for a day or two by spring storms. The entire plant—flowers, bracts, stem, scales, and roots—is fiery red. Its color should appeal to one's blood. Nevertheless, it is a singularly cold and unsympathetic plant. Everybody admires it as a wonderful curiosity, but nobody loves it as lilies, violets, roses, daisies are loved. Without fragrance, it stands beneath the pines and firs lonely and silent, as if unacquainted with any other plant in the world; never moving in the wildest storms; rigid as if lifeless, though covered with beautiful rosy flowers.

Far the most delightful and fragrant of the Valley flowers is the Washington lily, white, moderate in size, with from three- to ten-flowered racemes. I found one specimen in the lower end of the Valley at the foot of the Wawona grade that was eight feet high, the raceme two feet long, with fifty-two flowers, fifteen of them open; the others had faded or were still in the bud. This famous lily is distributed over the sunny portions of the sugar-pine woods, never in large meadow-garden companies like the large and the small tiger lilies (*pardalinum* and *parvum*), but widely scattered, standing up to the waist in dense ceanothus and manzanita chaparral, waving its lovely flowers above the blooming wilderness of brush, and giving their fragrance to the breeze. It is now becoming scarce in the most accessible parts of its range on account of the high price paid for its bulbs by gardeners through whom it has been distributed far and wide over the flower-loving world. For, on account of its pure color and delicate, delightful fragrance, all lily lovers at once adopted it as a favorite.

The principal shrubs are manzanita and ceanothus, several species of each, azalea, *Rubus nutkanus*, brier rose, choke-cherry, philadelphus, calycanthus, garrya, rhamnus, etc.

The manzanita never fails to attract particular attention. The species common in the Valley is usually about six or seven feet high, round-headed with innumerable branches, red or chocolate-color bark, pale green leaves set on edge, and a rich profusion of small, pink, narrow-throated, urn-shaped flowers, like those of arbutus. The knotty, crooked, angular branches are about as rigid as bones, and the red bark is so thin and smooth on both trunk and branches, they look as if they had been peeled and polished and painted. In the spring large areas on the mountain up to a height of eight or nine thousand feet are brightened with the rosy flowers, and in autumn with their red fruit. The pleasantly acid berries, about the size of peas, look like little apples, and a hungry mountaineer is glad to eat them, though half their bulk is made up of hard seeds. Indians, bears, coyotes, foxes, birds and other mountain people live on them for weeks and months. The different species of ceanothus usually associated with manzanita are flowery fragrant and altogether delightful shrubs, growing in glorious abundance, not only in the Valley, but high up in the forest on sunny or half-shaded ground. In the sugar-pine woods the most beautiful species is *C. integerrimus*, often called Californian lilac, or deer brush. It is five or six feet high with slender branches, glossy foliage, and abundance of blue flowers in close, showy panicles. Two species, *C. prostratus* and *C. procumbens*, spread smooth, blue-flowered mats and rugs beneath the pines, and offer fine beds to tired mountaineers. The commonest species, *C. cordulatus*, is most common in the silver-fir woods. It is white-flowered and thorny, and makes dense thickets of tangled chaparral, difficult to wade through or to walk over. But it is pressed flat every winter by ten or fifteen feet of snow. The western azalea makes glorious beds of bloom along the river bank and meadows. In the Valley it is from two to five feet high, has fine green leaves, mostly hidden beneath its rich profusion of large, fragrant white and yellow flowers, which are in their prime in June, July and August, according to the elevation, ranging from 3000 to 6000 feet. Near the azalea-

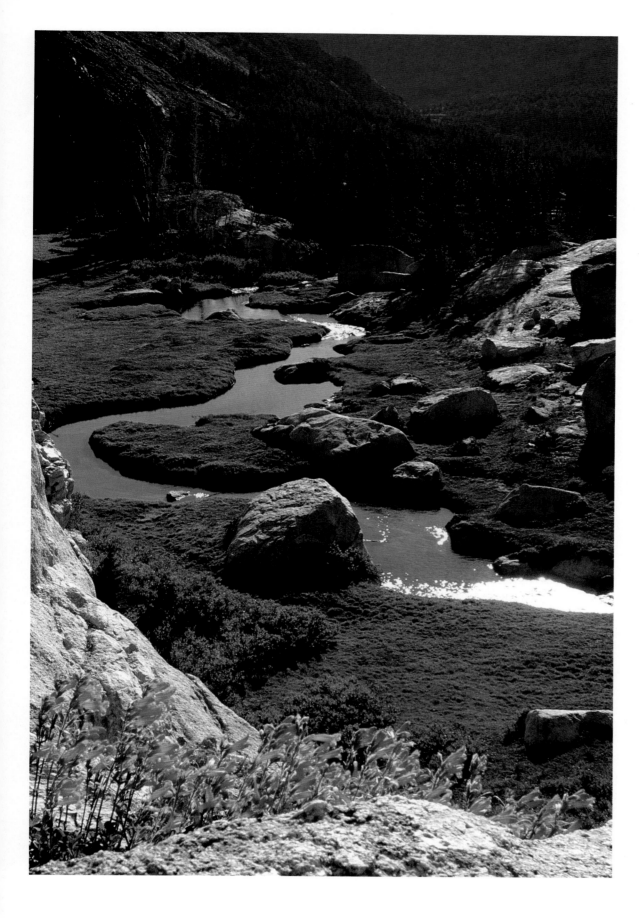

HANGING MEADOW ON MOUNT
CONNESS, 1987.

"The trees . . . seem unable to go a
step farther; but up and up, far
above the tree-line, these tender
plants climb, cheerily spreading
their gray and pink carpets right up
to the very edges of the snowbanks
in deep hollows and shadows."

*Edges in nature fascinate me: those
places where forest meets meadow,
meadow meets stream, and earth
meets sky. No single element by
itself creates such beauty or
fascination. In this scene the entire
transition from bare, glistening
granite to gravelly, flowered soil, to
fertile, stream-carved meadow, to
deep forest is displayed in just a few
hundred yards of mountainside.*

bordered streams the small wild rose, resembling *R. blanda*, makes large thickets deliciously fragrant, especially on a dewy morning and after showers. Not far from these azalea and rose gardens, *Rubus nutkanus* covers the ground with broad, soft, velvety leaves, and pure-white flowers as large as those of its neighbor and relative, the rose, and much finer in texture, followed at the end of summer by soft red berries good for everybody. This is the commonest and the most beautiful of the whole blessed, flowery, fruity *Rubus* genus.

There are a great many interesting ferns in the Valley and about it. Naturally enough the greater number are rock ferns—pellæa, cheilanthes, polypodium, adiantum, woodsia, cryptogramma, etc., with small tufted fronds, lining cool glens and fringing the seams of the cliffs. The most important of the larger species are woodwardia, aspidium, asplenium, and, above all, the common pteris. *Woodwardia radicans* is a superb, broad-shouldered fern five to eight feet high, growing in vase-shaped clumps where the ground is nearly level and on some of the benches of the north wall of the Valley where it is watered by a broad trickling stream. It thatches the sloping rocks, frond overlapping frond like roof shingles. The broad-fronded, hardy *Pteris aquilina*, the commonest of ferns, covers large areas on the floor of the Valley. No other fern does so much for the color glory of autumn, with its browns and reds and yellows, even after lying dead beneath the snow all winter. It spreads a rich brown mantle over the desolate ground in the spring before the grass has sprouted, and at the first touch of sun-heat its young fronds come rearing up full of faith and hope through the midst of the last year's ruins.

Of the five species of pellæa, *P. Breweri* is the hardiest as to enduring high altitudes and stormy weather and at the same time it is the most fragile of the genus. It grows in dense tufts in the clefts of storm-beaten rocks, high up on the mountainside on the very edge of the fern line. It is a handsome little fern about four or five inches high, has pale-green pinnate fronds, and shining bronze-colored stalks about as brittle as glass. Its companions on the lower part of its range are *Cryptogramma acrostichoides* and *Phegopteris alpestris*, the latter with soft, delicate fronds, not in the least like those of Rock fern, though it grows on the rocks where the snow lies longest. *Pellaea Bridgesii*, with blue-green, narrow, simply-pinnate fronds, is about the same size as Breweri and ranks next to it as a mountaineer, growing in fissures, wet or dry, and around the edges of boulders that are resting on glacier pavements with no fissures whatever. About a thousand feet lower we find the smaller, more abundant *P. densa* on ledges and boulder-strewn, fissured pavements, watered until late in summer from oozing currents, derived from lingering snowbanks. It is, or rather was, extremely abundant between the foot of the Nevada and the head of the Vernal Fall, but visitors with great industry have dug out almost every root, so that now one has to scramble in out-of-the-way places to find it. The three species of *Cheilanthes* in the Valley—*C. californica*, *C. gracillima*, and *C. myriophylla*, with beautiful two-to-four-pinnate fronds, an inch to five inches long, adorn the stupendous walls however dry and sheer. The exceedingly delicate californica is so rare that I have found it only once. The others are abundant and are sometimes accompanied by the little gold fern, *Gymnogramme triangularis*, and rarely by the curious little *Botrychium simplex*, some of them less than an inch high. The finest of all the rock ferns is *Adiantum pedatum*, lover of waterfalls and the finest spray-dust. The homes it loves best are over-leaning, cave-like hollows, beside the larger falls, where it can wet its fingers with their dewy spray. Many of these moss-lined

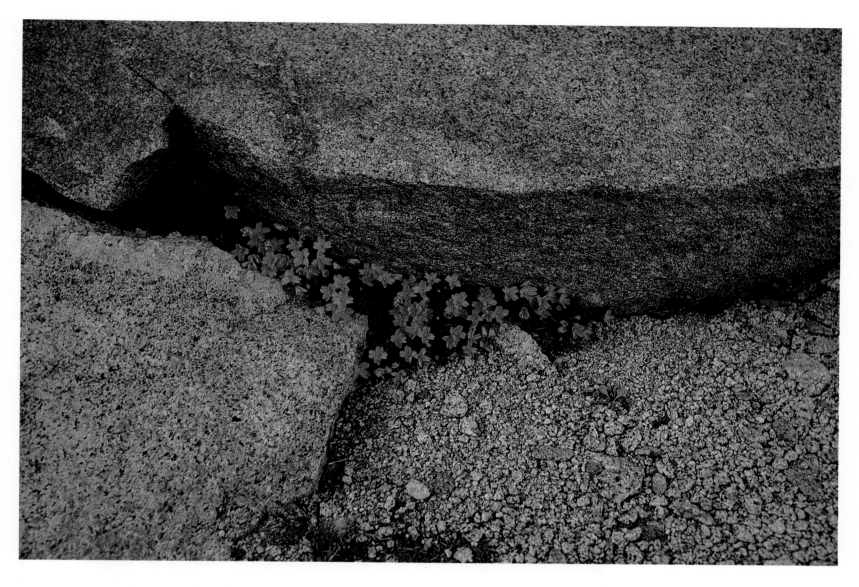

SIERRA PRIMROSES, CLOUDS REST,
1973.

"If my soul could get away from
this so-called prison, be granted all
the list of attributes generally
bestowed on spirits, my first ramble
on spirit-wings would not be among
the volcanoes of the moon. . . . My
first journeys would be into the
inner substance of flowers, and
among the folds and mazes of
Yosemite's falls."

*In the joint of a great slab of
exfoliating granite, I found a
crimson-purple cluster of Sierra
primroses. Just after the sun left, I
set up my camera in soft, even light
to record the full fabric, color, and
texture of the harsh environs of this
early-summer bloom.*

RED AND WHITE HEATHER ON THE
LYELL FORK, TUOLUMNE
RIVER, 1987.

"On my high mountain walks I
keep muttering, 'Cassiope,
cassiope.' This name, as Calvinists
say, is driven in upon me,
notwithstanding the glorious host
of plants that come about me
uncalled as soon as I show myself.
Cassiope seems the highest name of
all the small mountain-heath
people, and as if conscious of her
worth, keeps out of my way."

*No Sierra flower so captivated John
Muir as the tiny white bells of
cassiope, a type of mountain
heather. While ascending the John
Muir Trail toward Donohue Pass, I
spotted red and white heather
blooming together. As I singled out
the perfect, tiny bells through my
macro lens, I knew why Muir so
loved their shape and purity, even
when surrounded by larger, more
showy flora.*

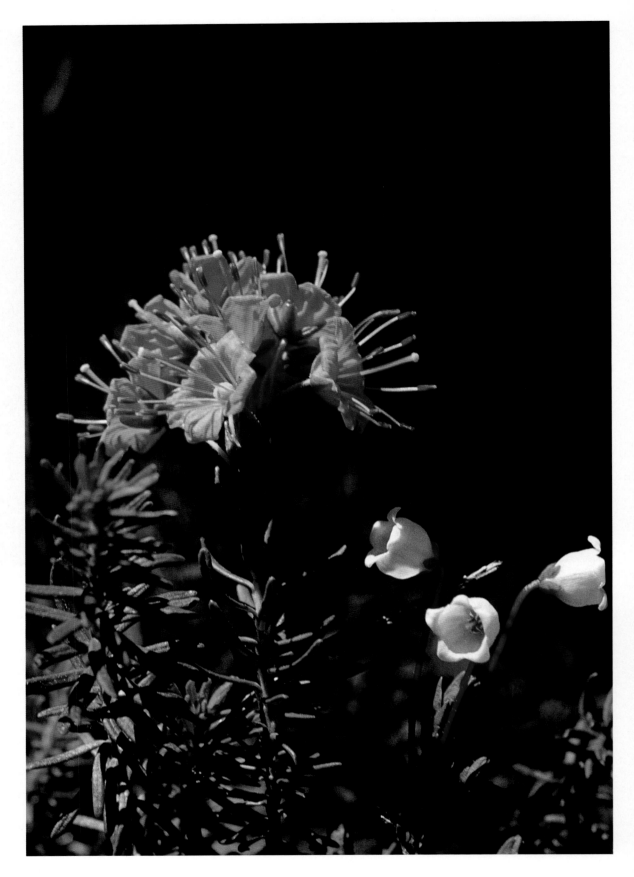

chambers contain thousands of these delightful ferns, clinging to mossy walls by the slightest hold, reaching out their delicate finger-fronds on dark, shining stalks, sensitive and tremulous, throbbing in unison with every movement and tone of the falling water, moving each division of the frond separately at times, as if fingering the music.

May and June are the main bloom-months of the year. Both the flowers and falls are then at their best. By the first of August the midsummer glories of the Valley are past their prime. The young birds are then out of their nests. Most of the plants have gone to seed; berries are ripe; autumn tints begin to kindle and burn over meadow and grove, and a soft mellow haze in the morning sunbeams heralds the approach of Indian summer. The shallow river is now at rest, its flood-work done. It is now but little more than a series of pools united by trickling, whispering currents that steal softly over brown pebbles and sand with scarce an audible murmur. Each pool has a character of its own and, though they are nearly currentless, the night air and tree shadows keep them cool. Their shores curve in and out in bay and promontory, giving the appearance of miniature lakes, their banks in most places embossed with brier and azalea, sedge and grass and fern; and above these in their glory of autumn colors a mingled growth of alder, willow, dogwood and balm-of-Gilead; mellow sunshine overhead, cool shadows beneath; light filtered and strained in passing through the ripe leaves like that which passes through colored windows. The surface of the water is stirred, perhaps, by whirling water-beetles, or some startled trout, seeking shelter beneath fallen logs or roots. The falls, too, are quiet; no wind stirs, and the whole Valley floor is a mosaic of greens and purples, yellows and reds. Even the rocks seem strangely soft and mellow, as if they, too, had ripened.

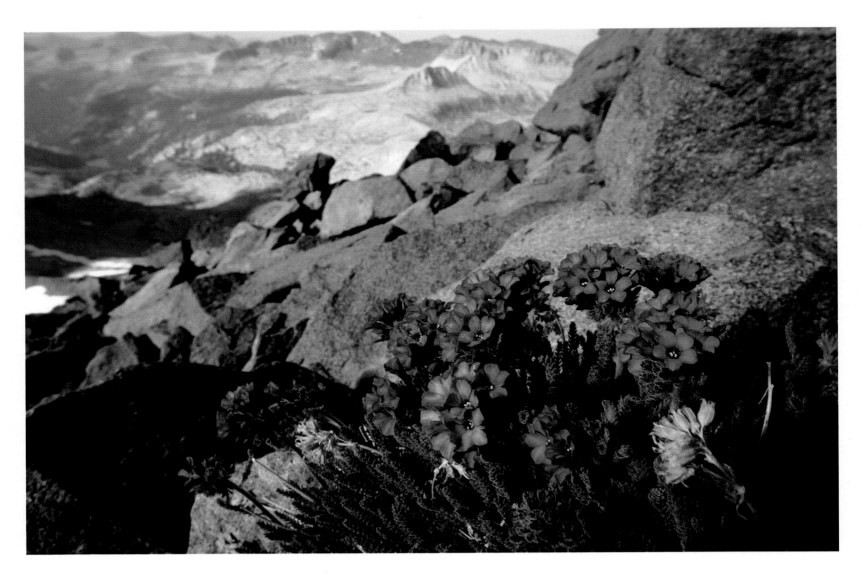

POLEMONIUM BLOSSOMS NEAR
THE SUMMIT OF MOUNT
LYELL, 1987.

"Day of climbing, scrambling,
sliding on the peaks around the
highest source of the Tuolumne and
Merced. Climbed three of the most
commanding of the mountains,
whose names I don't know . . . all
the immense round landscape seems
raw and lifeless as a quarry, yet the
most charming flowers were found
rejoicing in countless nooks and
garden-like patches everywhere."

*When I first climbed Mount Lyell as
a boy of fifteen in 1956, my Sierra
Club leader told me that I was now
entitled to pick a single
polemonium blossom. According to
tradition, only mountaineers who
climbed to thirteen thousand feet
could pick the flower. I later learned
of a far older "tradition."
Polemonium is a favorite browse for
those native Sierra mountaineers,
bighorn sheep. Finding untouched
blooms all over Mount Lyell today
is not only a result of enforcing laws
about picking flowers but also a sad
reminder that native bighorn
vanished from there during Muir's
time as a result of the domestic
sheep that he and other herdsmen
brought to the high
alpine meadows.*

CHAPTER IX

# The Birds

THE SONGS of the Yosemite winds and waterfalls are delightfully enriched with bird song, especially in the nesting time of spring and early summer. The most familiar and best known of all is the common robin, who may be seen every day, hopping about briskly on the meadows and uttering his cheery, enlivening call. The black-headed grosbeak, too, is here, with the Bullock oriole, and western tanager, brown song-sparrow, hermit thrush, the purple finch—a fine singer, with head and throat of a rosy-red hue—several species of warblers and vireos, kinglets, flycatchers, etc.

But the most wonderful singer of all the birds is the water-ouzel that dives into foaming rapids and feeds at the bottom, holding on in a wonderful way, living a charmed life.

Several species of humming-birds are always to be seen, darting and buzzing among the showy flowers. The little red-bellied nuthatches, the chickadees, and little brown creepers, threading the furrows of the bark of the pines, searching for food in the crevices. The large Steller's jay makes merry in the pine-tops; flocks of beautiful green swallows skim over the streams, and the noisy Clarke's crow may oftentimes be seen on the highest points around the Valley; and in the deep woods beyond the walls you may frequently hear and see the dusky grouse and the pileated woodpecker, or woodcock almost as large as a pigeon. The junco or snow-bird builds its nest on the floor of the Valley among the ferns; several species of sparrow are common and the beautiful lazuli bunting, a common bird in the underbrush, flitting about among the azalea and ceanothus bushes and enlivening the groves with his brilliant color; and on gravelly bars the spotted sandpiper is sometimes seen. Many woodpeckers dwell in the Valley; the familiar flicker, the Harris woodpecker and the species which so busily stores up acorns in the thick bark of the yellow pines.

The short, cold days of winter are also sweetened with the music and hopeful chatter of a considerable number of birds. No cheerier choir ever sang in snow. First and best of all is the water-ouzel, a dainty, dusky little bird about the size of a robin, that sings a sweet fluty song all winter and all summer, in storms and calms, sunshine and shadow, haunting the rapids and waterfalls with marvelous constancy, building his nest in the cleft of a rock bathed in spray. He is not web-footed, yet he dives fearlessly into foaming rapids, seeming to take the greater delight the more boisterous the stream, always as cheerful and calm as any linnet in a grove. All his gestures as he flits about amid the loud uproar of the falls bespeak the utmost simplicity and confidence—bird and stream one and inseparable. What a pair! yet they are well related. A finer bloom than the foam bell in an eddying pool is this little bird. We may miss the meaning of the loud-resounding torrent, but the flute-like voice of the bird—only love is in it.

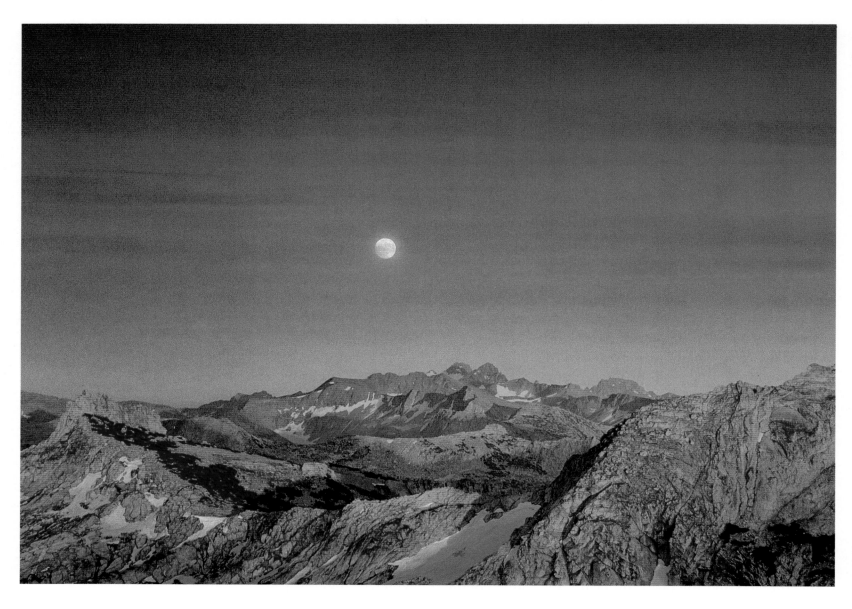

MOONRISE AT SUNSET FROM
CATHEDRAL PEAK, 1987.

"Now came the solemn, silent
evening. Long, blue, spiky shadows
crept out across the snow-fields,
while a rosy glow, at first scarce
discernible, gradually deepened and
suffused every mountain-top,
flushing the glaciers and the harsh
crags above them. This was the
alpenglow, to me one of the most
impressive of all the terrestrial
manifestations of God."

*I planned well in advance to be on
top of Cathedral Peak on the
evening of the full moon, knowing
that I would have to strike a
compromise between carrying a lot
of camera gear and climbing down*
*the steep mountain after sunset.
Unlike Muir's description of
alpenglow, the light on this evening
was awful until the last minute.
Clouds obscured the sun, and both
the moon and the high peaks were
bathed in a gray pallor rather than a
rosy glow. I considered going down
while there was still enough light to
walk the trail back to Tuolumne
Meadows, but finally decided to
wait it out and see. Minutes before
sunset, the sun popped below the
clouds and the landscape came alive
in multihued tones of red and
orange with the full moon glowing
over the summits of Mount Lyell
and its neighbors.*

A few robins, belated on their way down from the upper meadows, linger in the Valley and make out to spend the winter in comparative comfort, feeding on the mistletoe berries that grow on the oaks. In the depths of the great forests, on the high meadows, in the severest altitudes, they seem as much at home as in the fields and orchards about the busy habitations of man, ascending the Sierra as the snow melts, following the green footsteps of Spring, until in July or August the highest glacier meadows are reached on the summit of the Range. Then, after the short summer is over, and their work in cheering and sweetening these lofty wilds is done, they gradually make their way down again in accord with the weather, keeping below the snow-storms, lingering here and there to feed on huckleberries and frost-nipped wild cherries growing on the upper slopes. Thence down to the vineyards and orchards of the lowlands to spend the winter; entering the gardens of the great towns as well as parks and fields, where the blessed wanderers are too often slaughtered for food—surely a bad use to put so fine a musician to; better make stove wood of pianos to feed the kitchen fire.

The kingfisher winters in the Valley, and the flicker and, of course, the carpenter woodpecker, that lays up large stores of acorns in the bark of trees; wrens also, with a few brown and gray linnets, and flocks of the arctic bluebird, making lively pictures among the snow-laden mistletoe bushes. Flocks of pigeons are often seen, and about six species of ducks, as the river is never wholly frozen over. Among these are the mallard and the beautiful woodduck, now less common on account of being so often shot at. Flocks of wandering geese used to visit the Valley in March and April, and perhaps do so still, driven down by hunger or stress of weather while on their way across the Range. When pursued by the hunters I have frequently seen them try to fly over the walls of the Valley until tired out and compelled to re-alight. Yosemite magnitudes seem to be as deceptive to geese as to men, for after circling to a considerable height and forming regular harrow-shaped ranks they would suddenly find themselves in danger of being dashed against the face of the cliff, much nearer the bottom than the top. Then turning in confusion with loud screams they would try again and again until exhausted and compelled to descend. I have occasionally observed large flocks on their travels crossing the summits of the Range at a height of 12,000 to 13,000 feet above the level of the sea, and even in so rare an atmosphere as this they seemed to be sustaining themselves without extra effort. Strong, however, as they are of wind and wing, they cannot fly over Yosemite walls, starting from the bottom.

A pair of golden eagles have lived in the Valley ever since I first visited it, hunting all winter along the northern cliffs and down the river cañon. Their nest is on a ledge of the cliff over which pours the Nevada Fall. Perched on the top of a dead spar, they were always interested observers of the geese when they were being shot at. I once noticed one of the geese compelled to leave the flock on account of being sorely wounded, although it still seemed to fly pretty well. Immediately the eagles pursued it and no doubt struck it down, although I did not see the result of the hunt. Anyhow, it flew past me up the Valley, closely pursued.

One wild, stormy winter morning after five feet of snow had fallen on the floor of the Valley and the flying flakes driven by a strong wind still thickened the air, making darkness like the approach of night, I sallied forth to see what I might learn and enjoy. It was impossible to go very far without the aid of snow-shoes, but I found no great difficulty in making my way to a part of the river where one of my

HALF DOME RISING OUT OF A
WINTER STORM, 1986.

"When the sublime ice-floods of the
glacial period poured down the
flank of the range over what is now
Yosemite Valley . . . the South
Dome was, perhaps, the first to
emerge, burnished and shining like
a mirror above the surface of the icy
sea; and though it has sustained the
wear and tear of the elements tens
of thousands of years, it yet remains
a telling monument of the action of
the great glaciers that brought it
to light."

*Although Muir was surprisingly
astute for his time about the effects
of glaciation in Yosemite, he
overestimated the depth of the ice
that carved the Valley. Yosemite as
we know it was not glaciated in one
long, grand act, as Muir imagined,
but in a series of smaller events. The
maximum height of glaciation on
Half Dome was eight hundred feet
below the summit. One time my
wife, Barbara, flew me over
Yosemite when a blanket of cloud
enveloped the Valley; I realized that
its white bulk was positioned
approximately where the greatest
Yosemite glaciers must have flowed.
As we circled Half Dome, I reveled
in a private vision of Yosemite in
the Pleistocene.*

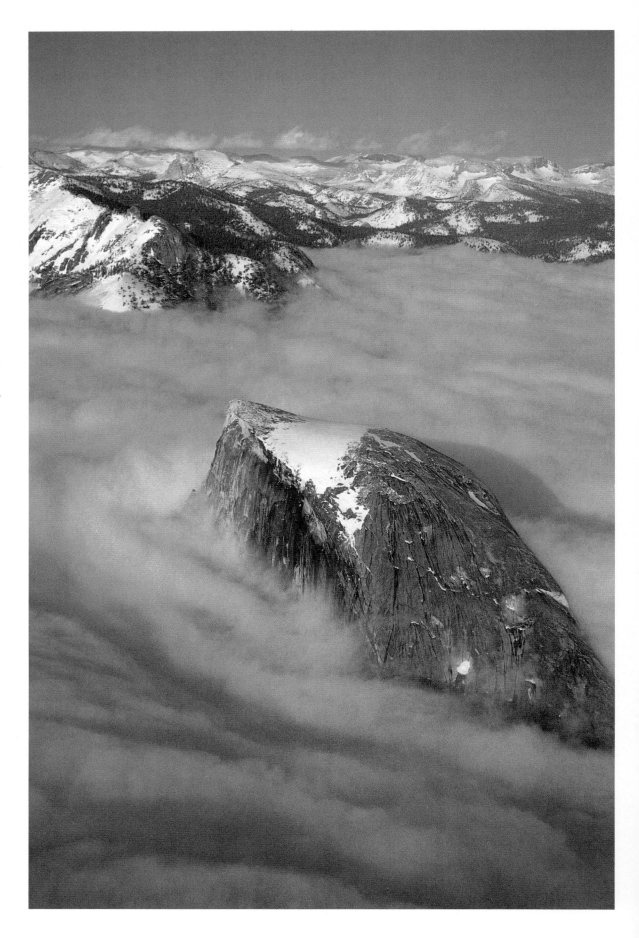

ouzels lived. I found him at home busy about his breakfast, apparently unaware of anything uncomfortable in the weather. Presently he flew out to a stone against which the icy current was beating, and turning his back to the wind, sang as delightfully as a lark in springtime.

After spending an hour or two with my favorite, I made my way across the Valley, boring and wallowing through the loose snow, to learn as much as possible about the way the other birds were spending their time. In winter one can always find them because they are then restricted to the north side of the Valley, especially the Indian Cañon groves, which from their peculiar exposure are the warmest.

I found most of the robins cowering on the lee side of the larger branches of the trees, where the snow could not fall on them, while two or three of the more venturesome were making desperate efforts to get at the mistletoe berries by clinging to the underside of the snow-crowned masses, back downward, something like woodpeckers. Every now and then some of the loose snow was dislodged and sifted down on the hungry birds, sending them screaming back to their companions in the grove, shivering and muttering like cold, hungry children.

Some of the sparrows were busy scratching and pecking at the feet of the larger trees where the snow had been shed off, gleaning seeds and benumbed insects, joined now and then by a robin weary of his unsuccessful efforts to get at the snow-covered mistletoe berries. The brave woodpeckers were clinging to the snowless sides of the larger boles and overarching branches of the camp trees, making short flights from side to side of the grove, pecking now and then at the acorns they had stored in the bark, and chattering aimlessly as if unable to keep still, evidently putting in the time in a very dull way. The hardy nuthatches were threading the open furrows of the barks in their usual industrious manner and uttering their quaint notes, giving no evidence of distress. The Steller's jays were, of course, making more noise and stir than all the other birds combined; ever coming and going with loud bluster, screaming as if each had a lump of melting sludge in his throat, and taking good care to improve every opportunity afforded by the darkness and confusion of the storm to steal from the acorn stores of the woodpeckers. One of the golden eagles made an impressive picture as he stood bolt upright on the top of a tall pine-stump, braving the storm, with his back to the wind and a tuft of snow piled on his broad shoulders, a monument of passive endurance. Thus every storm-bound bird seemed more or less uncomfortable, if not in distress. The storm was reflected in every gesture, and not one cheerful note, not to say song, came from a single bill. Their cowering, joyless endurance offered striking contrasts to the spontaneous, irrepressible gladness of the ouzel, who could no more help giving out sweet song than a rose sweet fragrance. He must sing, though the heavens fall.

NORTHWEST FACE OF HALF
DOME, 1971.

"At the head of the Valley, now
clearly revealed, stands the Half
Dome, the loftiest, most sublime
and the most beautiful of all the
rocks that guard this glorious
temple . . . finely sculptured and
poised in calm, deliberate majesty."

*During the winter of 1971, I
climbed the Four-Mile Trail to
Glacier Point armed with ice ax and
crampons for the final section where
snow had buried a part of the trail
that is etched into a sheer wall. I
carried a telephoto lens and waited
for the afternoon light to shine on
the sheer Northwest Face, which I
had climbed several times. Months
earlier I had succeeded on the first
climb of the South Face, an equally
high wall—with even fewer natural
flaws—just out of view on the right
beyond the skyline. My goal was
not to build drama with special
light or cloud effects, but to let the
Dome make its own display with
the tightest framing I could muster.*

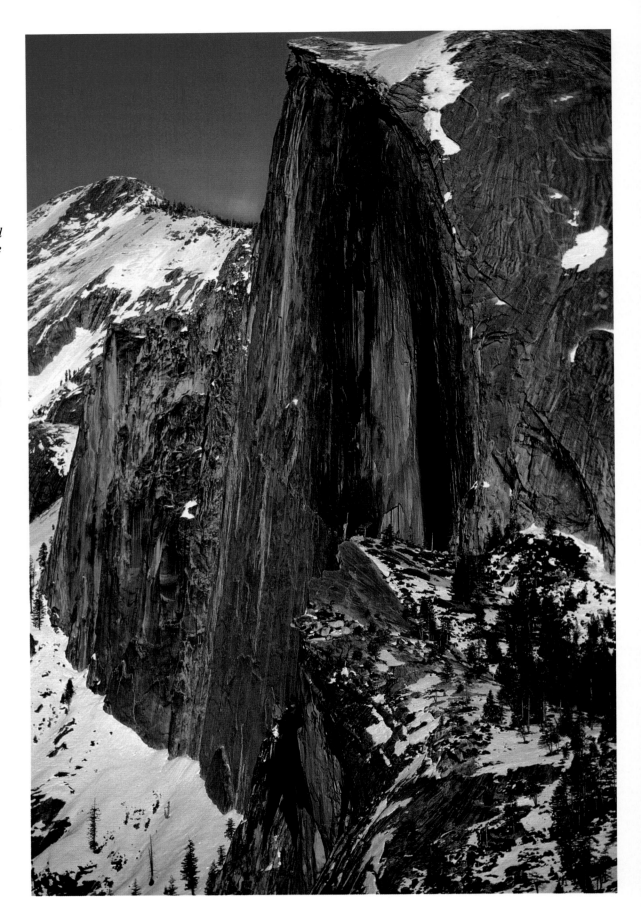

CHAPTER X

# The South Dome

WITH THE EXCEPTION of a few spires and pinnacles, the South Dome is the only rock about the Valley that is strictly inaccessible without artificial means, and its inaccessibility is expressed in severe terms. Nevertheless many a mountaineer, gazing admiringly, tried hard to invent a way to the top of its noble crown—all in vain, until in the year 1875, George Anderson, an indomitable Scotchman, undertook the adventure. The side facing Tenaya Cañon is an absolutely vertical precipice from the summit to a depth of about 1600 feet, and on the opposite side it is nearly vertical for about as great a depth. The southwest side presents a very steep and finely drawn curve from the top down a thousand feet or more, while on the northeast, where it is united with the Clouds' Rest Ridge, one may easily reach a point called the Saddle, about seven hundred feet below the summit. From the Saddle the Dome rises in a graceful curve a few degrees too steep for unaided climbing, besides being defended by overleaning ends of the concentric dome layers of the granite.

A year or two before Anderson gained the summit, John Conway, the master trail-builder of the Valley, and his little sons, who climbed smooth rocks like lizards, made a bold effort to reach the top by climbing barefooted up the grand curve with a rope which they fastened at irregular intervals by means of eye-bolts driven into joints of the rock. But finding that the upper part would require laborious drilling, they abandoned the attempt, glad to escape from the dangerous position they had reached, some 300 feet above the Saddle. Anderson began with Conway's old rope, which had been left in place, and resolutely drilled his way to the top, inserting eye-bolts five to six feet apart, and making his rope fast to each in succession, resting his feet on the last bolt while he drilled a hole for the next above. Occasionally some irregularity in the curve, or slight foothold, would enable him to climb a few feet without a rope, which he would pass and begin drilling again, and thus the whole work was accomplished in a few days. From this slender beginning he proposed to construct a substantial stairway which he hoped to complete in time for the next year's travel, but while busy getting out timber for his stairway and dreaming of the wealth he hoped to gain from tolls, he was taken sick and died all alone in his little cabin.

On the 10th of November, after returning from a visit to Mount Shasta, a month or two after Anderson had gained the summit, I made haste to the Dome, not only for the pleasure of climbing, but to see what I might learn. The first winter storm-clouds had blossomed and the mountains and all the high points about the Valley were mantled in fresh snow. I was, therefore, a little apprehensive of danger from the slipperiness of the rope and the rock. Anderson himself tried to prevent me from making the attempt, refusing to believe that any one could climb his rope in the snow-muffled condition in which it then was. Moreover, the sky was overcast and solemn snow-clouds began to curl around the summit, and my late experiences on icy Shasta came to mind. But reflecting that I had matches in my pocket, and that a little fire-wood might be found, I concluded that in case of a storm the night could be spent on the Dome without suffering anything worth minding, no matter what the clouds might bring forth. I therefore pushed on and gained the top.

It was one of those brooding, changeful days that come between Indian summer and winter, when the leaf colors have grown dim and the clouds come and go among the cliffs like living creatures looking for work: now hovering aloft, now caressing rugged rock-brows with great gentleness, or, wandering afar over the tops of the forests, touching the spires of fir and pine with their soft silken fringes as if trying to tell the glad news of the coming of snow.

The first view was perfectly glorious. A massive cloud of pure pearl luster, apparently as fixed and calm as the meadows and groves in the shadow beneath it, was arched across the Valley from wall to wall, one end resting on the grand abutment of El Capitan, the other on Cathedral Rock. A little later, as I stood on the tremendous verge overlooking Mirror Lake, a flock of smaller clouds, white as snow, came from the north, trailing their downy skirts over the dark forests, and entered the Valley with solemn god-like gestures through Indian Cañon and over the North Dome and Royal Arches, moving swiftly, yet with majestic deliberation. On they came, nearer and nearer, gathering and massing beneath my feet and filling the Tenaya Cañon. Then the sun shone free, lighting the pearly gray surface of the cloud-like sea and making it glow. Gazing, admiring, I was startled to see for the first time the rare optical phenomenon of the "Specter of the Brocken." My shadow, clearly outlined, about half a mile long, lay upon this glorious white surface with startling effect. I walked back and forth, waved my arms and struck all sorts of attitudes, to see every slightest movement enormously exaggerated. Considering that I have looked down so many times from mountain tops on seas of all sorts of clouds, it seems strange that I should have seen the "Brocken Specter" only this once. A grander surface and a grander standpoint, however, could hardly have been found in all the Sierra.

After this grand show the cloud-sea rose higher, wreathing the Dome, and for a short time submerging it, making darkness like night, and I began to think of looking for a camp-ground in a cluster of dwarf pines. But soon the sun shone free again, the clouds, sinking lower and lower, gradually vanished, leaving the Valley with its Indian-summer colors apparently refreshed, while to the eastward the summit-peaks, clad in new snow, towered along the horizon in glorious array.

Though apparently it is perfectly bald, there are four clumps of pines growing on the summit, representing three species, *Pinus albicaulis*, *P. contorta* and *P. ponderosa*, var. *Jeffreyi*—all three, of course, repressed and storm-beaten. The alpine spiræa grows here also and blossoms profusely with potentilla, erigeron, eriogonum, pentstemon, solidago, and an interesting species of onion, and four or five species of grasses and sedges. None of these differs in any respect from those of other summits of the same height, excepting the curious little narrow-leaved, waxen-bulbed onion, which I had not seen elsewhere.

Notwithstanding the enthusiastic eagerness of tourists to reach the crown of the Dome the views of the Valley from this lofty standpoint are less striking than from many other points comparatively low, chiefly on account of the foreshortening effect produced by looking down from so great a height. The North Dome is dwarfed almost beyond recognition, the grand sculpture of the Royal Arches is scarcely no-

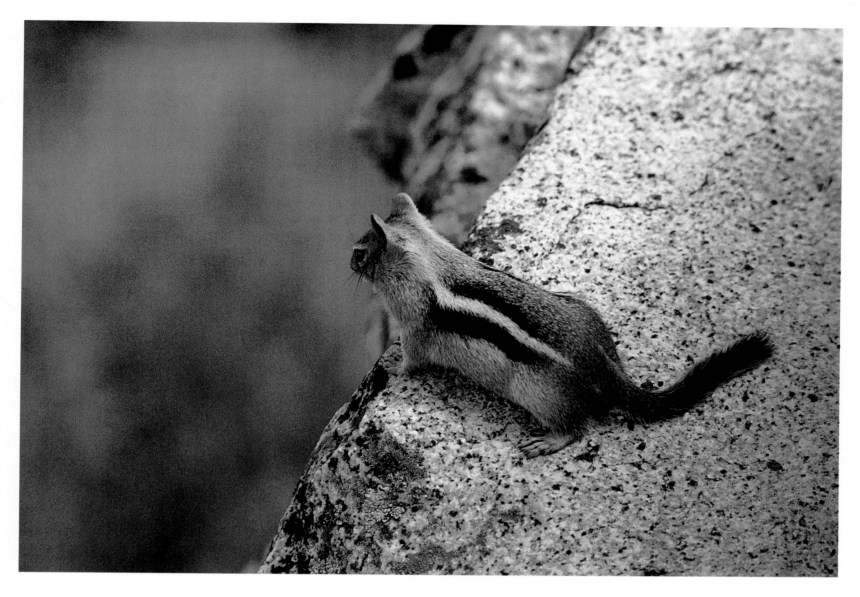

GOLDEN-MANTLED GROUND
SQUIRREL PEERING OVER HALF
DOME'S SUMMIT, 1987.

"Blue jays and Clarke's crows have
trodden the Dome for many a
day, and so have beetles and
chipmunks, and Tissiack would
hardly be more 'conquered' or
spoiled should man be added to her
list of visitors."

*While I was on a commercial
assignment to photograph the rock
singer David Lee Roth climbing on
the face of Half Dome, a few too
many onlookers arrived on top.
Dave's bodyguard had to gently
suggest that we wished privacy to
ensure no advance notice of how
the album cover would look.
As soon as the humans backed
away, a golden-mantled squirrel
purposefully ran to the
cliff's edge and peered down
at Dave.*

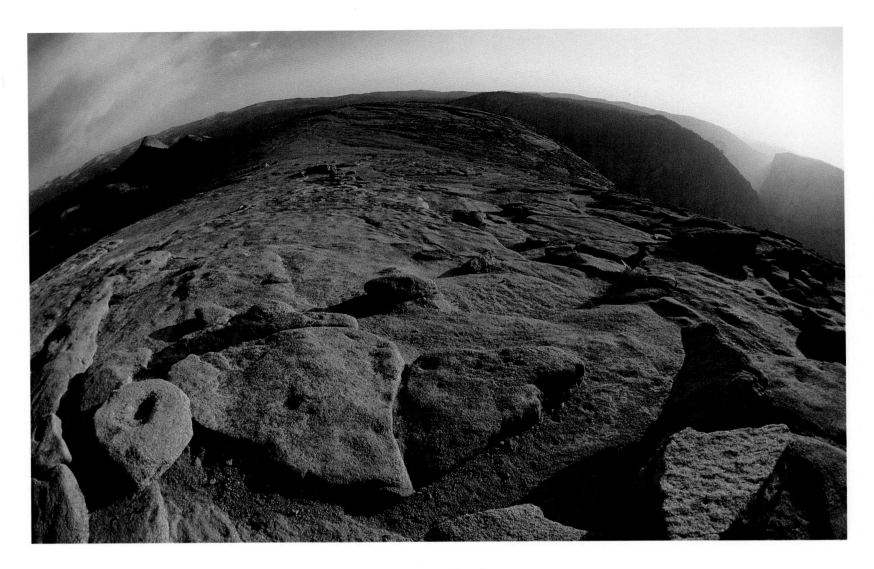

UNGLACIATED, ANCIENT EROSION SURFACE ON SUMMIT OF HALF DOME, 1987.

"No one has attempted to carry out Anderson's plan of making the Dome accessible. For my part I should prefer leaving it in pure wildness, though, after all, no great damage could be done by tramping over it. The surface would be strewn with tin cans and bottles, but the winter gales would blow the rubbish away."

*Since 1919, a cable stairway placed by the National Park Service has made the Dome accessible to any fit walker. As John Muir predicted, the summit is still quite pristine in appearance. His naiveté about future environmental impact, however, reflects an almost total lack of consciousness by his generation. Where would Half Dome's rubbish go if gales blew it away?*

ticeable, and the whole range of walls on both sides seem comparatively low, es-pecially when the Valley is flooded with noon sunshine; while the Dome itself, the most sublime feature of all the Yosemite views, is out of sight beneath one's feet. The view of Little Yosemite Valley is very fine, though inferior to one obtained from the base of the Starr King Cone, but the summit landscapes towards Mounts Ritter, Lyell, Dana, Conness, and the Merced Group, are very effective and complete.

No one has attempted to carry out Anderson's plan of making the Dome acces-sible. For my part I should prefer leaving it in pure wildness, though, after all, no great damage could be done by tramping over it. The surface would be strewn with tin cans and bottles, but the winter gales would blow the rubbish away. Avalanches might strip off any sort of stairway or ladder that might be built. Blue jays and Clarke's crows have trodden the Dome for many a day, and so have beetles and chipmunks, and Tissiack would hardly be more "conquered" or spoiled should man be added to her list of visitors. His louder scream and heavier scrambling would not stir a line of her countenance.

When the sublime ice-floods of the glacial period poured down the flank of the Range over what is now Yosemite Valley, they were compelled to break through a dam of domes extending across from Mount Starr King to North Dome; and as the period began to draw near a close the shallowing ice-currents were divided and the South Dome was, perhaps, the first to emerge, burnished and shining like a mirror above the surface of the icy sea; and though it has sustained the wear and tear of the elements tens of thousands of years, it yet remains a telling monument of the action of the great glaciers that brought it to light. Its entire surface is still covered with glacial hieroglyphics whose interpretation is the reward of all who devoutly study them.

GLACIAL POLISH, TUOLUMNE
MEADOWS, 1987.

"Tracing the ways of glaciers . . .
mysteriously influences every
human being. . . . The most striking
and attractive of the glacial
phenomena in the Upper Yosemite
region are the polished glacier
pavements, because they are so
beautiful, and their beauty is of so
rare a kind, so unlike any portion of
the loose, deeply weathered
lowlands where people make homes
and earn their bread. They are
simply flat or gently undulating
areas of hard resisting granite,
which present the unchanged
surface upon which with
enormous pressure the ancient
glaciers flowed."

*This fine little pocket of glacial
polish appears as freshly burnished
as it must have when the last ice
sheet retreated thousands of years
ago. I used to think of such spots as
remnants of some lost age, when the
entire high country emerged from
ice with a glassy surface, like the
polished granite facade of a
Manhattan building. My journeys
to other great granite ranges of the
world that remain locked in ice
convinced me otherwise. In the
Karakoram and in Patagonia, where
retreating modern glaciers are
exposing fresh granite as I write
these words, the surface is not more
evenly polished than this Tuolumne
Meadows dome today.*

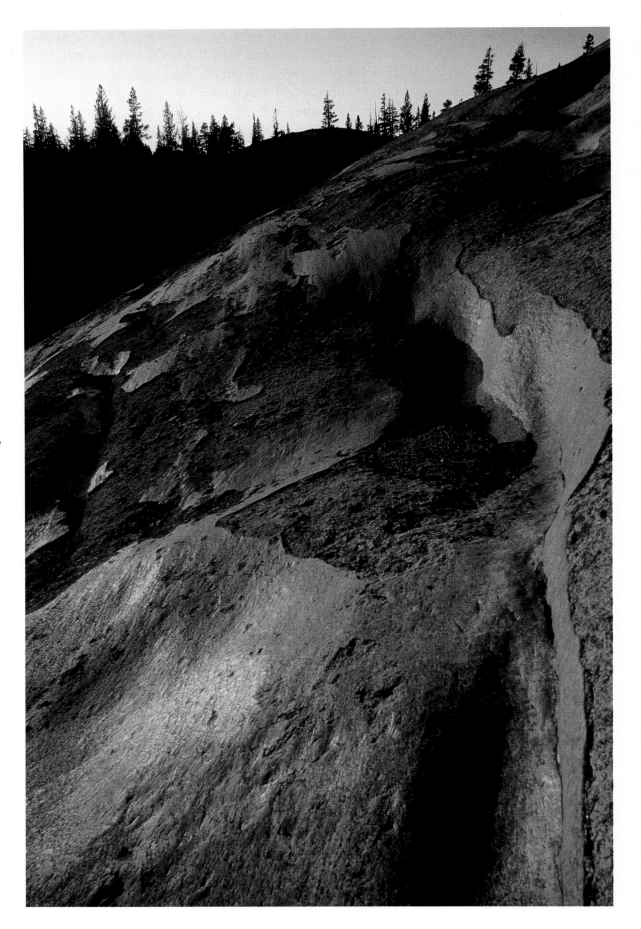

CHAPTER XI

# The Ancient Yosemite Glaciers:
# How the Valley Was Formed

ALL CALIFORNIA has been glaciated, the low plains and valleys as well as the mountains. Traces of an ice-sheet, thousands of feet in thickness, beneath whose heavy folds the present landscapes have been molded, may be found everywhere, though glaciers now exist only among the peaks of the High Sierra. No other mountain chain on this or any other of the continents that I have seen is so rich as the Sierra in bold, striking, well-preserved glacial monuments. Indeed, every feature is more or less tellingly glacial. Not a peak, ridge, dome, cañon, yosemite, lake-basin, stream or forest will you see that does not in some way explain the past existence and modes of action of flowing, grinding, sculpturing, soil-making, scenery-making ice. For, notwithstanding the post-glacial agents—the air, rain, snow, frost, river, avalanche, etc.—have been at work upon the greater portion of the Range for tens of thousands of stormy years, each engraving its own characters more and more deeply over those of the ice, the latter are so enduring and so heavily emphasized, they still rise in sublime relief, clear and legible, through every after-inscription. The landscapes of North Greenland, Antarctica, and some of those of our own Alaska, are still being fashioned beneath a slow-crawling mantle of ice, from a quarter of a mile to probably more than a mile in thickness, presenting noble illustrations of the ancient condition of California, when its sublime scenery lay hidden in process of formation. On the Himalaya, the mountains of Norway and Switzerland, the Caucasus, and on most of those of Alaska, their ice-mantle has been melted down into separate glaciers that flow river-like through the valleys, illustrating a similar past condition in the Sierra, when every cañon and valley was the channel of an ice-stream, all of which may be easily traced back to their fountains, where some sixty-five or seventy of their topmost residual branches still linger beneath protecting mountain shadows.

The change from one to another of those glacial conditions was slow as we count time. When the great cycle of snow years, called the Glacial Period, was nearly complete in California, the ice-mantle, wasting from season to season faster than it was renewed, began to withdraw from the lowlands and gradually became shallower everywhere. Then the highest of the Sierra domes and dividing ridges, containing distinct glaciers between them, began to appear above the icy sea. These first river-like glaciers remained united in one continuous sheet toward the summit of the Range for many centuries. But as the snow-fall diminished, and the climate became milder, this upper part of the ice-sheet was also in turn separated into smaller distinct glaciers, and these again into still smaller ones, while at the same time all were growing shorter and shallower, though fluctuations of the climate now and then occurred that brought their receding ends to a standstill, or even enabled them to advance for a few tens or hundreds of years.

Meanwhile, hardy, home-seeking plants and animals, after long waiting, flocked to their appointed places, pushing bravely on higher and higher, along every sun-warmed slope, closely following the retreating ice, which, like shreds of summer clouds, at length vanished from the new-born mountains, leaving them in all their main, telling features nearly as we find them now.

Tracing the ways of glaciers, learning how Nature sculptures mountain-waves in making scenery-beauty that so mysteriously influences every human being, is glorious work.

The most striking and attractive of the glacial phenomena in the upper Yosemite region are the polished glacier pavements, because they are so beautiful, and their beauty is of so rare a kind, so unlike any portion of the loose, deeply weathered lowlands where people make homes and earn their bread. They are simply flat or gently undulating areas of hard resisting granite, which present the unchanged surface upon which with enormous pressure the ancient glaciers flowed. They are found in most perfect condition in the subalpine region, at an elevation of from eight thousand to nine thousand feet. Some are miles in extent, only slightly interrupted by spots that have given way to the weather, while the best preserved portions reflect the sunbeams like calm water or glass, and shine as if polished afresh every day, notwithstanding they have been exposed to corroding rains, dew, frost, and snow measureless thousands of years.

The attention of wandering hunters and prospectors, who see so many mountain wonders, is seldom commanded by other glacial phenomena, moraines however regular and artificial-looking, cañons however deep or strangely modeled, rocks however high; but when they come to these shining pavements they stop and stare in wondering admiration, kneel again and again to examine the brightest spots, and try hard to account for their mysterious shining smoothness. They may have seen the winter avalanches of snow descending in awful majesty through the woods, scouring the rocks and sweeping away like weeds the trees that stood in their way, but conclude that this cannot be the work of avalanches, because the scratches and fine polished striæ show that the agent, whatever it was, moved along the sides of high rocks and ridges and up over the tops of them as well as down their slopes. Neither can they see how water may possibly have been the agent, for they find the same strange polish upon ridges and domes thousands of feet above the reach of any conceivable flood. Of all the agents of whose work they know anything, only the wind seems capable of moving across the face of the country in the directions indicated by the scratches and grooves. The Indian name of Lake Tenaya is "Py-weak"—the lake of shining rocks. One of the Yosemite tribe, Indian Tom, came to me and asked if I could tell him what had made the Tenaya rocks so smooth. Even dogs and horses, when first led up the mountains, study geology to this extent that they gaze wonderingly at the strange brightness of the ground and smell it, and place their feet cautiously upon it as if afraid of falling or sinking.

In the production of this admirable hard finish, the glaciers in many places flowed with a pressure of more than a thousand tons to the square yard, planing down granite, slate, and quartz alike, and bringing out the veins and crystals of the rocks

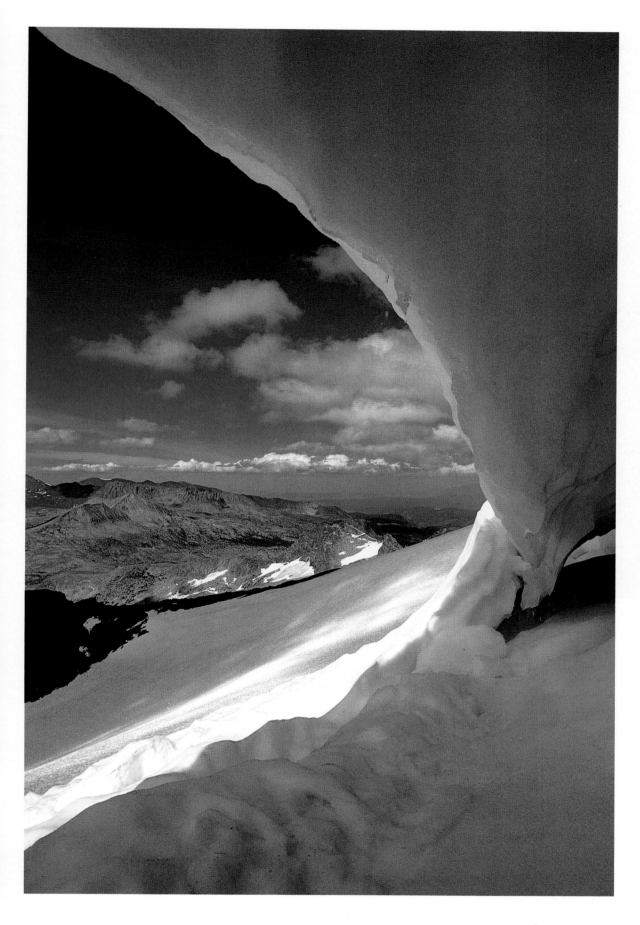

BERGSHRUND OF THE LYELL
GLACIER, MOUNT LYELL, 1987.

"A series of rugged zig-zags enabled
me to make my way down into the
weird ice world of the *Shrund*. Its
chambered hollows were hung with
a multitude of clustered icicles,
amidst which thin subdued light
pulsed and shimmered with
indescribable loveliness. Water
dripped and tinkled overhead, and
from far below there came strange
solemn murmurs from currents that
were feeling their way among veins
and fissures. . . . Ice creations of
this kind are perfectly enchanting."

*Muir's account of a Sierra glacier's
inner chamber so fascinated me
that I set out to explore the Lyell
Glacier's shrund a century later.
Even with modern expedition
boots, crampons, and ice ax the
descent was far from easy. I slipped
through a skylight-shaped opening
into a room filled with shimmering
ice forms. I had a camera, several
lenses, and a tripod, but
unfortunately the scene was far too
subtle in its lighting and too
complex in its forms to come across
well on film. As I crawled out
another opening beneath this
overhanging eave of glacial ice, I
saw the bold lines I was looking for,
with the improbable summer terrain
of the "Gentle Wilderness" in
the distance.*

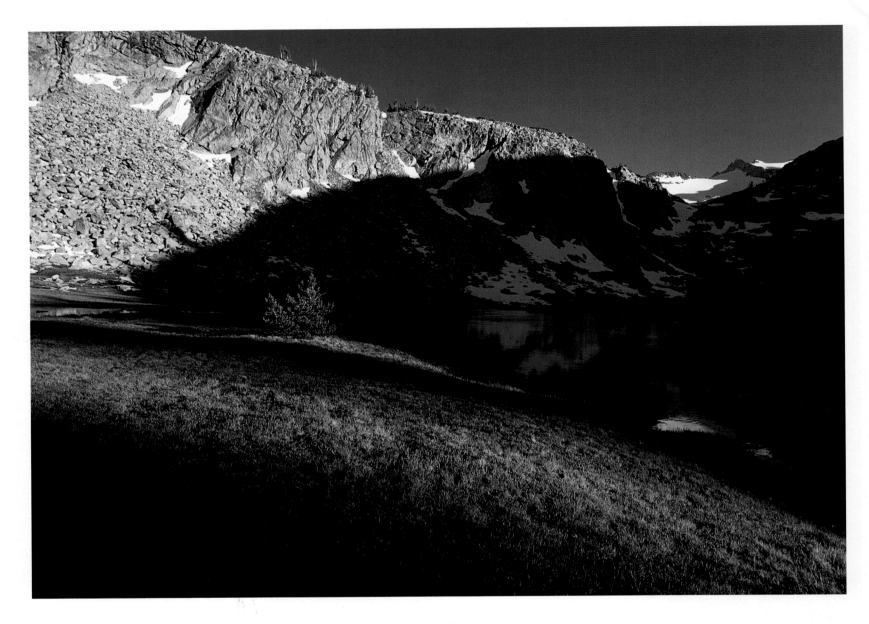

EVENING SHADOWS AT UPPER
LYELL BASE CAMP, 1988.

"These meadows are now in their
prime. How wonderful must be the
temper of the elastic leaves of
grasses and sedges to make curves
so perfect and fine. . . . All the
glacier meadows are beautiful, but
few are so perfect as this one.
Compared with it the most carefully
leveled, licked, snipped artificial
lawns of pleasure-grounds are
coarse things."

*During the second week of July, this
fine little meadow beside the John
Muir Trail comes into bloom. I
tried many ways of composing a
photograph here, but none satisfied
me until evening shadows came
across the meadow in broad arcs
that flowed with the contours of
Yosemite's highest peak, Mount
Lyell, overhead. I waited until the
light singled out a lone whitebark
pine sapling against a creeping
tongue of darkness. Holding that
vision, I moved back until I found
just the right spot, where a last
beam of light on the flowers and
grasses merged with the powerful
edges of land and light in
the distance.*

with beautiful distinctness. Over large areas below the sources of the Tuolumne and Merced the granite is porphyritic; feldspar crystals an inch or two in length in many places form the greater part of the rock, and these, when planed off level with the general surface, give rise to a beautiful mosaic on which the happy sunbeams plash and glow in passionate enthusiasm. Here lie the brightest of all the Sierra landscapes. The Range both to the north and south of this region was, perhaps, glaciated about as heavily, but because the rocks are less resisting, their polished surfaces have mostly given way to the weather, leaving only small imperfect patches. The lower remnants of the old glacial surface occur at an elevation of from 3000 to 5000 feet above the sea level, and twenty to thirty miles below the axis of the Range. The short, steeply inclined cañons of the eastern flank also contain enduring, brilliantly striated and polished rocks, but these are less magnificent than those of the broad western flank.

One of the best general views of the brightest and best of the Yosemite park landscapes that every Yosemite tourist should see, is to be had from the top of Fairview Dome, a lofty conoidal rock near Cathedral Peak that long ago I named the Tuolumne Glacier Monument, one of the most striking and best preserved of the domes. Its burnished crown is about 1500 feet above the Tuolumne Meadows and 10,000 above the sea. At first sight it seems inaccessible, though a good climber will find it may be scaled on the south side. About half-way up you will find it so steep that there is danger of slipping, but feldspar crystals, two or three inches long, of which the rock is full, having offered greater resistance to atmospheric erosion than the mass of the rock in which they are imbedded, have been brought into slight relief in some places, roughening the surface here and there, and affording helping footholds.

The summit is burnished and scored like the sides and base, the scratches and striæ indicating that the mighty Tuolumne Glacier swept over it as if it were only a mere boulder in the bottom of its channel. The pressure it withstood must have been enormous. Had it been less solidly built it would have been carried away, ground into moraine fragments, like the adjacent rock in which it lay imbedded; for, great as it is, it is only a hard residual knot like the Yosemite domes, brought into relief by the removal of less resisting rock about it; an illustration of the survival of the strongest and most favorably situated.

Hardly less wonderful is the resistance it has offered to the trying mountain weather since first its crown rose above the icy sea. The whole quantity of postglacial wear and tear it has suffered has not degraded it a hundredth of an inch, as may readily be shown by the polished portions of the surface. A few erratic boulders, nicely poised on its crown, tell an interesting story. They came from the summit-peaks twelve miles away, drifting like chips on the frozen sea, and were stranded here when the top of the monument emerged from the ice, while their companions, whose positions chanced to be above the slopes of the sides where they could not find rest, were carried farther on by falling back on the shallowing ice current.

The general view from the summit consists of a sublime assemblage of ice-born rocks and mountains, long wavering ridges, meadows, lakes, and forest-covered moraines, hundreds of square miles of them. The lofty summit-peaks rise grandly along the sky to the east, the gray pillared slopes of the Hoffman Range toward the west, and a billowy sea of shining rocks like the Monument, some of them almost as high and which from their peculiar sculpture seem to be rolling westward in the middle ground, something like breaking waves. Immediately beneath you are the Big Tuolumne Meadows, smooth lawns with large breadths of woods on either side, and watered by the young Tuolumne River, rushing cool and clear from its many snow- and ice-fountains. Nearly all the upper part of the basin of the Tuolumne Glacier is in sight, one of the greatest and most influential of all the Sierra ice-rivers. Lavishly flooded by many a noble affluent from the ice-laden flanks of Mounts Dana, Lyell, McClure, Gibbs, Conness, it poured its majestic outflowing current full against the end of the Hoffman Range, which divided and deflected it to right and left, just as a river of water is divided against an island in the middle of its channel. Two distinct glaciers were thus formed, one of which flowed through the great Tuolumne Cañon and Hetch Hetchy Valley, while the other swept upward in a deep current two miles wide across the divide, five hundred feet high between the basins of the Tuolumne and Merced, into the Tenaya Basin, and thence down through the Tenaya Cañon and Yosemite.

The map-like distinctness and freshness of this glacial landscape cannot fail to excite the attention of every beholder, no matter how little of its scientific significance may be recognized. These bald, westward-leaning rocks, with their rounded backs and shoulders toward the glacier fountains of the summit-mountains, and their split, angular fronts looking in the opposite direction, explain the tremendous grinding force with which the ice-flood passed over them, and also the direction of its flow. And the mountain peaks around the sides of the upper general Tuolumne Basin, with their sharp unglaciated summits and polished rounded sides, indicate the height to which the glaciers rose; while the numerous moraines, curving and swaying in beautiful lines, mark the boundaries of the main trunk and its tributaries as they existed toward the close of the glacial winter. None of the commerical highways of the land or sea, marked with buoys and lamps, fences, and guide-boards, is so unmistakably indicated as are these broad, shining trails of the vanished Tuolumne Glacier and its far-reaching tributaries.

I should like now to offer some nearer views of a few characteristic specimens of these wonderful old ice-streams, though it is not easy to make a selection from so vast a system intimately interblended. The main branches of the Merced Glacier are, perhaps, best suited to our purpose, because their basins, full of telling inscriptions, are the ones most attractive and accessible to the Yosemite visitors who like to look beyond the Valley walls. They number five, and may well be called Yosemite Glaciers, since they were the agents Nature used in developing and fashioning the grand Valley. The names I have given them are, beginning with the northernmost, Yosemite Creek, Hoffman, Tenaya, South Lyell, and Illilouette Glaciers. These all converged in admirable poise around from northeast to southeast, welded themselves together into the main Yosemite Glacier, which, grinding gradually deeper, swept down through the Valley, receiving small tributaries on its way from the Indian, Sentinel, and Pohono Cañons; and at length flowed out of the Valley, and on down the Range in a general westerly direction. At the time that the tributaries mentioned above were well defined as to their boundaries, the upper portion of the Valley walls, and the highest rocks about them, such as the Domes, the uppermost of the Three Brothers and the Sentinel, rose above the surface of the ice. But during the Valley's earlier history, all its rocks, however lofty, were buried beneath a continuous sheet, which swept on above and about them like the wind, the upper portion of the current flowing steadily, while the lower portion went mazing and swedging down in the crooked and dome-blocked cañons toward the head of the Valley.

Every glacier of the Sierra fluctuated in width and depth and length, and consequently in degree of individuality, down to the latest glacial days. It must, therefore, be borne in mind that the following description of the Yosemite glaciers applies only to their separate condition, and to that phase of their separate condition that they presented toward the close of the glacial period after most of their work was finished, and all the more telling features of the Valley and the adjacent region were brought into relief.

The comparatively level, many-fountained Yosemite Creek Glacier was about fourteen miles in length by four or five in width, and from five hundred to a thousand feet deep. Its principal tributaries, drawing their sources from the northern spurs of the Hoffman Range, at first pursued a westerly course; then, uniting with each other, and a series of short affluents from the western rim of the basin, the trunk thus formed swept around to the southward in a magnificent curve, and poured its ice over the north wall of Yosemite in cascades about two miles wide. This broad and comparatively shallow glacier formed a sort of crawling, wrinkled ice-cloud, that gradually became more regular in shape and river-like as it grew older. Encircling peaks began to overshadow its highest fountains, rock islets rose here and there amid its ebbing currents, and its picturesque banks, adorned with domes and round-backed ridges, extended in massive grandeur down to the brink of the Yosemite walls.

In the meantime the chief Hoffman tributaries, slowly receding to the shelter of the shadows covering their fountains, continued to live and work independently, spreading soil, deepening lake-basins and giving finishing touches to the sculpture in general. At length these also vanished, and the whole basin is now full of light. Forests flourish luxuriantly upon its ample moraines, lakes and meadows shine and bloom amid its polished domes, and a thousand gardens adorn the banks of its streams.

It is to the great width and even slope of the Yosemite Creek Glacier that we owe the unrivaled height and sheerness of the Yosemite Falls. For had the positions of the ice-fountains and the structure of the rocks been such as to cause down-thrusting concentration of the glacier as it approached the Valley, then, instead of a high vertical fall we should have had a long slanting cascade, which after all would perhaps have been as beautiful and interesting, if we only had a mind to see it so.

The short, comparatively swift-flowing Hoffman Glacier, whose fountains extend along the south slopes of the Hoffman Range, offered a striking contrast to the one just described. The erosive energy of the latter was diffused over a wide field of sunken, boulder-like domes and ridges. The Hoffman Glacier, on the contrary, moved right ahead on a comparatively even surface, making a descent of nearly five thousand feet in five miles, steadily contracting and deepening its current, and finally united with the Tenaya Glacier as one of its most influential tributaries in the development and sculpture of the great Half Dome, North Dome and the rocks adjacent to them about the head of the Valley.

The story of its death is not unlike that of its companion already described, though the declivity of its channel, and its uniform exposure to sun-heat prevented any considerable portion of its current from becoming torpid, lingering only well

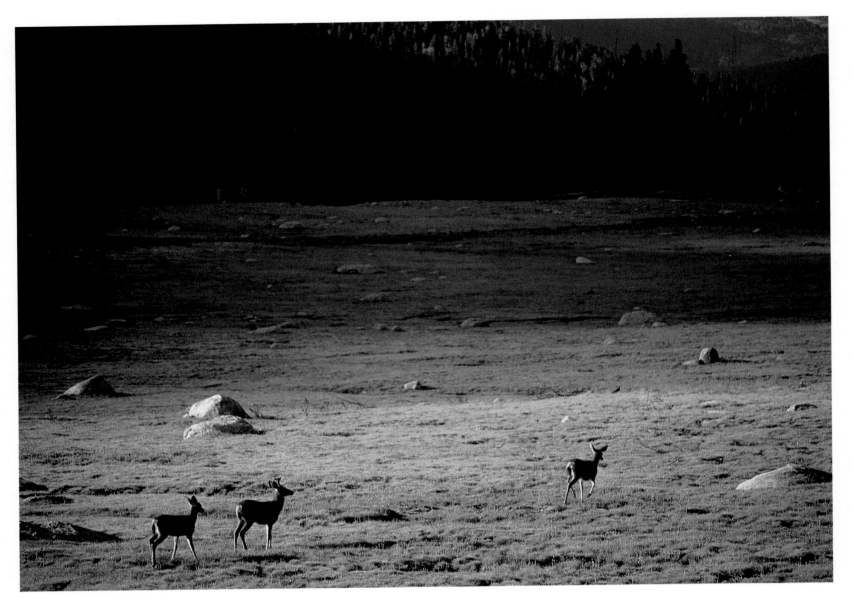

MULE DEER AT DAWN, TIOGA
PASS, 1987.

"Let children walk with Nature, let
them see the beautiful blendings
and communions of death and life,
their joyous inseparable unity, as
taught in woods and meadows,
plains and mountains and streams
of our blessed star, and they will
learn that death is stingless indeed,
and as beautiful as life. . . . All is
divine harmony."

*For me, this is not a photograph of
deer. The wild animals merely make
the landscape more alive. The
feeling I have is not a memory of
that specific moment in 1987 when
three deer happened to cross Dana*

*Meadow at dawn, but rather of a
distant, nebulous connection with
past experiences so early in my life
that I no longer remember their
sources. Appreciation of the natural
world is a communication with
nature in a language that, like any
language, is learned most fluently as
a child. Those who reach adulthood
without firm contacts with nature
must labor inexorably to absorb the
lessons children learn in a single
afternoon when the language of
nature is theirs for the taking
without phylum or genus or
explanation of any kind.*

up on the mountain slopes to finish their sculpture and encircle them with a zone of moraine soil for forests and gardens. Nowhere in all this wonderful region will you find more beautiful trees and shrubs and flowers covering the traces of ice.

The rugged Tenaya Glacier wildly crevassed here and there above the ridges it had to cross, instead of drawing its sources direct from the summit of the Range, formed, as we have seen, one of the outlets of the great Tuolumne Glacier, issuing from this noble fountain like a river from a lake, two miles wide, about fourteen miles long, and from 1500 to 2000 feet deep.

In leaving the Tuolumne region it crossed over the divide, as mentioned above, between the Tuolumne and Tenaya basins, making an ascent of five hundred feet. Hence, after contracting its wide current and receiving a strong affluent from the fountains about Cathedral Peak, it poured its massive flood over the northeastern rim of its basin in splendid cascades. Then, crushing heavily against the Clouds' Rest Ridge, it bore down upon the Yosemite domes with concentrated energy.

Toward the end of the ice period, while its Hoffman companion continued to grind rock-meal for coming plants, the main trunk became torpid, and vanished, exposing wide areas of rolling rock-waves and glistening pavements, on whose channel-less surface water ran wild and free. And because the trunk vanished almost simultaneously throughout its whole extent, no terminal moraines are found in its cañon channel; nor, since its walls are, in most places, too steeply inclined to admit of the deposition of moraine matter, do we find much of the two main laterals. The lowest of its residual glaciers lingered beneath the shadow of the Yosemite Half Dome; others along the base of Coliseum Peak above Lake Tenaya and along the precipitous wall extending from the lake to the Big Tuolumne Meadows. The latter, on account of the uniformity and continuity of their protecting shadows, formed moraines of considerable length and regularity that are liable to be mistaken for portions of the left lateral of the Tuolumne tributary glacier.

Spend all the time you can spare or steal on the tracks of this grand old glacier, charmed and enchanted by its magnificent cañon, lakes and cascades and resplendent glacier pavements.

The Nevada Glacier was longer and more symmetrical than the last, and the only one of the Merced system whose sources extended directly back to the main summits on the axis of the Range. Its numerous fountains were ranged side by side in three series, at an elevation of from 10,000 to 12,000 feet above the sea. The first, on the right side of the basin, extended from the Matterhorn to Cathedral Peak; that on the left through the Merced group, and these two parallel series were united by a third that extended around the head of the basin in a direction at right angles to the others.

The three ranges of high peaks and ridges that supplied the snow for these fountains, together with the Clouds' Rest Ridge, nearly inclose a rectangular basin, that was filled with a massive sea of ice, leaving an outlet toward the west through which flowed the main trunk glacier, three-fourths of a mile to a mile and a half wide, fifteen miles long, and from 1000 to 1500 feet deep, and entered Yosemite between the Half Dome and Mount Starr King.

Could we have visited Yosemite Valley at this period of its history, we should have found its ice cascades vastly more glorious than their tiny water representatives of the present day. One of the grandest of these was formed by that portion of the Nevada Glacier that poured over the shoulder of the Half Dome.

This glacier, as a whole, resembled an oak, with a gnarled swelling base and wide-spreading branches. Picturesque rocks of every conceivable form adorned its banks, among which glided the numerous tributaries, mottled with black and red and gray boulders, from the fountain peaks, while ever and anon, as the deliberate centuries passed away, dome after dome raised its burnished crown above the ice-flood to enrich the slowly opening landscapes.

The principal moraines occur in short irregular sections along the sides of the cañons, their fragmentary condition being due to interruptions caused by portions of the sides of the cañon walls being too steep for moraine matter to lie on, and to down-sweeping torrents and avalanches. The left lateral of the trunk may be traced about five miles from the mouth of the first main tributary to the Illilouette Cañon. The corresponding section of the right lateral, extending from Cathedral tributary to the Half Dome, is more complete because of the more favorable character of the north side of the cañon. A short side-glacier came in against it from the slopes of Clouds' Rest; but being fully exposed to the sun, it was melted long before the main trunk, allowing the latter to deposit this portion of its moraine undisturbed. Some conception of the size and appearance of this fine moraine may be gained by following the Clouds' Rest trail from Yosemite, which crosses it obliquely and conducts past several sections made by streams. Slate boulders may be seen that must have come from the Lyell group, twelve miles distant. But the bulk of the moraine is composed of porphyritic granite derived from Feldspar and Cathedral Valleys.

On the sides of the moraines we find a series of terraces, indicating fluctuations in the level of the glacier, caused by variations of snow-fall, temperature, etc., showing that the climate of the glacial period was diversified by cycles of milder or stormier seasons similar to those of post-glacial time.

After the depth of the main trunk diminished to about five hundred feet, the greater portion became torpid, as is shown by the moraines, and lay dying in its crooked channel like a wounded snake, maintaining for a time a feeble squirming motion in places of exceptional depth, or where the bottom of the cañon was more steeply inclined. The numerous fountain-wombs, however, continued fruitful long after the trunk had vanished, giving rise to an imposing array of short residual glaciers, extending around the rim of the general basin a distance of nearly twenty-four miles. Most of these have but recently succumbed to the new climate, dying in turn as determined by elevation, size, and exposure, leaving only a few feeble survivors beneath the coolest shadows, which are now slowly completing the sculpture of one of the noblest of the Yosemite basins.

The comparatively shallow glacier that at this time filled the Illilouette Basin, though once far from shallow, more resembled a lake than a river of ice, being nearly half as wide as it was long. Its greatest length was about ten miles, and its depth perhaps nowhere much exceeded 1000 feet. Its chief fountains, ranged along the west side of the Merced group, at an elevation of about 10,000 feet, gave birth to fine tributaries that flowed in a westerly direction, and united in the center of the basin. The broad trunk at first flowed northwestward, then curved to the northward, deflected by the lofty wall forming its western bank, and finally united with the grand Yosemite trunk, opposite Glacier Point.

All the phenomena relating to glacial action in this basin are remarkably simple and orderly, on account of the sheltered positions occupied by its ice-fountains, with reference to the disturbing effects of larger glaciers from the axis of the main

Range earlier in the period. From the eastern base of the Starr King cone you may obtain a fine view of the principal moraines sweeping grandly out into the middle of the basin from the shoulders of the peaks, between which the ice-fountains lay. The right lateral of the tributary, which took its rise between Red and Merced Mountains, measures two hundred and fifty feet in height at its upper extremity, and displays three well-defined terraces, similar to those of the South Lyell Glacier. The comparative smoothness of the uppermost terrace shows that it is considerably more ancient than the others, many of the boulders of which it is composed having crumbled. A few miles to the westward, this moraine has an average slope of twenty-seven degrees, and an elevation above the bottom of the channel of six hundred and sixty feet. Near the middle of the main basin, just where the regularly formed medial and lateral moraines flatten out and disappear, there is a remarkably smooth field of gravel, planted with arctostaphylos, that looks at the distance of a mile like a delightful meadow. Stream sections show the gravel deposit to be composed of the same material as the moraines, but finer, and more water-worn from the action of converging torrents issuing from the tributary glaciers after the trunk was melted. The southern boundary of the basin is a strikingly perfect wall, gray on the top, and white down the sides and at the base with snow, in which many a crystal brook takes rise. The northern boundary is made up of smooth undulating masses of gray granite, that lift here and there into beautiful domes of which the Starr King cluster is the finest, while on the east tower of the majestic fountain-peaks with wide cañons and névé amphitheaters between them, whose variegated rocks show out gloriously against the sky.

The ice-plows of this charming basin, ranged side by side in orderly gangs, furrowed the rocks with admirable uniformity, producing irrigating channels for a brood of wild streams, and abundance of rich soil adapted to every requirement of garden and grove. No other section of the Yosemite uplands is in so perfect a state of glacial cultivation. Its domes, and peaks, and swelling rock-waves, however majestic in themselves, are yet submissively subordinate to the garden center. The other basins we have been describing are combinations of sculptured rocks, embellished with gardens and groves; the Illilouette is one grand garden and forest, embellished with rocks, each of the five beautiful in its own way, and all as harmoniously related as are the five petals of a flower. After uniting in the Yosemite Valley, and expending the down-thrusting energy derived from their combined weight and the declivity of their channels, the grand trunk flowed on through and out of the Valley. In effecting its exit a considerable ascent was made, traces of which may still be seen on the abraded rocks at the lower end of the Valley, while the direction pursued after leaving the Valley is surely indicated by the immense lateral moraines extending from the ends of the walls at an elevation of from 1500 to 1800 feet. The right lateral moraine was disturbed by a large tributary glacier that occupied the basin of Cascade Creek, causing considerable complication in its structure. The left is simple in form for several miles of its length, or to the point where a tributary came in from the southeast. But both are greatly obscured by the forests and underbrush growing upon them, and by the denuding action of rains and melting snows, etc. It is, therefore, the less to be wondered at that these moraines, made up of material derived from the distant fountain-mountains, and from the Valley itself, were not sooner recognized.

The ancient glacier systems of the Tuolumne, San Joaquin, Kern, and Kings River

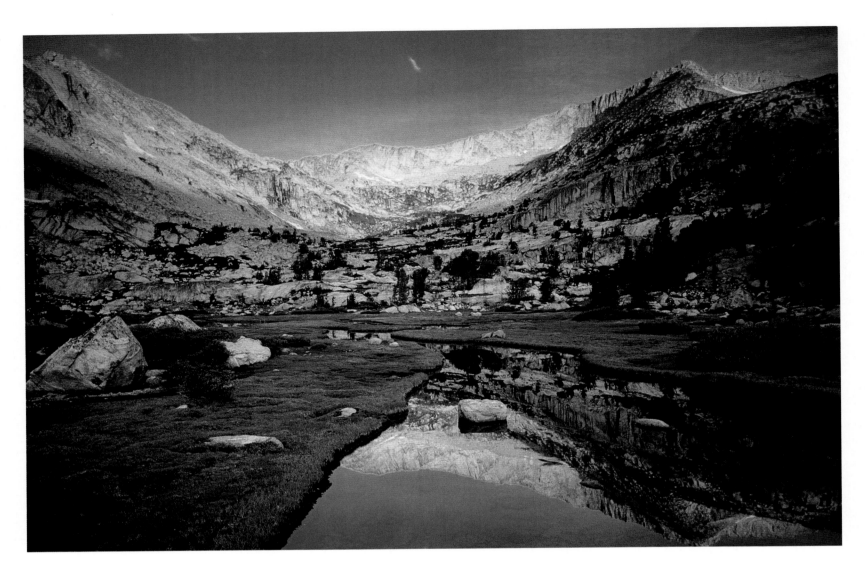

REFLECTION IN A GLACIAL TARN, MOUNT CONNESS, 1987.

"Here are the roots of all the life of the valleys, and here more simply than elsewhere is the eternal flux of Nature manifested. Ice changing to water, lakes to meadows, and mountains to plains. And while we thus contemplate Nature's methods of landscape creation, and, reading the records she has carved on the rocks, reconstruct, however imperfectly, the landscapes of the past, we also learn that as these we now behold have succeeded those of the pre-glacial age, so they in turn are withering and vanishing to be succeeded by others yet unborn."

*I visited this remote tarn twice within a matter of weeks. The first time I was ascending Mount Conness from the east. The tarn was beautiful, but its potential was far greater than a climber could record during random morning minutes well after dawn. Next time I positioned myself where I could capture dawn light dominating the water's reflection, yet hold a clear vision of the land before me in predawn shadows. Thus light and form converge on a landscape in transition.*

basins were developed on a still grander scale and are so replete with interest that the most sketchy outline descriptions of each, with the works they have accomplished, would fill many a volume. Therefore I can do but little more than invite everybody who is free to go and see for himself.

The action of flowing ice, whether in the form of river-like glaciers or broad mantles, especially the part it played in sculpturing the earth, is as yet but little understood. Water rivers work openly where people dwell, and so does the rain, and the sea, thundering on all the shores of the world; and the universal ocean of air, though invisible, speaks aloud in a thousand voices, and explains its modes of working and its power. But glaciers, back in their white solitudes, work apart from men, exerting their tremendous energies in silence and darkness. Outspread, spirit-like, they brood above the predestined landscapes, work on unwearied through immeasurable ages, until, in the fullness of time, the mountains and valleys are brought forth, channels furrowed for rivers, basins made for lakes and meadows, and arms of the sea, soils spread for forests and fields; then they shrink and vanish like summer clouds.

NEARING THE SUMMIT OF
CATHEDRAL PEAK, 1987.

"The mountains are fountains of
men as well as of rivers, of glaciers,
of fertile soil. The great poets,
philosophers, prophets, able men
whose thoughts and deeds have
moved the world, have come down
from the mountains—mountain-
dwellers who have grown strong
there with the forest trees in
Nature's work-shops."

*Muir himself was not only one of
those very mountain-dwellers
whose great thoughts and deeds
have moved the world, but also a
man whose life's work, play, and
philosophy were amazingly
interconnected. Climbing
mountains has definitely affected
the way I think about the world,
and long ago I recognized that
many of the strongest voices in the
environmental movement—people
such as Ansel Adams, David
Brower, and Dick Leonard—gained
their power from having climbed
mountains, from having put
themselves in situations where they
had to actively adapt themselves to
their natural surroundings instead
of change the environment to suit
their needs, as in everyday life. By
immersing themselves both
physically and mentally in
situations of risk where the very
essence of their experience was the
natural character of the land, they
each discovered, as I did in my own
time, a new way of viewing the
world that profoundly changed their
lives. I'm convinced that this
process, which Muir first
experienced in Yosemite, gave birth
to the environmental movement and
has continued to nurture the
movement into the best of what it
has become today.*

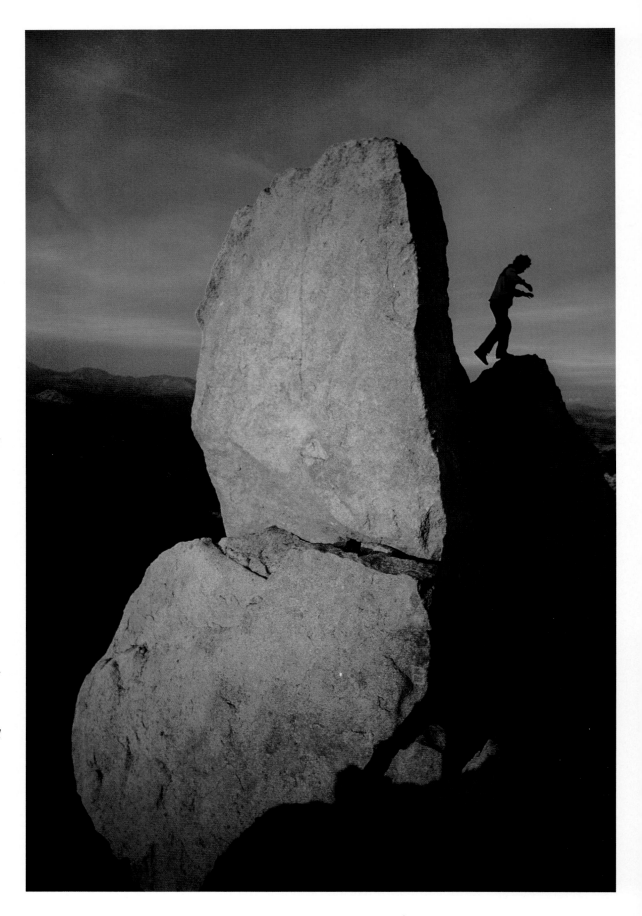

CHAPTER XII

# How Best to Spend One's
Yosemite Time

ONE-DAY EXCURSIONS: NO. I.

IF I WERE so time-poor as to have only one day to spend in Yosemite I should start at daybreak, say at three o'clock in midsummer, with a pocketful of any sort of dry breakfast stuff, for Glacier Point, Sentinel Dome, the head of Illilouette Fall, Nevada Fall, the top of Liberty Cap, Vernal Fall and the wild boulder-choked River Cañon. The trail leaves the Valley at the base of the Sentinel Rock, and as you slowly saunter from point to point along its many accommodating zigzags nearly all the Valley rocks and falls are seen in striking, ever-changing combinations. At an elevation of about five hundred feet a particularly fine, wide-sweeping view down the Valley is obtained, past the sheer face of the Sentinel and between the Cathedral Rocks and El Capitan. At a height of about 1500 feet the great Half Dome comes full in sight, overshadowing every other feature of the Valley to the eastward. From Glacier Point you look down 3000 feet over the edge of its sheer face to the meadows and groves and innumerable yellow pine spires, with the meandering river sparkling and spangling through the midst of them. Across the Valley a great telling view is presented of the Royal Arches, North Dome, Indian Cañon, Three Brothers and El Capitan, with the dome-paved basin of Yosemite Creek and Mount Hoffman in the background. To the eastward, the Half Dome close beside you looking higher and more wonderful than ever; southeastward the Starr King, girdled with silver firs, and the spacious garden-like basin of the Illilouette and its deeply sculptured fountain-peaks, called "The Merced Group"; and beyond all, marshaled along the eastern horizon, the icy summits on the axis of the Range and broad swaths of forests growing on ancient moraines, while the Nevada, Vernal and Yosemite Falls are not only full in sight but are distinctly heard as if one were standing beside them in their spray.

The views from the summit of Sentinel Dome are still more extensive and telling. Eastward the crowds of peaks at the head of the Merced, Tuolumne and San Joaquin Rivers are presented in bewildering array; westward, the vast forests, yellow foothills and the broad San Joaquin plains and the Coast Ranges, hazy and dim in the distance.

From Glacier Point go down the trail into the lower end of the Illilouette Basin, cross Illilouette Creek and follow it to the Fall where from an outjutting rock at its

DIFFRACTION FRINGE IN CLEAR
MOUNTAIN AIR, MOUNT
CONNESS, 1987.

"Walk away quietly in any direction
and taste the freedom of the
mountaineer. Camp out among the
grasses and gentians of glacial
meadows, in craggy garden nooks
full of Nature's darlings. Climb the
mountains and get their good
tidings. Nature's peace will flow
into you as sunshine flows into
trees. The winds will blow their
own freshness into you, and the
storms their energies, while cares
will drop off like autumn leaves."

*On a clear day in the High Sierra,
the light has a purity almost never
seen in the lowlands. Thin high-
altitude air, lacking moisture and
dust, makes for sharp-edged
shadows that are extremely dark
because so little light is being
scattered in the sky. Thus when a
beam of pure sunlight struck a
climber on top of Mount Conness, a
strange aura of diffraction, not
visible in hazy air, isolated him
from his world of mountain, sky,
and shadow.*

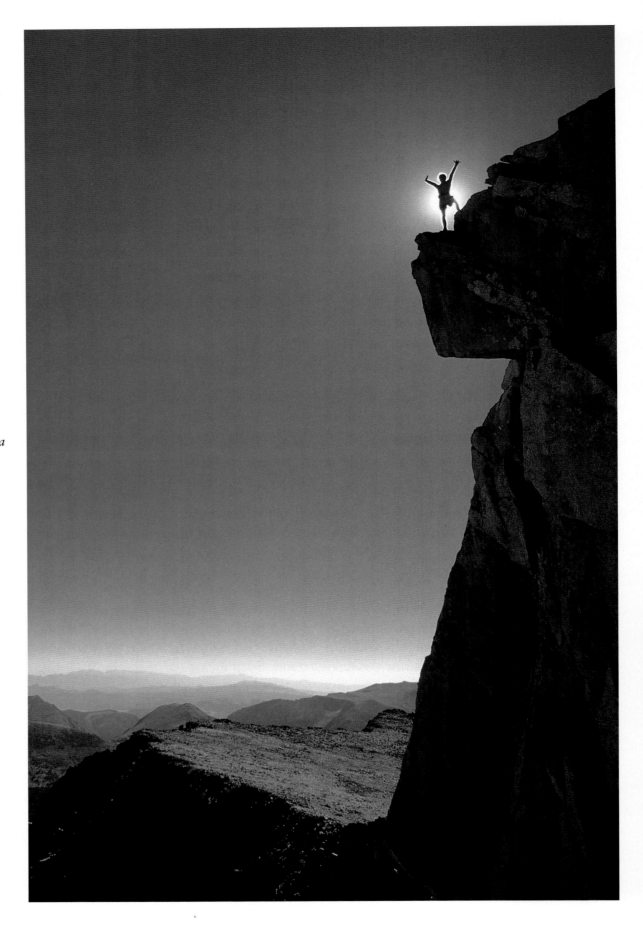

head you will get a fine view of its rejoicing waters and wild cañon and the Half Dome. Thence returning to the trail, follow it to the head of the Nevada Fall. Linger here an hour or two, for not only have you glorious views of the wonderful fall, but of its wild, leaping, exulting rapids and, greater than all, the stupendous scenery into the heart of which the white passionate river goes wildly thundering, surpassing everything of its kind in the world. After an unmeasured hour or so of this glory, all your body aglow, nerve currents flashing through you never before felt, go to the top of the Liberty Cap, only a glad saunter now that your legs as well as head and heart are awake and rejoicing with everything. The Liberty Cap, a companion of the Half Dome, is sheer and inaccessible on three of its sides but on the east a gentle, ice-burnished, juniper-dotted slope extends to the summit where other wonderful views are displayed where all are wonderful: the south side and shoulders of Half Dome and Clouds' Rest, the beautiful Little Yosemite Valley and its many domes, the Starr King cluster of domes, Sentinel Dome, Glacier Point, and, perhaps the most tremendously impressive of all, the views of the hopper-shaped cañon of the river from the head of the Nevada Fall to the head of the Valley.

Returning to the trail you descend between the Nevada Fall and the Liberty Cap with fine side views of both the fall and the rock, pass on through clouds of spray and along the rapids to the head of the Vernal Fall, about a mile below the Nevada. Linger here if night is still distant, for views of this favorite fall and the stupendous rock scenery about it. Then descend a stairway by its side, follow a dim trail through its spray, and a plain one along the border of the boulder-dashed rapids and so back to the wide, tranquil Valley.

### ONE-DAY EXCURSIONS: NO. 2.

Another grand one-day excursion is to the Upper Yosemite Fall, the top of the highest of the Three Brothers, called Eagle Peak on the Geological Survey maps; the brow of El Capitan; the head of the Ribbon Fall; across the beautiful Ribbon Creek Basin; and back to the Valley by the Big Oak Flat wagon-road.

The trail leaves the Valley on the east side of the largest of the earthquake taluses immediately opposite the Sentinel Rock and as it passes within a few rods of the foot of the great Fall, magnificent views are obtained as you approach it and pass through its spray, though when the snow is melting fast you will be well drenched. From the foot of the Fall the trail zigzags up a narrow cañon between the Fall and a plain mural cliff that is burnished here and there by glacial action.

You should stop a while on a flat iron-fenced rock a little below the head of the Fall beside the enthusiastic throng of starry comet-like waters to learn something of their strength, their marvelous variety of forms, and above all, their glorious music, gathered and composed from the snow-storms, hail-, rain- and wind-storms that have fallen on their glacier-sculptured, domey, ridgy basin. Refreshed and exhilarated, you follow your trail-way through silver fir and pine woods to Eagle Peak, where the most comprehensive of all the views to be had on the north-wall heights are displayed. After an hour or two of gazing, dreaming, studying the tremendous topography, etc., trace the rim of the Valley to the grand El Capitan ridge and go down to its brow, where you will gain everlasting impressions of Nature's steadfastness and power combined with ineffable fineness of beauty.

Dragging yourself away, go to the head of the Ribbon Fall, thence across the beautiful Ribbon Creek Basin to the Big Oak Flat stage-road, and down its fine grades to the Valley, enjoying glorious Yosemite scenery all the way to the foot of El Capitan and your camp.

## TWO-DAY EXCURSIONS: NO. I

For a two-day trip I would go straight to Mount Hoffman, spend the night on the summit, next morning go down by May Lake to Tenaya Lake and return to the Valley by Clouds' Rest and the Nevada and Vernal Falls. As on the foregoing excursion, you leave the Valley by the Yosemite Falls trail and follow it to the Tioga wagon-road, a short distance east of Porcupine Flat. From that point push straight up to the summit. Mount Hoffman is a mass of gray granite that rises almost in the center of the Yosemite Park, about eight or ten miles in a straight line from the Valley. Its southern slopes are low and easily climbed, and adorned here and there with castle-like crumbling piles and long jagged crests that look like artificial masonry; but on the north side it is abruptly precipitous and banked with lasting snow. Most of the broad summit is comparatively level and thick sown with crystals, quartz, mica, hornblende, feldspar, granite, zircon, tourmaline, etc., weathered out and strewn closely and loosely as if they had been sown broadcast. Their radiance is fairly dazzling in sunlight, almost hiding the multitude of small flowers that grow among them. At first sight only these radiant crystals are likely to be noticed, but looking closely you discover a multitude of very small gilias, phloxes, mimulus, etc., many of them with more petals than leaves. On the borders of little streams larger plants flourish—lupines, daisies, asters, goldenrods, hairbell, mountain columbine, potentilla, astragalus and a few gentians; with charming heathworts—bryanthus, cassiope, kalmia, vaccinium in boulder-fringing rings or bank covers. You saunter among the crystals and flowers as if you were walking among stars. From the summit nearly all the Yosemite Park is displayed like a map: forests, lakes, meadows, and snowy peaks. Northward lies Yosemite's wide basin with its domes and small lakes, shining like larger crystals; eastward the rocky, meadowy Tuolumne region, bounded by its snowy peaks in glorious array; southward Yosemite and westward the vast forest. On no other Yosemite Park mountain are you more likely to linger. You will find it a magnificent sky camp. Clumps of dwarf pine and mountain hemlock will furnish resin roots and branches for fuel and light, and the rills, sparkling water. Thousands of the little plant people will gaze at your camp-fire with the crystals and stars, companions and guardians as you lie at rest in the heart of the vast serene night.

The most telling of all the wide Hoffman views is the basin of the Tuolumne with its meadows, forests and hundreds of smooth rock-waves that appear to be coming rolling on towards you like high heaving waves ready to break, and beyond these the great mountains. But best of all are the dawn and the sunrise. No mountain top could be better placed for this most glorious of mountain views—to watch and see the deepening colors of the dawn and the sunbeams streaming through the snowy High Sierra passes, awakening the lakes and crystals, the chilled plant people and winged people, and making everything shine and sing in pure glory.

With your heart aglow, spangling Lake Tenaya and Lake May will beckon you away for walks on their ice-burnished shores. Leave Tenaya at the west end, cross to the south side of the outlet, and gradually work your way up in an almost straight south direction to the summit of the divide between Tenaya Creek and the main upper Merced River or Nevada Creek and follow the divide to Clouds' Rest. After

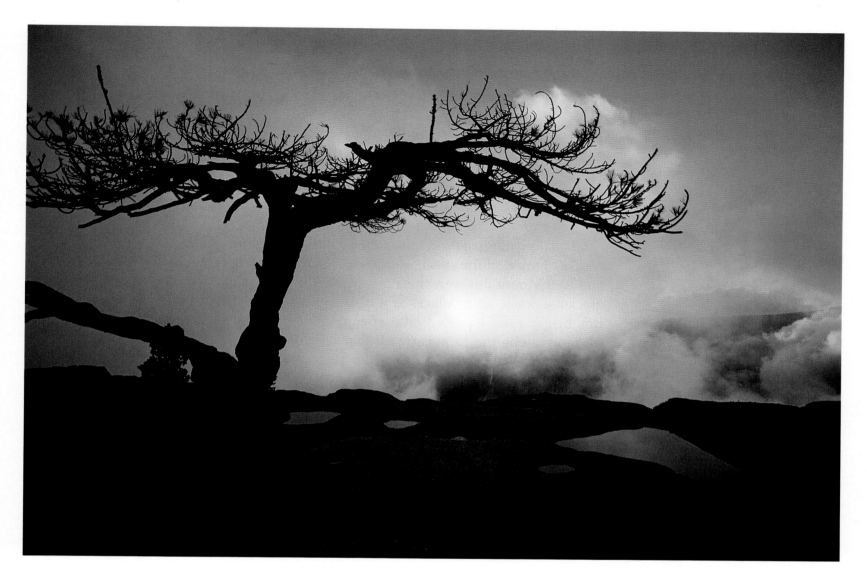

JEFFREY PINE ON SENTINEL
DOME, 1978.

". . . a sturdy storm-enduring
mountaineer of a tree, living on
sunshine and snow, maintaining
tough health on this diet for
perhaps more than a thousand
years."

*For more than a century, Yosemite
visitors marveled at a tenacious
lone pine clinging to life atop
Sentinel Dome. The tree, like a
tough old mountain man, was
gnarled, wiry, photogenic, and very
much alive. In 1976 and 1977
California suffered two years of
extreme drought. The patriarch
died, and as its last dry needles
were falling to the ground the
following year, I waited out a wet
storm, which might have brought
life to the tree a year earlier, to
catch the evening sun bursting
through clouds below the broad
sweep of its curving limbs.*

a glorious view from the crest of this lofty granite wave you will find a trail on its western end that will lead you down past Nevada and Vernal Falls to the Valley in good time, provided you left your Hoffman sky camp early.

TWO-DAY EXCURSIONS: NO. 2.

Another grand two-day excursion is the same as the first of the one-day trips, as far as the head of Illilouette Fall. From there trace the beautiful stream up through the heart of its magnificent forests and gardens to the cañons between the Red and Merced Peaks, and pass the night where I camped forty-one years ago. Early next morning visit the small glacier on the north side of Merced Peak, the first of the sixty-five that I discovered in the Sierra.

Glacial phenomena in the Illilouette Basin are on the grandest scale, and in the course of my explorations I found that the cañon and moraines between the Merced and Red Mountains were the most interesting of them all. The path of the vanished glacier shone in many places as if washed with silver, and pushing up the cañon on this bright road I passed lake after lake in solid basins of granite and many a meadow along the cañon stream that links them together. The main lateral moraines that bound the view below the cañon are from a hundred to nearly two hundred feet high and wonderfully regular, like artificial embankments, covered with a magnificent growth of silver fir and pine. But this garden and forest luxuriance is speedily left behind, and patches of bryanthus, cassiope and arctic willows begin to appear. The small lakes which a few miles down the Valley are so richly bordered with flowery meadows have at an elevation of 10,000 feet only small brown mats of carex, leaving bare rocks around more than half their shores. Yet, strange to say, amid all this arctic repression the mountain pine on ledges and buttresses of Red Mountain seems to find the climate best suited to it. Some specimens that I measured were over a hundred feet high and twenty-four feet in circumference, showing hardly a trace of severe storms, looking as fresh and vigorous as the giants of the lower zones. Evening came on just as I got fairly into the main cañon. It is about a mile wide and a little less than two miles long. The crumbling spurs of Red Mountain bound it on the north, the somber cliffs of Merced Mountain on the south and a deeply-serrated, splintered ridge curving around from mountain to mountain shuts it in on the east. My camp was on the brink of one of the lakes in a thicket of mountain hemlock, partly sheltered from the wind. Early next morning I set out to trace the ancient glacier to its head. Passing around the north shore of my camp lake I followed the main stream from one lakelet to another. The dwarf pines and hemlocks disappeared and the stream was bordered with icicles. The main lateral moraines that extend from the mouth of the cañon are continued in straggling masses along the walls. Tracing the streams back to the highest of its little lakes, I noticed a deposit of fine gray mud, something like the mud worn from a grindstone. This suggested its glacial origin, for the stream that was carrying it issued from a raw-looking moraine that seemed to be in process of formation. It is from sixty to over a hundred feet high in front, with a slope of about thirty-eight degrees. Climbing to the top of it, I discovered a very small but well-characterized glacier swooping down from the shadowy cliffs of the mountain to its terminal moraine. The ice appeared on all the lower portion of the glacier; farther up it was covered with snow. The uppermost crevasse or "bergschrund" was from twelve to fourteen feet wide. The melting snow and ice formed a network of rills that ran gracefully down the

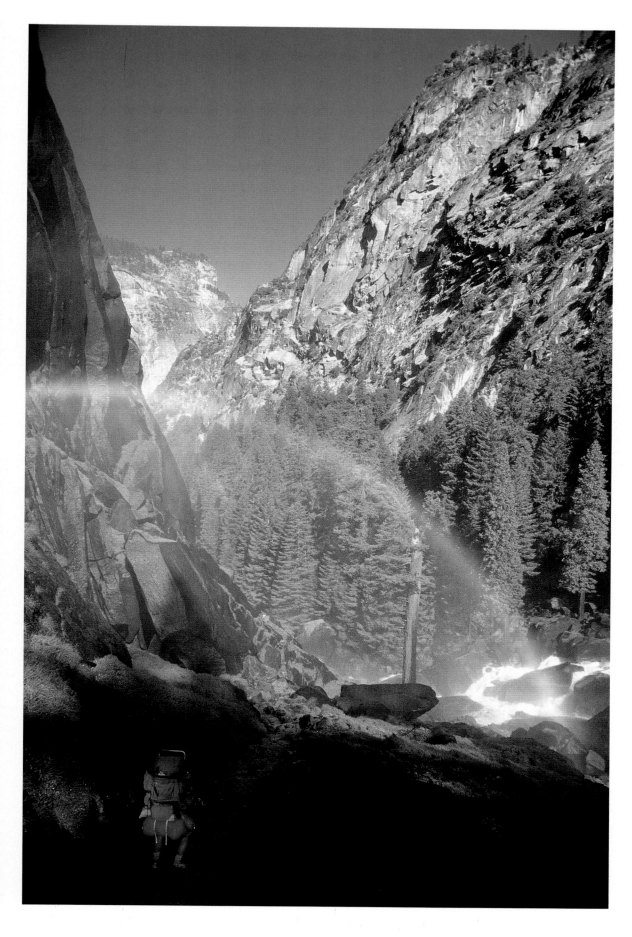

"Our crude civilization engenders a multitude of wants, and lawgivers are ever at their wit's end devising. The hall and the theater and the church have been invented, and compulsory education. Why not add compulsory recreation? Our forefathers forged chains of duty and habit, which bind us notwithstanding our boasted freedom. . . . How hard to pull or shake people out of town! Earthquakes cannot do it, nor even plagues. These only cause the civilized to pray and ring bells and cower in corners of bedrooms and churches."

*The Mist Trail above Happy Isles is the quickest path from the Valley floor to instant wilderness gratification. During the spring and early summer, the amphitheater below Vernal Fall is filled with rolling mists and rainbows. Here one meets tourists out for an hour's stroll as well as hikers with huge packs on the home stretch of the John Muir Trail, which traverses 211 miles of roadless Sierra wilderness.*

surface of the glacier, merrily singing in their shining channels. After this discovery I made excursions over all the High Sierra and discovered that what at first sight looked like snow-fields were in great part glaciers which were completing the sculpture of the summit peaks.

Rising early—which will be easy, as your bed will be rather cold and you will not be able to sleep much anyhow—after visiting the glacier, climb the Red Mountain and enjoy the magnificent views from the summit. I counted forty lakes from one standpoint on this mountain, and the views to the westward over the Illilouette Basin, the most superbly forested of all the basins whose waters drain into Yosemite, and those of the Yosemite rocks, especially the Half Dome and the upper part of the north wall, are very fine. But, of course, far the most imposing view is the vast array of snowy peaks along the axis of the Range. Then from the top of this peak, light and free and exhilarated with mountain air and mountain beauty, you should run lightly down the northern slope of the mountain, descend the cañon between Red and Gray Mountains, thence northward along the bases of Gray Mountain and Mount Clark and go down into the head of Little Yosemite, and thence down past the Nevada and Vernal Falls to the Valley, a truly glorious two-day trip!

### A THREE-DAY EXCURSION

The best three-day excursion, as far as I can see, is the same as the first of the two-day trips until you reach Lake Tenaya. There instead of returning to the Valley, follow the Tioga road around the northwest side of the lake, over to the Tuolumne Meadows and up to the west base of Mount Dana. Leave the road there and make straight for the highest point on the timber-line between Mounts Dana and Gibbs and camp there.

On the morning of the third day go to the top of Mount Dana in time for the glory of the dawn and the sunrise over the gray Mono Desert and the sublime forest of High Sierra peaks. When you leave the mountain go far enough down the north side for a view of the Dana Glacier, then make your way back to the Tioga road, follow it along the Tuolumne Meadows to the crossing of Budd Creek where you will find the Sunrise trail branching off up the mountain-side through the forest in a southwesterly direction past the west side of Cathedral Peak, which will lead you down to the Valley by the Vernal and Nevada Falls. If you are a good walker you can leave the trail where it begins to descend a steep slope in the silver fir woods, and bear off to the right and make straight for the top of Clouds' Rest. The walking is good and almost level and from the west end of Clouds' Rest take the Clouds' Rest trail which will lead direct to the Valley by the Nevada and Vernal Falls. To any one not desperately time-poor this trip should have four days instead of three; camping the second night at the Soda Springs; thence to Mount Dana and return to the Soda Springs, camping the third night there; thence by the Sunrise trail to Cathedral Peak, visiting the beautiful Cathedral Lake which lies about a mile to the west of Cathedral Peak, eating your luncheon, and thence to Clouds' Rest and the Valley as above. This is one of the most interesting of all the comparatively short trips that can be made in the whole Yosemite region. Not only do you see all the grandest of the Yosemite rocks and waterfalls and the High Sierra with their glaciers, glacier lakes and glacier meadows, etc., but sections of the magnificent silver fir, two-leaved pine, and dwarf pine zones; with the principal alpine flowers and shrubs, especially sods of dwarf vaccinium covered with flowers and fruit though less than an inch high, broad mats of dwarf willow scarce an inch high with catkins that rise straight from the ground, and glorious beds of blue gentians—grandeur enough and beauty enough for a lifetime.

### THE UPPER TUOLUMNE EXCURSION

We come now to the grandest of all the Yosemite excursions, one that requires at least two or three weeks. The best time to make it is from about the middle of July. The visitor entering the Yosemite in July has the advantage of seeing the falls not, perhaps, in their very flood prime but next thing to it; while the glacier-meadows will be in their glory and the snow on the mountains will be firm enough to make climbing safe. Long ago I made these Sierra trips, carrying only a sackful of bread with a little tea and sugar and was thus independent and free, but now that trails or carriage roads lead out of the Valley in almost every direction it is easy to take a pack animal, so that the luxury of a blanket and a supply of food can easily be had.

The best way to leave the Valley will be by the Yosemite Fall trail, camping the first night on the Tioga road opposite the east end of the Hoffman Range. Next morning climb Mount Hoffman; thence push on past Tenaya Lake into the Tuolumne Meadows and establish a central camp near the Soda Springs, from which glorious excursions can be made at your leisure. For here in this upper Tuolumne Valley is the widest, smoothest, most serenely spacious, and in every way the most delightful summer pleasure-park in all the High Sierra. And since it is connected with Yosemite by two good trails, and a fairly good carriage road that passes between Yosemite and Mount Hoffman, it is also the most accessible. It is in the heart of the High Sierra east of Yosemite, 8500 to 9000 feet above the level of the sea. The gray, picturesque Cathedral Range bounds it on the south; a similar range or spur, the highest peak of which is Mount Conness, on the north; the noble Mounts Dana, Gibbs, Mammoth, Lyell, McClure and others on the axis of the Range on the east; a heaving, billowing crowd of glacier-polished rocks and Mount Hoffman on the west. Down through the open sunny meadow-levels of the Valley flows the Tuolumne River, fresh and cool from its many glacial fountains, the highest of which are the glaciers that lie on the north sides of Mount Lyell and Mount McClure.

Along the river a series of beautiful glacier-meadows extend with but little interruption, from the lower end of the Valley to its head, a distance of about twelve miles, forming charming sauntering-grounds from which the glorious mountains may be enjoyed as they look down in divine serenity over the dark forests that clothe their bases. Narrow strips of pine woods cross the meadow-carpet from side to side, and it is somewhat roughened here and there by moraine boulders and dead trees brought down from the heights by snow avalanches; but for miles and miles it is so smooth and level that a hundred horsemen may ride abreast over it.

The main lower portion of the meadows is about four miles long and from a quarter to half a mile wide, but the width of the Valley is, on an average, about eight miles. Tracing the river, we find that it forks a mile above the Soda Springs, the main fork turning southward to Mount Lyell, the other eastward to Mount Dana and Mount Gibbs. Along both forks strips of meadow extend almost to their heads. The most beautiful portions of the meadows are spread over lake basins, which have been filled up by deposits from the river. A few of these river-lakes still exist, but they are now shallow and are rapidly approaching extinction. The sod in most places is exceedingly fine and silky and free from weeds and bushes; while charming flowers abound, especially gentians, dwarf daisies, potentillas, and the pink bells of dwarf vaccinium. On the banks of the river and its tributaries cassiope and bryanthus may be found, where the sod curls over stream banks and around boulders. The principal grass of these meadows is a delicate calamagrostis with very slender filiform leaves, and when it is in flower the ground seems to be covered with a faint purple mist, the stems of the panicles being so fine that they are almost invisible, and offer no appreciable resistance in walking through them. Along the edges of the meadows beneath the pines and throughout the greater part of the Valley tall ribbon-leaved grasses grow in abundance, chiefly bromus, triticum and agrostis.

In October the nights are frosty, and then the meadows at sunrise, when every leaf is laden with crystals, are a fine sight. The days are still warm and calm, and bees and butterflies continue to waver and hum about the late-blooming flowers until the coming of the snow, usually in November. Storm then follows storm in quick succession, burying the meadows to a depth of from ten to twenty feet, while magnificent avalanches descend through the forests from the laden heights, depositing huge piles of snow mixed with uprooted trees and boulders. In the open sunshine the snow usually lasts until the end of June but the new season's vegetation is not generally in bloom until late in July. Perhaps the best all round excursion-time after winters of average snowfall is from the middle of July to the middle or end of August. The snow is then melted from the woods and southern slopes of the mountains and the meadows and gardens are in their glory, while the weather is mostly all-reviving, exhilarating sunshine. The few clouds that rise now and then and the showers they yield are only enough to keep everything fresh and fragrant.

The groves about the Soda Springs are favorite camping-grounds on account of the cold, pleasant-tasting water charged with carbonic acid, and because of the views of the mountains across the meadow—the Glacier Monument, Cathedral Peak, Cathedral Spires, Unicorn Peak and a series of ornamental nameless companions, rising in striking forms and nearness above a dense forest growing on the left lateral moraine of the ancient Tuolumne Glacier, which, broad, deep, and far-reaching, exerted vast influence on the scenery of this portion of the Sierra. But there are fine camping-grounds all along the meadows, and one may move from grove to grove every day all summer, enjoying new homes and new beauty to satisfy every roving desire for change.

There are five main capital excursions to be made from here—to the summits of Mounts Dana, Lyell and Conness, and through the Bloody Cañon Pass to Mono Lake and the volcanoes, and down the Tuolumne Cañon, at least as far as the foot of the wonderful series of river cataracts. All of these excursions are sure to be made memorable with joyful health-giving experiences; but perhaps none of them will be remembered with keener delight than the days spent in sauntering on the broad velvet lawns by the river, sharing the sky with the mountains and trees, gaining something of their strength and peace.

The excursion to the top of Mount Dana is a very easy one; for though the mountain is 13,000 feet high, the ascent from the west side is so gentle and smooth that one may ride a mule to the very summit. Across many a busy stream, from meadow to meadow, lies your flowery way; mountains all about you, few of them hidden by irregular foregrounds. Gradually ascending, other mountains come in sight, peak

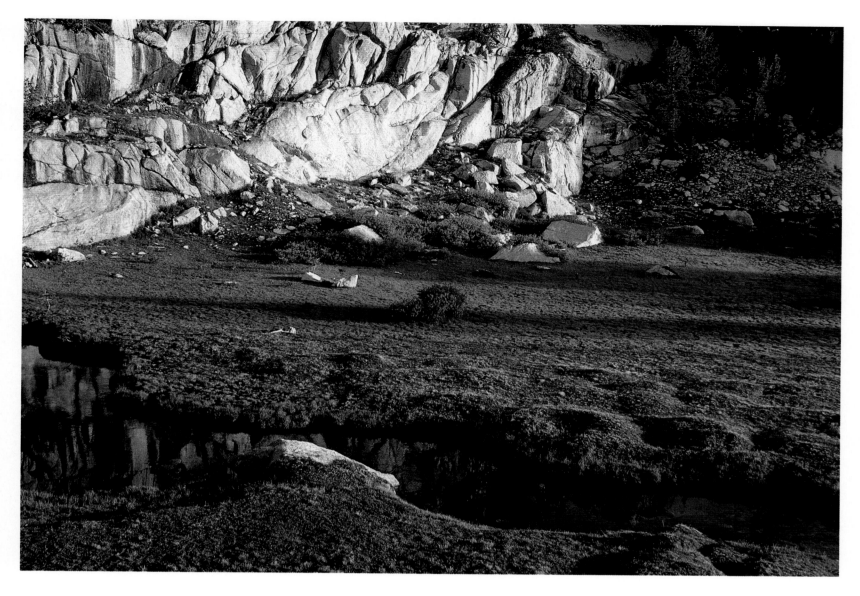

TIMBERLINE CREEK, MOUNT
CONNESS, 1987.

"One is constantly reminded of the
infinite lavishness and fertility of
Nature—inexhaustible abundance
amid what seems enormous waste.
And yet when we look into any of
her operations that lie within reach
of our minds, we learn that no
particle of her material is wasted or
worn out. It is eternally flowing
from use to use, beauty to yet
higher beauty . . . its next
appearance will be better and more
beautiful than the last."

*In early summer I headed out before
daylight to climb Mount Conness.
Within the hour I was stopped in
my tracks by the clarity and
simplicity of this rockbound
meadow. Vivid new grass sprouted
evenly from a carpet of soil recently
exposed by the melting snow. I
decided to postpone my ascent and
wait for first light to hit this little
alpine paradise. With my camera
perched on a stack of rocks instead
of on the tripod I had left behind, I
was able to make as carefully
controlled a photograph as I could
have made with a full load of gear,
the difference being that I never
would have happened on this
remote scene at dawn had I been
burdened with more gear.*

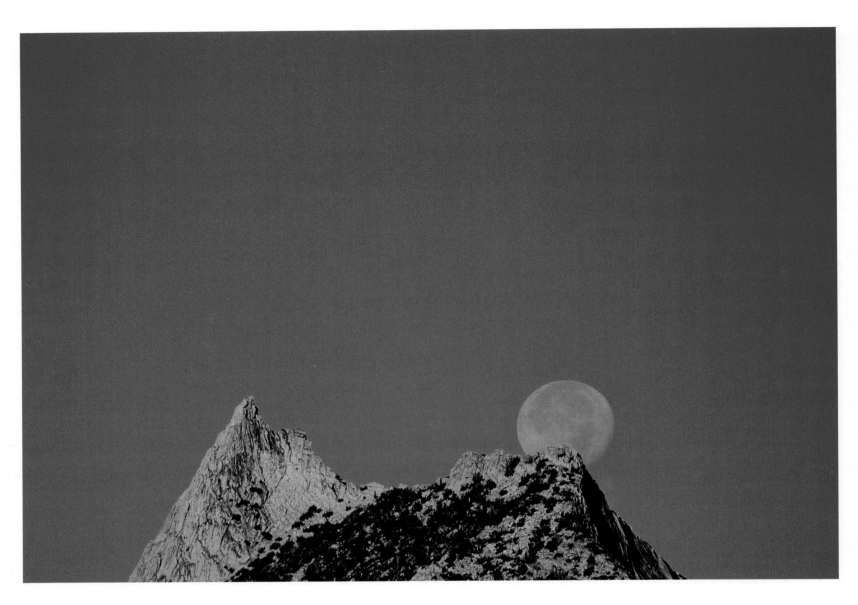

MOONSET OVER CATHEDRAL
PEAK, 1987.

"The grand Sierra Cathedral [is] a
building of one stone, hewn from
the living rock, with sides, roof,
gable, spire and ornamental
pinnacles, fashioned and finished
symmetrically like a work of
art. . . . From every direction its
peculiar form and graceful, majestic
beauty of expression never fail
to charm."

*The sight of a moon in a mountain
sky is not only an evening or
twilight phenomenon. On clear
days the sky is so dark that the
moon stays visible well into the day.
One morning long after the flush of
dawn had given way to the full light
of day, I spotted a nearly full moon
hanging low in the sky and chased
it across Tuolumne Meadows
until it touched the spire of
Cathedral Peak.*

rising above peak with their snow and ice in endless variety of grouping and sculpture. Now your attention is turned to the moraines, sweeping in beautiful curves from the hollows and cañons, now to the granite waves and pavements rising here and there above the heathy sod, polished a thousand years ago and still shining. Towards the base of the mountain you note the dwarfing of the trees, until at a height of about 11,000 feet you find patches of the tough, white-barked pine, pressed so flat by the ten or twenty feet of snow piled upon them every winter for centuries that you may walk over them as if walking on a shaggy rug. And, if curious about such things, you may discover specimens of this hardy tree-mountaineer not more than four feet high and about as many inches in diameter at the ground, that are from two hundred to four hundred years old, still holding bravely to life, making the most of their slender summers, shaking their tasseled needles in the breeze right cheerily, drinking the thin sunshine and maturing their fine purple cones as if they meant to live forever. The general view from the summit is one of the most extensive and sublime to be found in all the Range. To the eastward you gaze far out over the desert plains and mountains of the "Great Basin," range beyond range extending with soft outlines, blue and purple in the distance. More than six thousand feet below you lies Lake Mono, ten miles in diameter from north to south, and fourteen from west to east, lying bare in the treeless desert like a disk of burnished metal, though at times it is swept by mountain storm-winds and streaked with foam. To the southward there is a well-defined range of pale-gray extinct volcanoes, and though the highest of them rises nearly two thousand feet above the lake, you can look down from here into their circular, cup-like craters, from which a comparatively short time ago ashes and cinders were showered over the surrounding sage plains and glacier-laden mountains.

To the westward the landscape is made up of exceedingly strong, gray, glaciated domes and ridge waves, most of them comparatively low, but the largest high enough to be called mountains; separated by cañons and darkened with lines and fields of forest, Cathedral Peak and Mount Hoffman in the distance; small lakes and innumerable meadows in the foreground. Northward and southward the great snowy mountains, marshaled along the axis of the Range, are seen in all their glory, crowded together in some places like trees in groves, making landscapes of wild, extravagant, bewildering magnificence, yet calm and silent as the sky.

Some eight glaciers are in sight. One of these is the Dana Glacier on the north side of the mountain, lying at the foot of a precipice about a thousand feet high, with a lovely pale-green lake a little below it. This is one of the many, small, shrunken remnants of the vast glacial system of the Sierra that once filled the hollows and valleys of the mountains and covered all the lower ridges below the immediate summit-fountains, flowing to right and left away from the axis of the Range, lavishly fed by the snows of the glacial period.

In the excursion to Mount Lyell the immediate base of the mountain is easily reached on meadow walks along the river. Turning to the southward above the forks of the river, you enter the narrow Lyell branch of the Valley, narrow enough and deep enough to be called a cañon. It is about eight miles long and from 2000 to 3000 feet deep. The flat meadow bottom is from about three hundred to two hundred yards wide, with gently curved margins about fifty yards wide from which rise the simple massive walls of gray granite at an angle of about thirty-three degrees, mostly timbered with a light growth of pine and streaked in many places with avalanche channels. Towards the upper end of the cañon the Sierra crown comes in sight, forming a finely balanced picture framed by the massive cañon walls. In the foreground, when the grass is in flower, you have the purple meadow willow-thickets on the river banks; in the middle distance huge swelling bosses of granite that form the base of the general mass of the mountain, with fringing lines of dark woods marking the lower curves, smoothly snow-clad except in the autumn.

If you wish to spend two days on the Lyell trip you will find a good camp-ground on the east side of the river, about a mile above a fine cascade that comes down over the cañon wall in telling style and makes good camp music. From here to the top of the mountains is usually an easy day's work. At one place near the summit careful climbing is necessary, but it is not so dangerous or difficult as to deter any one of ordinary skill, while the views are glorious. To the northward are Mammoth Mountain, Mounts Gibbs, Dana, Warren, Conness and others, unnumbered and unnamed; to the southeast the indescribably wild and jagged range of Mount Ritter and the Minarets; southwestward stretches the dividing ridge between the north fork of the San Joaquin and the Merced, uniting with the Obelisk or Merced group of peaks that form the main fountains of the Illilouette branch of the Merced; and to the northwestward extends the Cathedral spur. These spurs like distinct ranges meet at your feet; therefore you look at them mostly in the direction of their exten-sion, and their peaks seem to be massed and crowded against one another, while immense amphitheaters, cañons and subordinate ridges with their wealth of lakes, glaciers, and snow-fields, maze and cluster between them. In making the ascent in June or October the glacier is easily crossed, for then its snow mantle is smooth or mostly melted off. But in midsummer the climbing is exceedingly tedious because the snow is then weathered into curious and beautiful blades, sharp and slender, and set on edge in a leaning position. They lean towards the head of the glacier and extend across from side to side in regular order in a direction at right angles to the direction of greatest declivity, the distance between the crests being about two or three feet, and the depth of the troughs between them about three feet. A more interesting problem than a walk over a glacier thus sculptured and adorned is sel-dom presented to the mountaineer.

The Lyell Glacier is about a mile wide and less than a mile long, but presents, nevertheless, all the essential characters of large, river-like glaciers—moraines, earth-bands, blue veins, crevasses, etc., while the streams that issue from it are, of course, turbid with rock-mud, showing its grinding action on its bed. And it is all the more interesting since it is the highest and most enduring remnant of the great Tuolumne Glacier, whose traces are still distinct fifty miles away, and whose influ-ence on the landscape was so profound. The McClure Glacier, once a tributary of the Lyell, is smaller. Thirty-eight years ago I set a series of stakes in it to determine its rate of motion. Towards the end of summer in the middle of the glacier it was only a little over an inch in twenty-four hours.

The trip to Mono from the Soda Springs can be made in a day, but many days may profitably be spent near the shores of the lake, out on its islands and about the volcanoes.

In making the trip down the Big Tuolumne Cañon, animals may be led as far as a small, grassy, forested lake-basin that lies below the crossing of the Virginia Creek trail. And from this point any one accustomed to walking on earthquake boulders, carpeted with cañon chaparral, can easily go down as far as the big cascades and

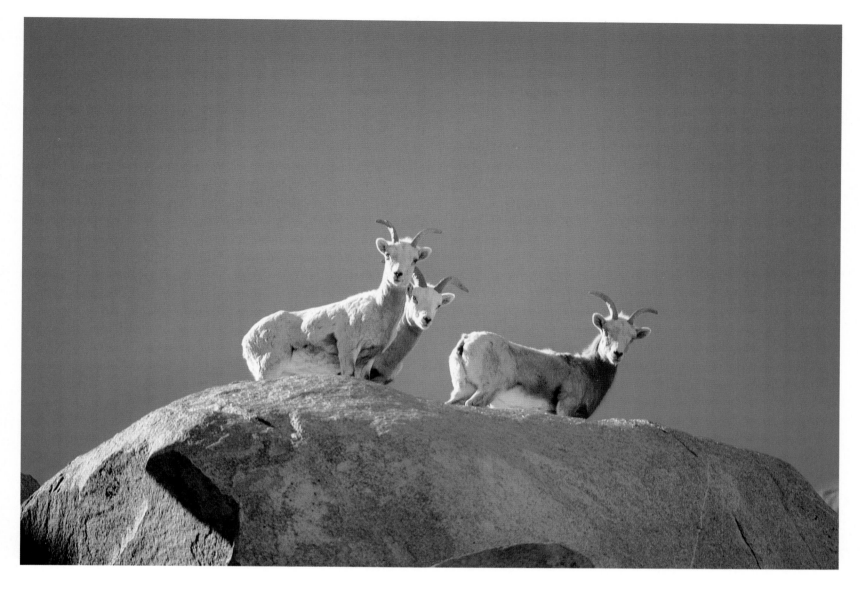

CALIFORNIA BIGHORN SHEEP,
BAXTER PASS HERD, 1972.

"The domestic sheep . . . is
expressionless, like a dull bundle of
something only half alive, while the
wild is as elegant and graceful as a
deer, every movement manifesting
admirable strength and character.
The tame is timid; the wild is bold.
The tame is always more or less
ruffled and dirty; while the wild is
as smooth and clean as the flowers
of his mountain pastures."

*John Muir found bighorn skulls in
the Yosemite high country, but
never saw a live animal until he
ventured south, out of what is now
the national park, into regions
where the sheep had not been
disturbed by the grazing of
domestic herds. I made twelve
unsuccessful outings to photograph
some of the last two-hundred-odd
animals remaining in the High
Sierra before the lucky winter
morning when I suddenly became
aware of three sheep staring at me
from the safety of a cliff just a
hundred feet away. Since then a few
members of the same herd have
been transplanted to Lee Vining
Canyon, just east of Tioga Pass, and
sheep may again be seen on
Yosemite's high peaks in years
to come.*

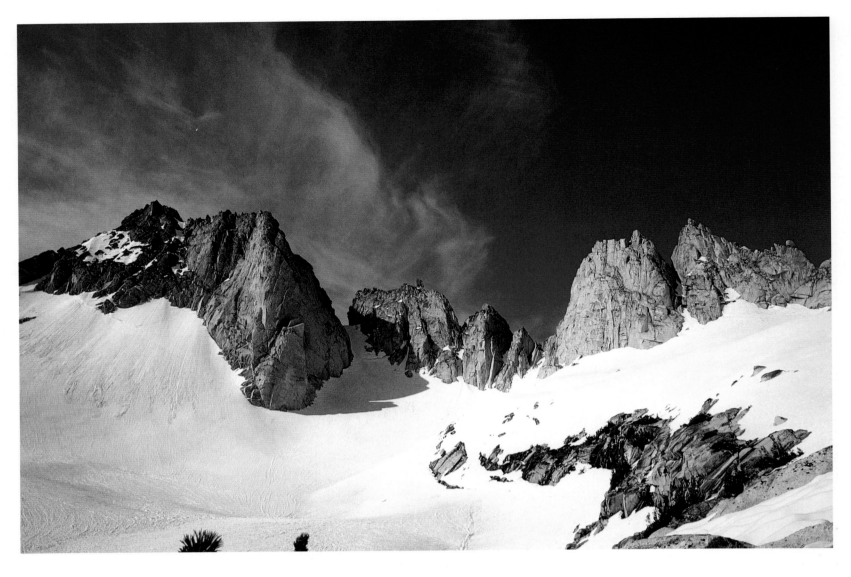

SAWTOOTH RANGE, NORTHERN
YOSEMITE, 1969.

"Looking northward and
southward along the axis of the
range, you see the glorious array of
high mountains, crags and peaks
and snow, the fountain-heads of
rivers that are flowing west to
the sea."

*The spires of the Sawtooth Range in
the little-visited northeast corner of
the park are reminiscent of the
aiguilles of Chamonix, in the French
Alps. In this midsummer scene,
during one of the snowiest years in
history, the spires remain
snowbound in late July.*

return to camp in one day. Many, however, are not able to do this, and it is better to go leisurely, prepared to camp anywhere, and enjoy the marvelous grandeur of the place.

The cañon begins near the lower end of the meadows and extends to the Hetch Hetchy Valley, a distance of about eighteen miles, though it will seem much longer to any one who scrambles through it. It is from twelve hundred to about five thousand feet deep, and is comparatively narrow, but there are several roomy, park-like openings in it, and throughout its whole extent Yosemite features are displayed on a grand scale—domes, El Capitan rocks, gables, Sentinels, Royal Arches, Glacier Points, Cathedral Spires, etc. There is even a Half Dome among its wealth of rock forms, though far less sublime than the Yosemite Half Dome. Its falls and cascades are innumerable. The sheer falls, except when the snow is melting in early spring, are quite small in volume as compared with those of Yosemite and Hetch Hetchy; though in any other country many of them would be regarded as wonders. But it is the cascades or sloping falls on the main river that are the crowning glory of the cañon, and these in volume, extent and variety surpass those of any other cañon in the Sierra. The most showy and interesting of them are mostly in the upper part of the cañon, above the point of entrance of Cathedral Creek and Hoffman Creek. For miles the river is one wild, exulting, on-rushing mass of snowy purple bloom, spreading over glacial waves of granite without any definite channel, gliding in magnificent silver plumes, dashing and foaming through huge boulder-dams, leaping high into the air in wheel-like whirls, displaying glorious enthusiasm, tossing from side to side, doubling, glinting, singing in exuberance of mountain energy.

Every one who is anything of a mountaineer should go on through the entire length of the cañon, coming out by Hetch Hetchy. There is not a dull step all the way. With wide variations, it is a Yosemite Valley from end to end.

Besides these main, far-reaching, much-seeing excursions from the main central camp, there are numberless, lovely little saunters and scrambles and a dozen or so not so very little. Among the best of these are to Lambert and Fair View Domes; to the topmost spires of Cathedral Peak, and to those of the North Church, around the base of which you pass on your way to Mount Conness; to one of the very loveliest of the glacier-meadows imbedded in the pine woods about three miles north of the Soda Springs, where forty-two years ago I spent six weeks. It trends east and west, and you can find it easily by going past the base of Lambert's Dome to Dog Lake and thence up northward through the woods about a mile or so; to the shining rock-waves full of ice-burnished, feldspar crystals at the foot of the meadows; to Lake Tenaya; and, last but not least, a rather long and very hearty scramble down by the end of the meadow along the Tioga road toward Lake Tenaya to the crossing of Cathedral Creek, where you turn off and trace the creek down to its confluence with the Tuolumne. This is a genuine scramble much of the way but one of the most wonderfully telling in its glacial rock-forms and inscriptions.

If you stop and fish at every tempting lake and stream you come to, a whole month, or even two months, will not be too long for this grand High Sierra excursion. My own Sierra trip was ten years long.

## OTHER TRIPS FROM THE VALLEY

Short carriage trips are usually made in the early morning to Mirror Lake to see its wonderful reflections of the Half Dome and Mount Watkins; and in the afternoon

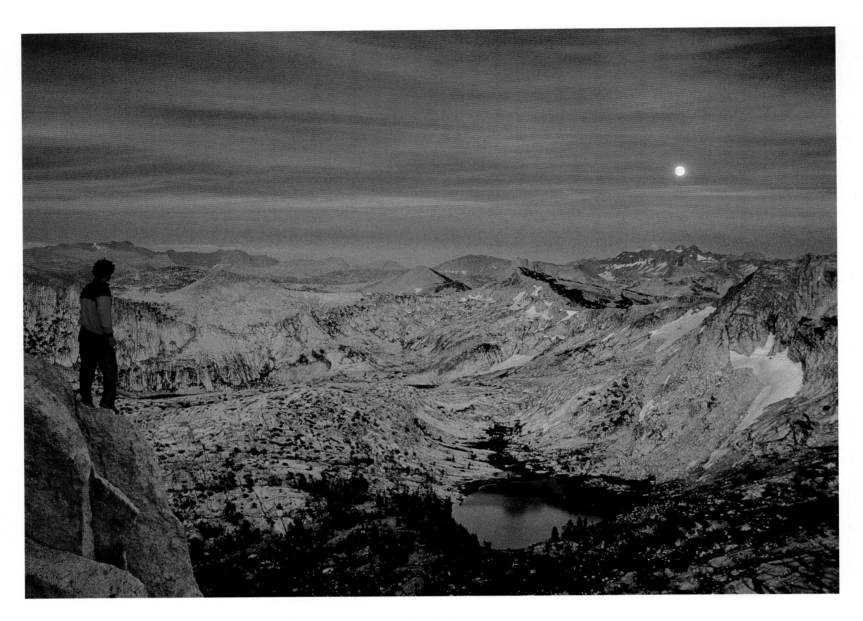

CLIMBER AND MOONRISE,
CATHEDRAL PEAK, 1987.

"No feature, however, of all the
noble landscape as seen from here
seems more wonderful than the
Cathedral itself, a temple displaying
Nature's best masonry and sermons
in stones. . . . This I may say is the
first time I have been in church in
California."

*Perhaps even more wonderful than
Muir's midday vision from atop
Cathedral Peak in 1869 after a
remarkable solo first ascent of steep
granite is this modern climber's
view of moonrise at twilight from
the same summit rocks.*

many ride down the Valley to see the Bridal Veil rainbows or up the river cañon to see those of the Vernal Fall; where, standing in the spray, not minding getting drenched, you may see what are called round rainbows, when the two ends of the ordinary bow are lengthened and meet at your feet, forming a complete circle which is broken and united again and again as determined by the varying wafts of spray. A few ambitious scramblers climb to the top of the Sentinel Rock, others walk or ride down the Valley and up to the once-famous Inspiration Point for a last grand view; while a good many appreciative tourists, who have only a day or two, do no climbing or riding but spend their time sauntering on the meadows by the river, watching the falls, and the play of light and shade among the rocks from morning to night, perhaps gaining more than those who make haste up the trails in large noisy parties. Those who have unlimited time find something worth while all the year round on every accessible part of the vast, deeply sculptured walls. At least so I have found it after making the Valley my home for years.

Here are a few specimens selected from my own short trips which walkers may find useful.

One, up the river cañon, across the bridge between the Vernal and Nevada Falls, through chaparral beds and boulders to the shoulder of Half Dome, along the top of the shoulder to the dome itself, down by a crumbling slot gully and close along the base of the tremendous split front (the most awfully impressive, sheer, precipice view I ever found in all my cañon wanderings), thence up the east shoulder and along the ridge to Clouds' Rest—a glorious sunset—then a grand starry run back home to my cabin; down through the junipers, down through the firs, now in black shadows, now in white light, past roaring Nevada and Vernal, glowering ghost-like beneath their huge frowning cliffs; down the dark, gloomy cañon, through the pines of the Valley, dreamily murmuring in their calm, breezy sleep—a fine wild little excursion for good legs and good eyes—so much sun-, moon- and star-shine in it, and sublime, up-and-down rhythmical, glacial topography.

Another, to the head of Yosemite Fall by Indian Cañon; thence up the Yosemite Creek, tracing it all the way to its highest sources back of Mount Hoffman, then a wide sweep around the head of its dome-paved basin, passing its many little lakes and bogs, gardens and groves, trilling, warbling rills, and back by the Fall Cañon. This was one of my Sabbath walk, run-and-slide excursions long ago before any trail had been made on the north side of the Valley.

Another fine trip was up, bright and early, by Avalanche Cañon to Glacier Point, along the rugged south wall, tracing all its far outs and ins to the head of the Bridal Veil Fall, thence back home, bright and late, by a brushy, bouldery slope between Cathedral rocks and Cathedral spires and along the level Valley floor. This was one of my long, bright-day and bright-night walks thirty or forty years ago when, like river and ocean currents, time flowed undivided, uncounted—a fine free, sauntery, scrambly, botanical, beauty-filled ramble. The walk up the Valley was made glorious by the marvelous brightness of the morning star. So great was her light, she made every tree cast a well-defined shadow on the smooth sandy ground.

Everybody who visits Yosemite wants to see the famous Big Trees. Before the railroad was constructed, all three of the stage-roads that entered the Valley passed through a grove of these trees by the way; namely, the Tuolumne, Merced and Mariposa groves. The Tuolumne grove was passed on the Big Oak Flat road, the Merced grove by the Coulterville road and the Mariposa grove by the Raymond and Wawona road. Now, to see any one of these groves, a special trip has to be made. Most visitors go to the Mariposa grove, the largest of the three. On this Sequoia trip you see not only the giant Big Trees but magnificent forests of silver fir, sugar pine, yellow pine, libocedrus and Douglas spruce. The trip need not require more than two days, spending a night in a good hotel at Wawona, a beautiful place on the south fork of the Merced River, and returning to the Valley or to El Portal, the terminus of the railroad. This extra trip by stage costs fifteen dollars. All the High Sierra excursions that I have sketched cost from a dollar a week to anything you like. None of mine when I was exploring the Sierra cost over a dollar a week, most of them less.

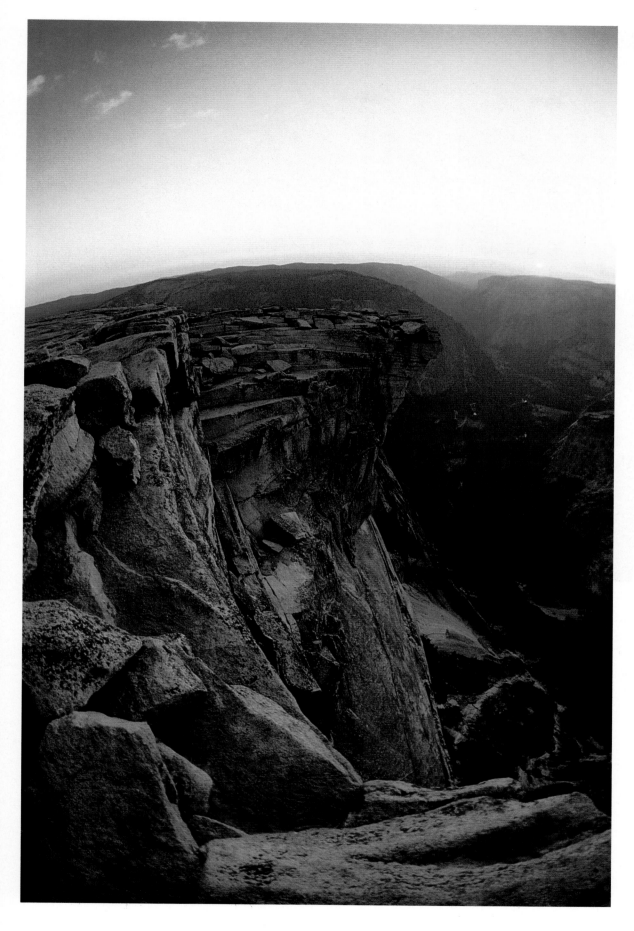

VIEW INTO YOSEMITE VALLEY
FROM HALF DOME, 1987.

"Bathed in the purple light of
evening, and beating time to the
tones of the falls, the whole seems a
work of enchantment."

*Because the effect of watching
sunset from Half Dome's summit
defies any single plane of vision, I
chose an extreme wide-angle to
capture the Dome beneath my feet,
the yawning chasm of the
Northwest Face, the Valley far
below, and the evening sky glowing
in the distance. Even with the
obvious wide-angle distortion, this
view remains truest to my
perception of being there at the
edge of the abyss, alone, bathed in
purple light.*

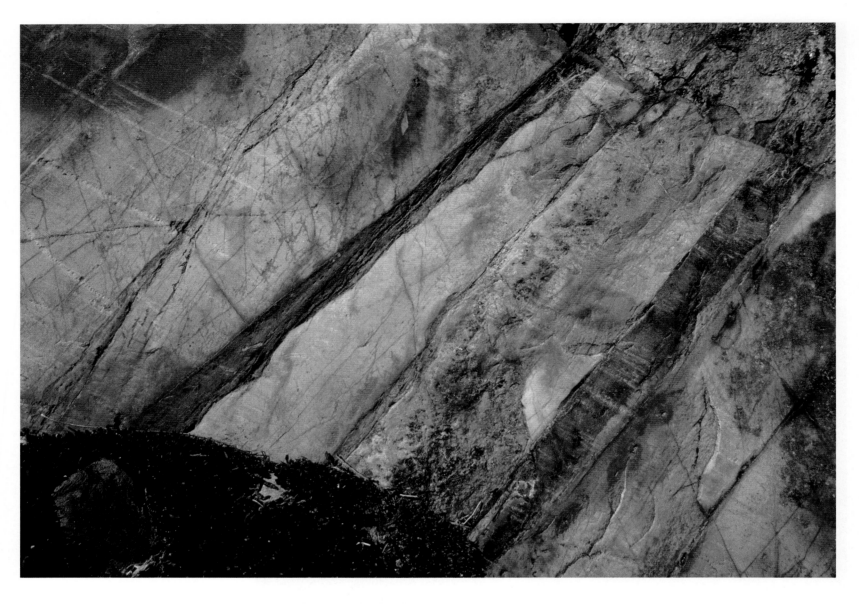

GLACIER-POLISHED DIKE
PATTERNS, TIOGA PASS, 1987.

"The cleanness of the ground
suggests Nature taking pains like a
housewife, the rock pavements seem
as if carefully swept and dusted and
polished every day. No wonder one
feels a magic exhilaration when
these pavements are touched."

*The ancient metamorphic rocks
atop Tioga Pass take on an entirely
different look from their normal
hackly appearance where ice has
ground their surfaces into works of
natural art that somehow remain as
clean and complete as on that day
long ago when a glacier melted
back to expose its handiwork.*

CHAPTER XIII

# Early History of the Valley

IN THE WILD GOLD YEARS of 1849 and '50, the Indian tribes along the western Sierra foothills became alarmed at the sudden invasion of their acorn orchard and game fields by miners, and soon began to make war upon them, in their usual murdering, plundering style. This continued until the United States Indian Commissioners succeeded in gathering them into reservations, some peacefully, others by burning their villages and stores of food. The Yosemite or Grizzly Bear tribe, fancying themselves secure in their deep mountain stronghold, were the most troublesome and defiant of all, and it was while the Mariposa battalion, under command of Major Savage, was trying to capture this war-like tribe and conduct them to the Fresno reservation that their deep mountain home, the Yosemite Valley, was discovered. From a camp on the south fork of the Merced, Major Savage sent Indian runners to the bands who were supposed to be hiding in the mountains, instructing them to tell the Indians that if they would come in and make treaty with the Commissioners they would be furnished with food and clothing and be protected, but if they did not come in he would make war upon them and kill them all. None of the Yosemite Indians responded to this general message, but when a special messenger was sent to the chief he appeared the next day. He came entirely alone and stood in dignified silence before one of the guards until invited to enter the camp. He was recognized by one of the friendly Indians as Tenaya, the old chief of the Grizzlies, and, after he had been supplied with food, Major Savage, with the aid of Indian interpreters, informed him of the wishes of the Commissioners. But the old chief was very suspicious of Savage and feared that he was taking this method of getting the tribe into his power for the purpose of revenging his personal wrong. Savage told him if he would go to the Commissioners and make peace with them as the other tribes had done there would be no more war. Tenaya inquired what was the object of taking all the Indians to the San Joaquin plain. "My people," said he, "do not want anything from the Great Father you tell me about. The Great Spirit is our father and he has always supplied us with all we need. We do not want anything from white men. Our women are able to do our work. Go, then. Let us remain in the mountains where we were born, where the ashes of our fathers have been given to the wind. I have said enough."

To this the Major answered abruptly in Indian style: "If you and your people have all you desire, why do you steal our horses and mules? Why do you rob the miners' camps? Why do you murder the white men and plunder and burn their houses?"

Tenaya was silent for some time. He evidently understood what the Major had said, for he replied, "My young men have sometimes taken horses and mules from the whites. This was wrong. It is not wrong to take the property of enemies who have wronged my people. My young men believed that the gold diggers were our enemies. We now know they are not and we shall be glad to live in peace with them. We will stay here and be friends. My people do not want to go to the plains. Some of the tribes who have gone there are very bad. We cannot live with them. Here we can defend ourselves."

To this Major Savage firmly said, "Your people must go to the Commissioners. If they do not your young men will again steal horses and kill and plunder the whites. It was your people who robbed my stores, burned my houses and murdered my men. If they do not make a treaty, your whole tribe will be destroyed. Not one of them will be left alive."

To this the old chief replied, "It is useless to talk to you about who destroyed your property and killed your people. I am old and you can kill me if you will, but it is useless to lie to you who know more than all the Indians. Therefore I will not lie to you but if you will let me return to my people I will bring them in." He was allowed to go. The next day he came back and said his people were on the way to our camp to go with the men sent by the Great Father, who was so good and rich.

Another day passed but no Indians from the deep Valley appeared. The old chief said that the snow was so deep and his village was so far down that it took a long time to climb out of it. After waiting still another day the expedition started for the Valley. When Tenaya was questioned as to the route and distance he said that the snow was so deep that the horses could not go through it. Old Tenaya was taken along as guide. When the party had gone about half-way to the Valley they met the Yosemites on their way to the camp on the south fork. There were only seventy-two of them and when the old chief was asked what had become of the rest of his band, he replied, "This is all of my people that are willing to go with me to the plains. All the rest have gone with their wives and children over the mountains to the Mono and Tuolumne tribes." Savage told Tenaya that he was not telling the truth, for Indians could not cross the mountains in the deep snow, and that he knew they must still be at his village or hiding somewhere near it. The tribe had been estimated to number over two hundred. Major Savage then said to him, "You may return to camp with your people and I will take one of your young men with me to your village to see your people who will not come. They will come if I find them." "You will not find any of my people there," said Tenaya; "I do not know where they are. My tribe is small. Many of the people of my tribe have come from other tribes and if they go to the plains and are seen they will be killed by the friends of those with whom they have quarreled. I was told that I was growing old and it was well that I should go, but that young and strong men can find plenty in the mountains: therefore, why should they go to the hot plains to be penned up like horses and cattle? My heart has been sore since that talk but I am now willing to go, for it is best for my people."

Pushing ahead, taking turns in breaking a way through the snow, they arrived in sight of the great Valley early in the afternoon and, guided by one of Tenaya's In-

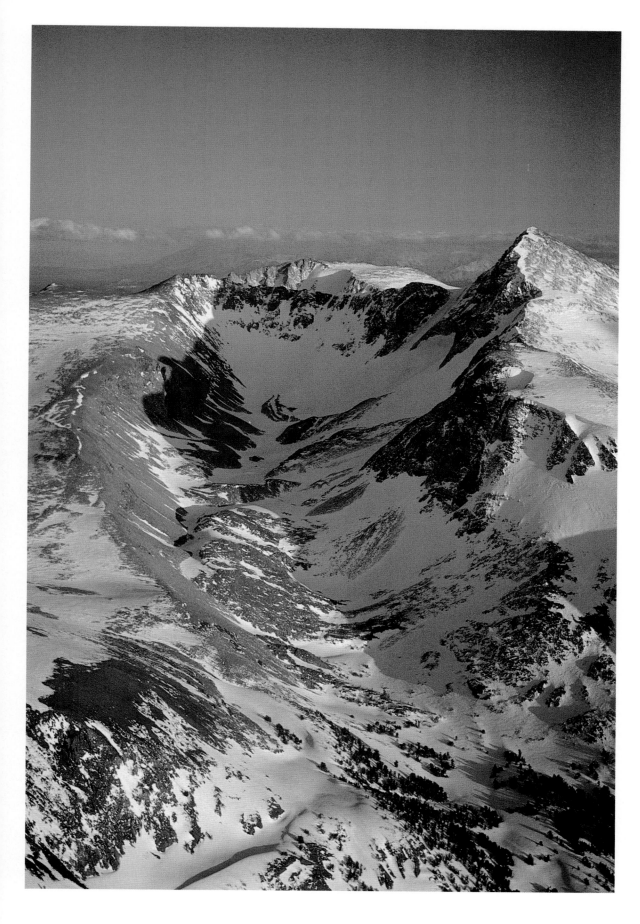

AERIAL VIEW OF MOUNT DANA AND ITS GLACIER, 1984.

"Two years ago, when picking flowers in the mountains back of Yosemite Valley, I found a book. It was blotted and storm-beaten; all of its outer pages were mealy and crumbly, the paper seemed to dissolve like the snow beneath which it had been buried; but many of the inner pages were well preserved, and though all were more or less stained and torn, whole chapters were easily readable. In this condition is the great open book of Yosemite glaciers today; its granite pages have been torn and blurred by the same storms that wasted the castaway book."

*Although I had climbed Mount Dana by several routes, I had never made sense of its whole—the way glaciers, past and present, have influenced its shape—until I flew low over the peak after a dusting of fall snow had etched its contours in bold relief. And Dana is one of the cleaner pages in the book of Yosemite prehistory.*

MOUNT DANA AT DAWN OVER
MONO LAKE, 1988.

"Eastward, the whole region seems
a land of desolation covered with
beautiful light. The torrid volcanic
basin of Mono, with its one bare
lake fourteen miles long; Owen's
Valley and the broad lava table-land
at its head, dotted with craters, and
the massive Inyo Range, rivaling
even the Sierra in height; these are
spread, map-like, beneath you, with
countless ranges beyond, passing
and overlapping one another and
fading on the glowing horizon."

*Mono Lake today presents an
otherworldly appearance of alkaline
tufa towers emerging from briny
waters that are receding year by
year because of the insatiable thirst
of the city of Los Angeles. Long
ago, however, Mono Lake had an
even more incongruous look.
Geologists have discovered
overlapping fossil shorelines and
glacial moraines. Several thousand
years ago, when human beings
might possibly have been there to
see it, the Tioga Glacier was one
continuous stream of ice from
Mount Dana in Yosemite down to
the shore of the lake, where icebergs
calved off and floated across the
waters to melt or run aground on
the arid desert shores.*

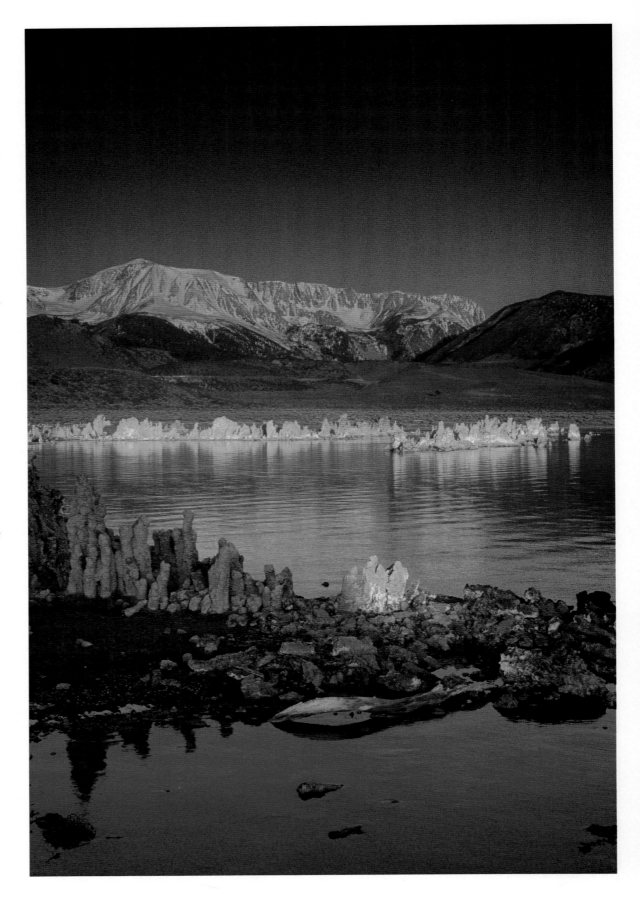

dians, descended by the same route as that followed by the Mariposa trail, and the weary party went into camp on the river bank opposite El Capitan. After supper, seated around a big fire, the wonderful Valley became the topic of conversation and Dr. Bunell suggested giving it a name. Many were proposed, but after a vote had been taken the name Yosemite, proposed by Dr. Bunell, was adopted almost unanimously to perpetuate the name of the tribe who so long had made their home there. The Indian name of the Valley, however, is Ahwahnee. The Indians had names for all the different rocks and streams of the Valley, but very few of them are now in use by the whites, Pohono, the Bridal Veil, being the principal one. The expedition remained only one day and two nights in the Valley, hurrying out on the approach of a storm and reached the south-fork headquarters on the evening of the third day after starting out. Thus, in three days the round trip had been made to the Valley, most of it had been explored in a general way and some of its principal features had been named. But the Indians had fled up the Tenaya Cañon trail and none of them were seen, except an old woman unable to follow the fugitives.

A second expedition was made in the same year under command of Major Boling. When the Valley was entered no Indians were seen, but the many wigwams with smoldering fires showed that they had been hurriedly abandoned that very day. Later, five young Indians who had been left to watch the movements of the expedition were captured at the foot of the Three Brothers after a lively chase. Three of the five were sons of the old chief and the rock was named for them. All of these captives made good their escape within a few days, except the youngest son of Tenaya, who was shot by his guard while trying to escape. That same day the old chief was captured on the cliff on the east side of Indian Cañon by some of Boling's scouts. As Tenaya walked toward the camp his eye fell upon the dead body of his favorite son. Captain Boling through an interpreter, expressed his regret at the occurrence, but not a word did Tenaya utter in reply. Later, he made an attempt to escape but was caught as he was about to swim across the river. Tenaya expected to be shot for this attempt and when brought into the presence of Captain Boling he said in great emotion, "Kill me, Sir Captain, yes, kill me as you killed my son, as you would kill my people if they were to come to you. You would kill all my tribe if you had the power. Yes, Sir America, you can now tell your warriors to kill the old chief. You have made my life dark with sorrow. You killed the child of my heart. Why not kill the father? But wait a little and when I am dead I will call my people to come and they shall hear me in their sleep and come to avenge the death of their chief and his son. Yes, Sir America, my spirit will make trouble for you and your people, as you have made trouble to me and my people. With the wizards I will follow the white people and make them fear me. You may kill me, Sir Captain, but you shall not live in peace. I will follow in your footsteps. I will not leave my home, but be with the spirits among the rocks, the waterfalls, in the rivers and in the winds; wherever you go I will be with you. You will not see me but you will fear the spirit of the old chief and grow cold. The Great Spirit has spoken. I am done."

This expedition finally captured the remnants of the tribes at the head of Lake Tenaya and took them to the Fresno reservation, together with their chief, Tenaya. But after a short stay they were allowed to return to the Valley under restrictions. Tenaya promised faithfully to conform to everything required, joyfully left the hot and dry reservation, and with his family returned to his Yosemite home.

The following year a party of miners was attacked by the Indians in the Valley

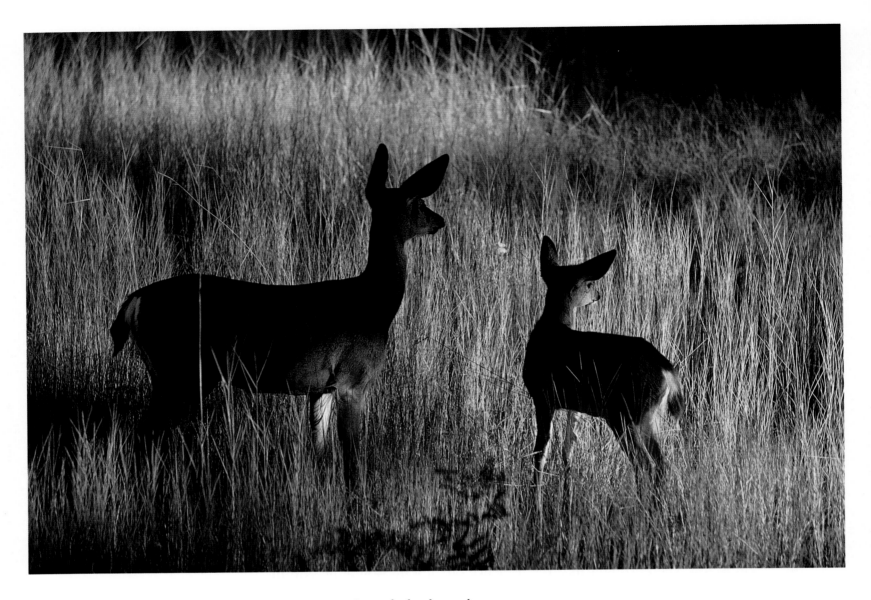

MULE DEER IN LAST LIGHT,
YOSEMITE VALLEY, 1976.

"How many hearts with warm red
blood in them are beating under
cover of the woods, and how many
teeth and eyes are shining! A
multitude of animal people,
intimately related to us, but of
whose lives we know almost
nothing, are as busy about their
own affairs as we are about ours."

*One evening I watched a doe and
her fawn meander through a
meadow in last light, all too aware
of my presence for a good
photograph. After a while they
relaxed, and I kept them focused in
my telephoto lens, hoping for an
opportune moment. Something in
the grass startled the doe. The fawn
ran to her side and peered at the
same spot, just close enough to be a
separate form with a visual and
emotional connection to its mother.
I clicked my shutter a moment
before the animals darted off. Then
a coyote stepped out of the grass.*

and two of them were killed. This led to another Yosemite expedition. A detachment of regular soldiers from Fort Miller under Lieutenant Moore, U.S.A., was at once dispatched to capture or punish the murderers. Lieutenant Moore entered the Valley in the night and surprised and captured a party of five Indians, but an alarm was given and Tenaya and his people fled from their huts and escaped to the Monos on the east side of the Range. On examination of the five prisoners in the morning it was discovered that each of them had some article of clothing that belonged to the murdered men. The bodies of the two miners were found and buried on the edge of the Bridal Veil meadow. When the captives were accused of the murder of the two white men they admitted that they had killed them to prevent white men from coming to their Valley, declaring that it was their home and that white men had no right to come there without their consent. Lieutenant Moore told them through his interpreter that they had sold their lands to the Government, that it belonged to the white men now, and that they had agreed to live on the reservation provided for them. To this they replied that Tenaya had never consented to the sale of their Valley and had never received pay for it. The other chief, they said, had no right to sell their territory. The lieutenant being fully satisfied that he had captured the real murderers, promptly pronounced judgment and had them placed in line and shot. Lieutenant Moore pursued the fugitives to Mono but was not successful in finding any of them. After being hospitably entertained and protected by the Mono and Paute tribes, they stole a number of stolen horses from their entertainers and made their way by a long, obscure route by the head of the north fork of the San Joaquin, reached their Yosemite home once more, but early one morning, after a feast of horse-flesh, a band of Monos surprised them in their huts, killing Tenaya and nearly all his tribe. Only a small remnant escaped down the river cañon. The Tenaya Cañon and Lake were named for the famous old chief.

Very few visits were made to the Valley before the summer of 1855, when Mr. J. M. Hutchings, having heard of its wonderful scenery, collected a party and made the first regular tourist's visit to the Yosemite and in his California magazine described it in articles illustrated by a good artist, who was taken into the Valley by him for that purpose. This first party was followed by another from Mariposa the same year, consisting of sixteen or eighteen persons. The next year the regular pleasure travel began and a trail on the Mariposa side of the Valley was opened by Mann Brothers. This trail was afterwards purchased by the citizens of the county and made free to the public. The first house built in the Yosemite Valley was erected in the autumn of 1856 and was kept as a hotel the next year by G. A. Hite and later by J. H. Neal and S. M. Cunningham. It was situated directly opposite the Yosemite Fall. A little over half a mile farther up the Valley a canvas house was put up in 1858 by G. A. Hite. Next year a frame house was built and kept as a hotel by Mr. Peck, afterward by Mr. Longhurst and since 1864 by Mr. Hutchings. All these hotels have vanished except the frame house built in 1859, which has been changed beyond recognition. A large hotel built on the brink of the river in front of the old one is now the only hotel in the Valley. A large hotel built by the State and located farther up the Valley was burned. To provide for the overflow of visitors there are three camps with board floors, wood frame, and covered with canvas, well furnished, some of them with electric light. A large first-class hotel is very much needed.

Travel of late years has been rapidly increasing, especially after the establishment, by Act of Congress in 1890, of the Yosemite National Park and the recession in 1905 of the original reservation to the Federal Government by the State. The greatest increase, of course, was caused by the construction of the Yosemite Valley railroad from Merced to the border of the Park, eight miles below the Valley.

It is eighty miles long, and the entire distance, except the first twenty-four miles from the town of Merced, is built through the precipitous Merced River Cañon. The roadbed was virtually blasted out of the solid rock for the entire distance in the cañon. Work was begun in September, 1905, and the first train entered El Portal, the terminus, April 15, 1907. Many miles of the road cost as much as $100,000 per mile. Its business has increased from 4000 tourists in the first year it was operated to 15,000 in 1910.

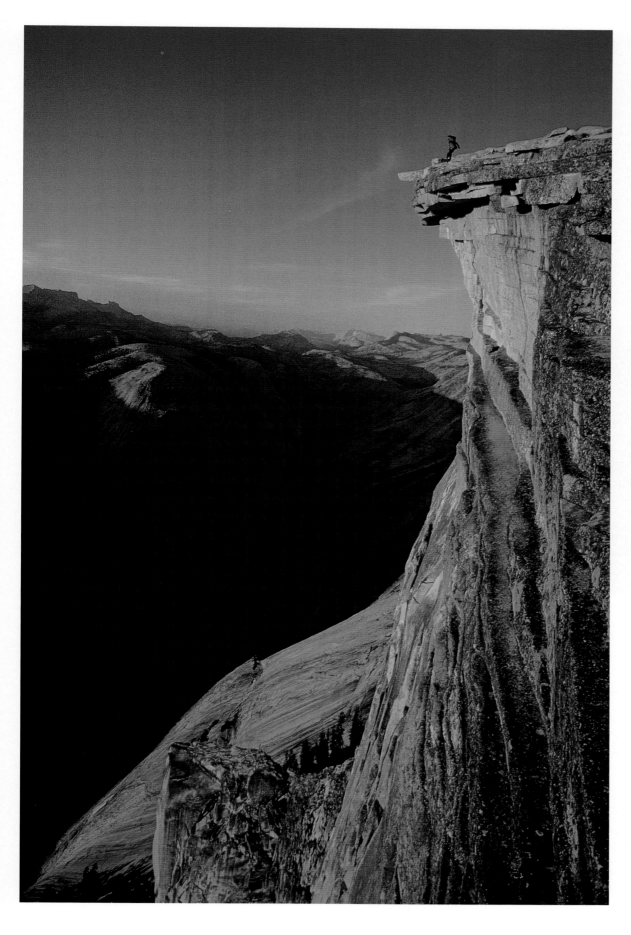

BACKPACKER ATOP
HALF DOME, 1973.

"The regular Yosemite pleasure
travel began in 1856, and has
gradually increased until the present
time. The regular tourist, ever in
motion, is one of the most
characteristic productions of the
present century; and however
frivolous and inappreciative the
poorer specimens may appear,
viewed comprehensively they are a
hopeful and significant sign of the
times, indicating at least a
beginning of our return to nature;
for going to the mountains is
going home."

*Despite Muir's condescension
toward regular tourists, he
recognized that the increased
awareness they gained through their
limited travels in Yosemite was the
key to preserving the natural values
he treasured. Had Muir chosen to
remain silent and keep the
wilderness experience to himself,
there might not be a Yosemite
National Park today. Instead of a
single backpacker at sunset
surveying a natural scene, the top of
Half Dome in 1973 might have
been a mob scene at a tramway
station, once a serious proposal.*

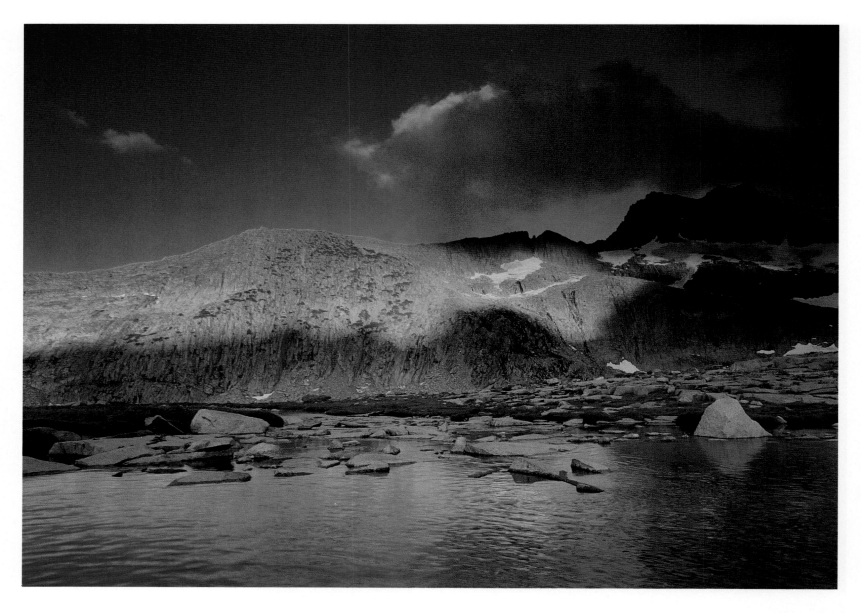

SUNSET ON UPPER LYELL FORK OF
THE TUOLUMNE RIVER, 1987.

"Lakes, the eyes of the wilderness,
are seen gleaming in every
direction—round or square, or oval
like mirrors; others narrow and
sinuous, drawn close about the
peaks like silver girdles; the highest
reflecting only rock and snow and
sky. But neither these nor the
glaciers, nor yet the brown bits of
moorland that occur here and there,
are large enough to make any
marked impression upon the mighty
host of peaks."

*After climbing Mount Lyell I had
plenty of time to return to a
comfortable camp in the lower
canyon, but when I passed this
shallow lakelet sprawled across old
glacier pavement, I decided to
spend the night and see how the
alpenglow would mingle with the
water, the granite, and the clouds.
The trade-off of ten hours of tossing
and turning on a bed of granite for
five minutes of splendid light was
well worth it.*

CHAPTER XIV

# Lamon

THE GOOD OLD PIONEER, Lamon, was the first of all the early Yosemite set-
tlers who cordially and unreservedly adopted the Valley as his home.
He was born in the Shenandoah Valley, Virginia, May 10, 1817, emigrated
to Illinois with his father, John Lamon, at the age of nineteen; afterwards went to
Texas and settled on the Brazos, where he raised melons and hunted alligators for
a living. "Right interestin' business," he said; "especially the alligator part of it."
From the Brazos he went to the Comanche Indian country between Gonzales and
Austin, twenty miles from his nearest neighbor. During the first summer, the only
bread he had was the breast meat of wild turkeys. When the formidable Comanche
Indians were on the war-path he left his cabin after dark and slept in the woods.
From Texas he crossed the plains to California and worked in the Calaveras and
Mariposa gold-fields.

He first heard Yosemite spoken of as a very beautiful mountain valley and after
making two excursions in the summers of 1857 and 1858 to see the wonderful
place, he made up his mind to quit roving and make a permanent home in it. In
April, 1859, he moved into it, located a garden opposite the Half Dome, set out a
lot of apple, pear and peach trees, planted potatoes, etc., that he had packed in on
a "contrary old mule," and worked for his board in building a hotel which was
afterwards purchased by Mr. Hutchings. His neighbors thought he was very foolish
in attempting to raise crops in so high and cold a valley, and warned him that he
could raise nothing and sell nothing, and would surely starve.

For the first year or two lack of provisions compelled him to move out on the
approach of winter, but in 1862 after he had succeeded in raising some fruit and
vegetables he began to winter in the Valley.

The first winter he had no companions, not even a dog or cat, and one evening
was greatly surprised to see two men coming up the Valley. They were very glad to
see him, for they had come from Mariposa in search of him, a report having been
spread that he had been killed by Indians. He assured his visitors that he felt safer
in his Yosemite home, lying snug and squirrel-like in his 10 × 12 cabin, than in Mariposa. When the avalanches began to slip, he wondered where all the wild roaring
and booming came from, the flying snow preventing them from being seen. But,

upon the whole, he wondered most at the brightness, gentleness, and sunniness of the weather, and hopefully employed the calm days in clearing ground for an orchard and vegetable garden.

In the second winter he built a winter cabin under the Royal Arches, where he enjoyed more sunshine. But no matter how he praised the weather he could not induce any one to winter with him until 1864.

He liked to describe the great flood of 1867, the year before I reached California, when all the walls were striped with thundering waterfalls.

He was a fine, erect, whole-souled man, between six and seven feet high, with a broad, open face, bland and guileless as his pet oxen. No stranger to hunger and weariness, he knew well how to appreciate suffering of a like kind in others, and many there be, myself among the number, who can testify to his simple, unostentatious kindness that found expression in a thousand small deeds.

After gaining sufficient means to enjoy a long afternoon of life in comparative affluence and ease, he died in the autumn of 1876. He sleeps in a beautiful spot near Galen Clark and a monument hewn from a block of Yosemite granite marks his grave.

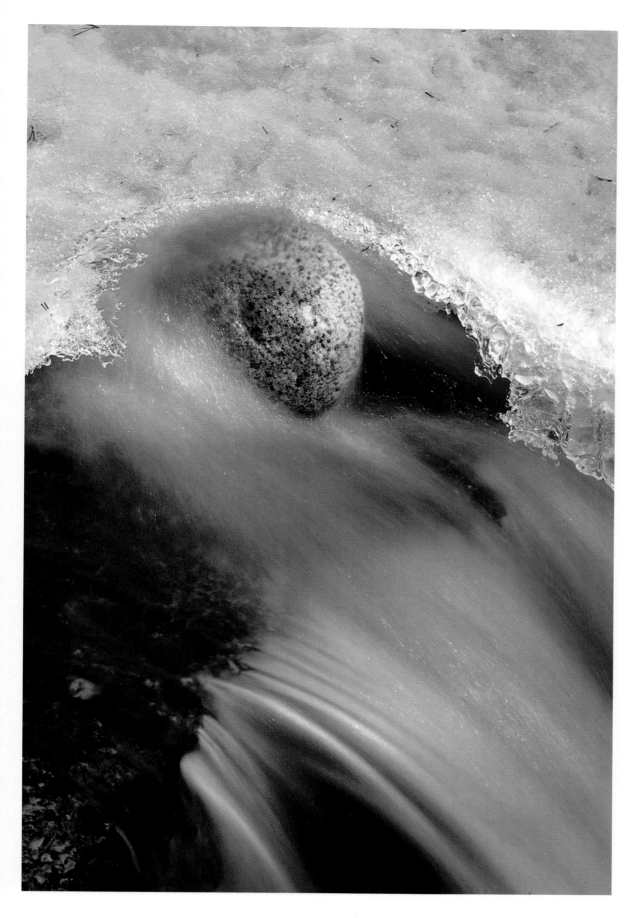

APRIL ICE HOLE IN THE
TUOLUMNE RIVER, TUOLUMNE
MEADOWS, 1977.

"The glacier flowed over its ground
as a river flows over a boulder . . .
from all those deadly, crushing,
bitter experiences comes this
delicate life and beauty, to teach us
that what we in our faithless
ignorance and fear call destruction
is creation."

*While the Tuolumne River was still
frozen solidly enough to walk
across, I spotted a boulder, with a
rapid flowing over it, exposed
through an ice hole. On closer
inspection I figured out that it was
no random event. The boulder had
forced water to spray up under the
ice, creating this first melt hole. For
only a few days of the year could I
have had this intimate experience:
crawling out onto the ice in the
middle of the river to peer into this
hole singled out, it seemed, by
natural forces for my camera
and me.*

CLOUDS ABOVE THE
GRAND CANYON OF THE
TUOLUMNE, 1972.

"It would require years of
enthusiastic study to master the
English alphabet, if it were carved
upon the flank of the Sierra in
letters sixty or seventy miles long,
their bases set in the foothills, their
tops leaning back among the
glaciers and shattered peaks of the
summit, often veiled with forests
and thickets, and their continuity
often broken by cross-gorges
and hills."

*To the casual visitor, Yosemite's
features and landmarks are separate
entities. This scene is a cliff, a
cloud, and a canyon. But to a
person who spends time looking,
feeling, and experiencing the land,
these elements unite into a whole
that speaks at once of past, present,
and future. The cloud brings storms
that presently fill the canyon below
with water; long ago, storms
created glaciers that sculpted the
cliff and canyon. In a very real way,
Yosemite is the sum of its parts
rather than a collection of unusual
natural features.*

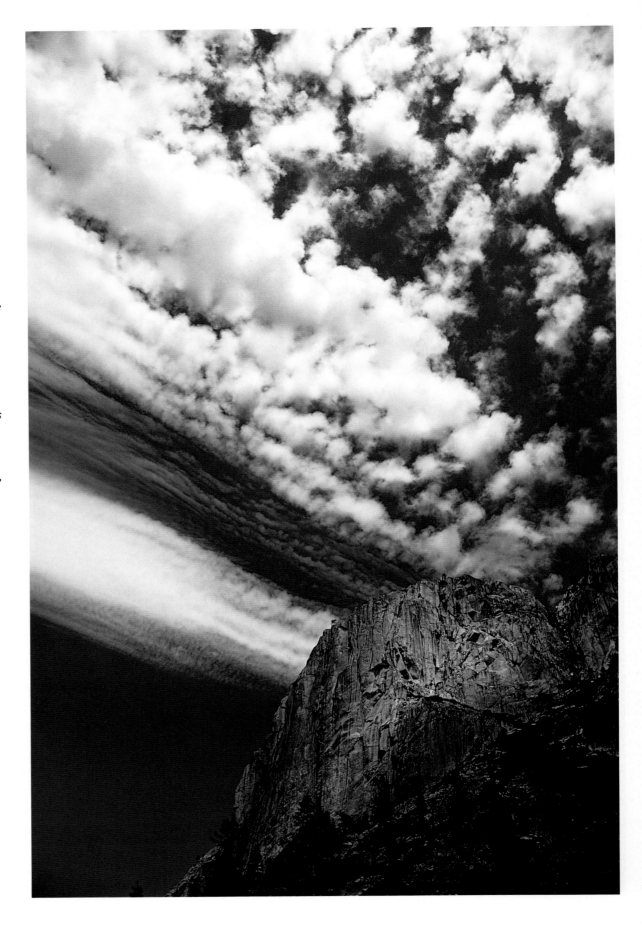

CHAPTER XV

# Galen Clark

GALEN CLARK was the best mountaineer I ever met, and one of the kindest and most amiable of all my mountain friends. I first met him at his Wawona ranch forty-three years ago on my first visit to Yosemite. I had entered the Valley with one companion by way of Coulterville, and returned by what was then known as the Mariposa trail. Both trails were buried in deep snow where the elevation was from 5000 to 7000 feet above sea level in the sugar pine and silver fir regions. We had no great difficulty, however, in finding our way by the trends of the main features of the topography. Botanizing by the way, we made slow, plodding progress, and were again about out of provisions when we reached Clark's hospitable cabin at Wawona. He kindly furnished us with flour and a little sugar and tea, and my companion, who complained of the benumbing poverty of a strictly vegetarian diet, gladly accepted Mr. Clark's offer of a piece of a bear that had just been killed. After a short talk about bears and the forests and the way to the Big Trees, we pushed on up through the Wawona firs and sugar pines, and camped in the now-famous Mariposa grove.

Later, after making my home in the Yosemite Valley, I became well acquainted with Mr. Clark, while he was guardian. He was elected again and again to this important office by different Boards of Commissioners on account of his efficiency and his real love of the Valley.

Although nearly all my mountaineering has been done without companions, I had the pleasure of having Galen Clark with me on three excursions. About thirty-five years ago I invited him to accompany me on a trip through the Big Tuolumne Cañon from Hetch Hetchy Valley. The cañon up to that time had not been explored, and knowing that the difference in the elevation of the river at the head of the cañon and in Hetch Hetchy was about 5000 feet, we expected to find some magnificent cataracts or falls; nor were we disappointed. When we were leaving Yosemite an ambitious young man begged leave to join us. I strongly advised him not to attempt such a long, hard trip, for it would undoubtedly prove very trying to an inexperienced climber. He assured us, however, that he was equal to anything, would gladly meet every difficulty as it came, and cause us no hindrance or trouble of any sort. So at last, after repeating our advice that he give up the trip, we consented to his joining us. We entered the cañon by way of Hetch Hetchy Valley, each carrying his own provisions, and making his own tea, porridge, bed, etc.

In the morning of the second day out from Hetch Hetchy we came to what is now known as "Muir Gorge," and Mr. Clark without hesitation prepared to force a way through it, wading and jumping from one submerged boulder to another through the torrent, bracing and steadying himself with a long pole. Though the river was then rather low, the savage, roaring, surging song it was singing was rather nerve-trying, especially to our inexperienced companion. With careful assistance, however, I managed to get him through, but this hard trial, naturally enough, proved too much and he informed us, pale and trembling, that he could go no farther. I gathered some wood at the upper throat of the gorge, made a fire for him and ad-

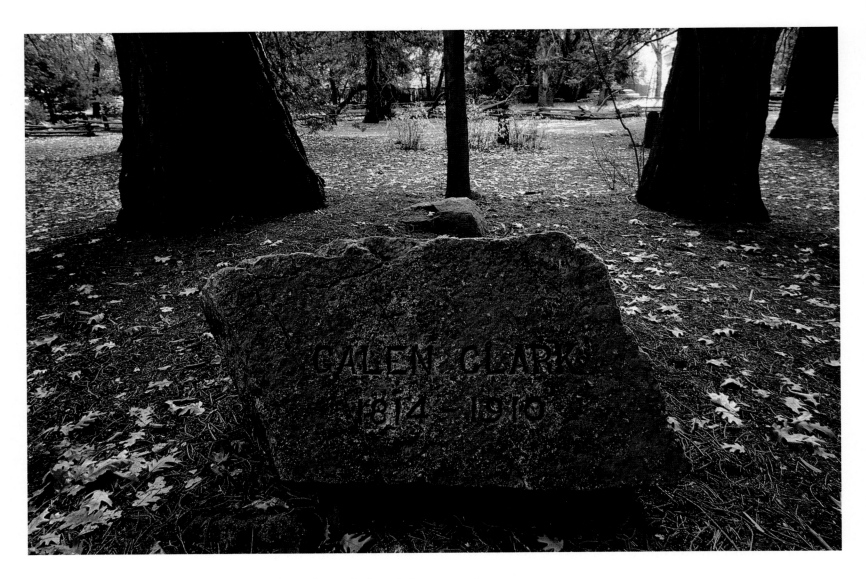

GALEN CLARK'S GRAVE, YOSEMITE
VILLAGE, 1987.

"Galen Clark was the best
mountaineer I ever met, and one of
the kindest and most amiable of all
my mountain friends. . . . The value
of the mountain air in prolonging
life is well exemplified in Mr.
Clark's case. While working in the
mines he contracted a severe cold
that settled on his lungs and finally
caused severe inflammation and
bleeding, and none of his friends
thought he would ever recover. The
physicians told him he had but a
short time to live. . . . About
twenty years before his death he
made choice of a plot in the
Yosemite cemetery on the north side
of the Valley, not far from the
Yosemite Fall, and selecting a dozen
or so of seedling sequoias in the
Mariposa Grove he brought them to
the Valley and planted them around
the spot he had chosen for his last
rest. . . . Doubtless they will long
shade the grave of their blessed
lover and friend."

*As I set up to photograph the old
headstone beneath a stand of still-
youthful sequoias, my mind
wandered far from my immediate
task. Would my life have been the
same if my mother had not spent
those college summers in Yosemite
Valley, and if Galen Clark's name
and character had not made such an
impression on her?*

vised him to feel at home and make himself comfortable, hoped he would enjoy the grand scenery and the songs of the water-ouzels which haunted the gorge, and assured him that we would return some time in the night, though it might be late, as we wished to go on through the entire cañon if possible. We pushed our way through the dense chaparral and over the earthquake taluses with such speed that we reached the foot of the upper cataract while we had still an hour or so of daylight for the return trip. It was long after dark when we reached our adventurous, but nerve-shaken companion who, of course, was anxious and lonely, not being accustomed to solitude, however kindly and flowery and full of sweet bird-song and stream-song. Being tired we simply lay down in restful comfort on the river bank beside a good fire, instead of trying to go down the gorge in the dark or climb over its high shoulder to our blankets and provisions, which we had left in the morning in a tree at the foot of the gorge. I remember Mr. Clark remarking that if he had his choice that night between provisions and blankets he would choose his blankets.

The next morning in about an hour we had crossed over the ridge through which the gorge is cut, reached our provisions, made tea, and had a good breakfast. As soon as we had returned to Yosemite I obtained fresh provisions, pushed off alone up to the head of Yosemite Creek basin, entered the cañon by a side cañon, and completed the exploration up to the Tuolumne Meadows.

It was on this first trip from Hetch Hetchy to the upper cataracts that I had convincing proofs of Mr. Clark's daring and skill as a mountaineer, particularly in fording torrents, and in forcing his way through thick chaparral. I found it somewhat difficult to keep up with him in dense, tangled brush, though in jumping on boulder taluses and slippery cobble-beds I had no difficulty in leaving him behind.

After I had discovered the glaciers on Mount Lyell and Mount McClure, Mr. Clark kindly made a second excursion with me to assist in establishing a line of stakes across the McClure glacier to measure its rate of flow. On this trip we also climbed Mount Lyell together, when the snow which covered the glacier was melted into upleaning, icy blades which were extremely difficult to cross, not being strong enough to support our weight, nor wide enough apart to enable us to stride across each blade as it was met. Here again I, being lighter, had no difficulty in keeping ahead of him. While resting after wearisome staggering and falling he stared at the marvelous ranks of leaning blades, and said, "I think I have traveled all sorts of trails and cañons, through all kinds of brush and snow, but this gets me."

Mr. Clark at my urgent request joined my small party on a trip to the Kings River yosemite by way of the high mountains, most of the way without a trail. He joined us at the Mariposa Big Tree grove and intended to go all the way, but finding that, on account of the difficulties encountered, the time required was much greater than he expected, he turned back near the head of the north fork of the Kings River.

In cooking his mess of oatmeal porridge and making tea, his pot was always the first to boil, and I used to wonder why, with all his skill in scrambling through brush in the easiest way, and preparing his meals, he was so utterly careless about his beds. He would lie down anywhere on any ground, rough or smooth, without taking pains even to remove cobbles or sharp-angled rocks protruding through the grass or gravel, saying that his own bones were as hard as any stones and could do him no harm.

His kindness to all Yosemite visitors and mountaineers was marvelously constant and uniform. He was not a good business man, and in building an extensive hotel and barns at Wawona, before the travel to Yosemite had been greatly developed, he borrowed money, mortgaged his property and lost it all.

Though not the first to see the Mariposa Big Tree grove, he was the first to explore it, after he had heard from a prospector, who had passed through the grove and who gave him the indefinite information, that there were some wonderful big trees up there on the top of the Wawona hill and that he believed they must be of the same kind that had become so famous and well-known in the Calaveras grove farther north. On this information, Galen Clark told me, he went up and thoroughly explored the grove, counting the trees and measuring the largest, and becoming familiar with it. He stated also that he had explored the forest to the southward and had discovered the much larger Fresno grove of about two square miles, six or seven miles distant from the Mariposa grove. Unfortunately most of the Fresno grove has been cut and flumed down to the railroad near Madera.

Mr. Clark was truly and literally a gentle-man. I never heard him utter a hasty, angry, fault-finding word. His voice was uniformly pitched at a rather low tone, perfectly even, although glances of his eyes and slight intonations of his voice often indicated that something funny or mildly sarcastic was coming, but upon the whole he was serious and industrious, and, however deep and fun-provoking a story might be, he never indulged in boisterous laughter.

He was very fond of scenery and once told me after I became acquainted with him that he liked "nothing in the world better than climbing to the top of a high ridge or mountain and looking off." He preferred the mountain ridges and domes in the Yosemite regions on account of the wealth and beauty of the forests. Oftentimes he would take his rifle, a few pounds of bacon, a few pounds of flour, and a single blanket and go off hunting, for no other reason than to explore and get acquainted with the most beautiful points of view within a journey of a week or two from his Wawona home. On these trips he was always alone and could indulge in tranquil enjoyment of Nature to his heart's content. He said that on those trips, when he was a sufficient distance from home in a neighborhood where he wished to linger, he always shot a deer, sometimes a grouse, and occasionally a bear. After diminishing the weight of a deer or bear by eating part of it, he carried as much as possible of the best of the meat to Wawona, and from his hospitable well-supplied cabin no weary wanderer ever went away hungry or unrested.

The value of the mountain air in prolonging life is well exemplified in Mr. Clark's case. While working in the mines he contracted a severe cold that settled on his lungs and finally caused severe inflammation and bleeding, and none of his friends thought he would ever recover. The physicians told him he had but a short time to live. It was then that he repaired to the beautiful sugar pine woods at Wawona and took up a claim, including the fine meadows there, and building his cabin, began his life of wandering and exploring in the glorious mountains about him, usually going bareheaded. In a remarkably short time his lungs were healed.

He was one of the most sincere tree-lovers I ever knew. About twenty years before his death he made choice of a plot in the Yosemite cemetery on the north side of the Valley, not far from the Yosemite Fall, and selecting a dozen or so of seedling sequoias in the Mariposa grove he brought them to the Valley and planted them around the spot he had chosen for his last rest. The ground there is gravelly and dry; by careful watering he finally nursed most of the seedlings into good, thrifty trees, and doubtless they will long shade the grave of their blessed lover and friend.

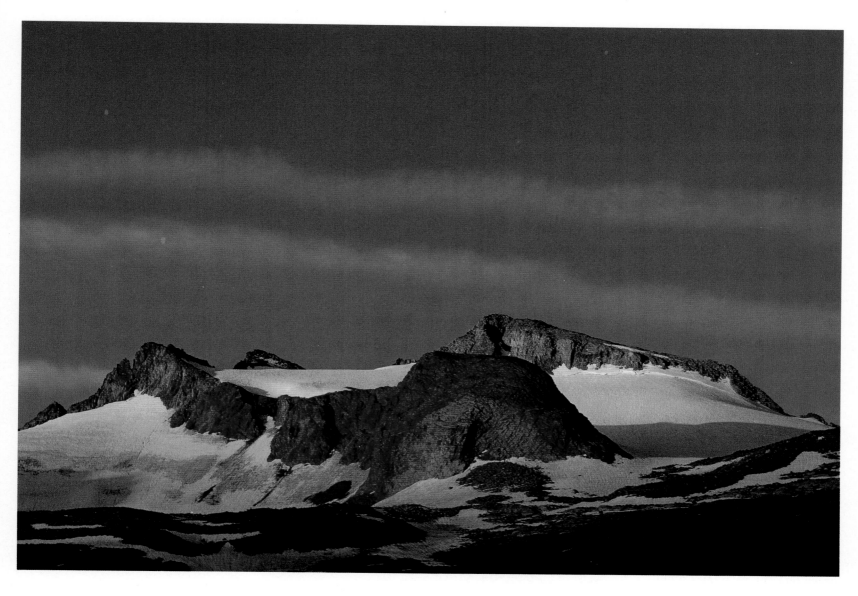

MOUNT LYELL AND ITS
GLACIER, 1987.

"The Lyell Glacier is about a mile
wide and less than a mile long, but
presents, nevertheless, all the
essential characters of large, river-
like glaciers—moraines, earth-
bands, blue veins, crevasses, etc.,
while the streams that issue from it
are, of course, turbid with rock-
mud, showing its grinding action on
its bed. And it is all the more
interesting since it is the highest and
most enduring remnant of the great
Tuolumne Glacier, whose traces are
still distinct fifty miles away, and
whose influence on the landscape
was so profound."

*I like to think of Mount Lyell as an
alpine counterpart of an Egyptian
pyramid. It rises far above the
surrounding terrain, and secrets of
the past are chambered beneath its
surface. Here Muir found the source
of the architecture of his beloved
Tuolumne peaks, domes, and
canyons. Here in more modern
times an entire bighorn sheep,
mummified after a fall into a
crevasse centuries ago, emerged
from its icy tomb at the toe of
the glacier.*

MELTWATER POOL ON THE LYELL
GLACIER, 1987.

"Mr. [Galen] Clark kindly made a
second excursion with me to assist
in establishing a line of stakes
across the McClure glacier to
measure its rate of flow. On this trip
we also climbed Mount Lyell
together, when the snow which
covered the glacier was melted into
upleaning, icy blades which were
extremely difficult to cross. . . .
While resting after wearisome
staggering and falling he stared at
the marvelous ranks of leaning
blades and said, 'I think I have
traveled all sorts of trails and
canyons, through all kinds of brush
and snow, but this gets me.'"

*The surface of Lyell Glacier is
forever changing. In winter, deep
powder snow hides its contours. In
spring, the snow firms up into a
smooth, white surface. In early
summer, when this image was
made, differential melting begins to
pock the surface with pits, while
meltwater gathers into turquoise
ponds. Later, the sun cups deepen
into the awful leaning blades that
hindered Galen Clark's progress.
They also hinder the surface runoff
of the meltwater, and the ponds
disappear. In the fall, except in very
heavy snow years, surface snow
melts away, exposing the bones of
the ice, with annual rings of
deposition that gradually move
down from above.*

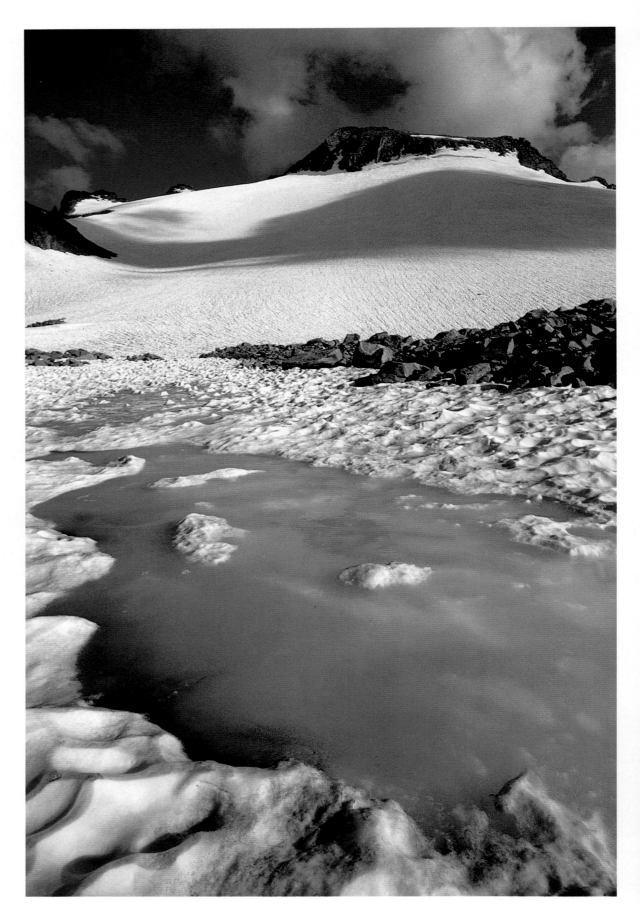

CHAPTER XVI

# Hetch Hetchy Valley

YOSEMITE IS SO WONDERFUL that we are apt to regard it as an exceptional creation, the only valley of its kind in the world; but Nature is not so poor as to have only one of anything. Several other yosemites have been discovered in the Sierra that occupy the same relative positions on the Range and were formed by the same forces in the same kind of granite. One of these, the Hetch Hetchy Valley, is in the Yosemite National Park about twenty miles from Yosemite and is easily accessible to all sorts of travelers by a road and trail that leaves the Big Oak Flat road at Bronson Meadows a few miles below Crane Flat, and to mountaineers by way of Yosemite Creek basin and the head of the middle fork of the Tuolumne.

It is said to have been discovered by Joseph Screech, a hunter, in 1850, a year before the discovery of the great Yosemite. After my first visit to it in the autumn of 1871, I have always called it the "Tuolumne Yosemite," for it is a wonderfully exact counterpart of the Merced Yosemite, not only in its sublime rocks and waterfalls but in the gardens, groves and meadows of its flowery park-like floor. The floor of Yosemite is about 4000 feet above the sea; the Hetch Hetchy floor about 3700 feet. And as the Merced River flows through Yosemite, so does the Tuolumne through Hetch Hetchy. The walls of both are of gray granite, rise abruptly from the floor, are sculptured in the same style and in both every rock is a glacier monument.

Standing boldly out from the south wall is a strikingly picturesque rock called by the Indians, Kolana, the outermost of a group 2300 feet high, corresponding with the Cathedral Rocks of Yosemite both in relative position and form. On the opposite side of the Valley, facing Kolana, there is a counterpart of the El Capitan that rises sheer and plain to a height of 1800 feet, and over its massive brow flows a stream which makes the most graceful fall I have ever seen. From the edge of the cliff to the top of an earthquake talus it is perfectly free in the air for a thousand feet before it is broken into cascades among talus boulders. It is in all its glory in June, when the snow is melting fast, but fades and vanishes toward the end of summer. The only fall I know with which it may fairly be compared is the Yosemite Bridal Veil; but it excels even that favorite fall both in height and airy-fairy beauty and behavior. Lowlanders are apt to suppose that mountain streams in their wild career over cliffs lose control of themselves and tumble in a noisy chaos of mist and spray. On the contrary, on no part of their travels are they more harmonious and self-controlled. Imagine yourself in Hetch Hetchy on a sunny day in June, standing waist-deep in grass and flowers (as I have often stood), while the great pines sway dreamily with scarcely perceptible motion. Looking northward across the Valley you see a plain, gray granite cliff rising abruptly out of the gardens and groves to a height of 1800 feet, and in front of it Tueeulala's silvery scarf burning with irised sun-fire. In the first white outburst at the head there is abundance of visible energy, but it is speedily hushed and concealed in divine repose, and its tranquil progress to the base of the cliff is like that of a downy feather in a still room. Now observe the fineness and marvelous distinctness of the various sun-illumined fabrics into which the water is woven; they sift and float from form to form down the face of that grand gray rock in so leisurely and unconfused a manner that you can examine their texture, and patterns and tones of color as you would a piece of embroidery held in the hand. Toward the top of the fall you see groups of booming, comet-like masses, their solid, white heads separate, their tails like combed silk interlacing among delicate gray and purple shadows, ever forming and dissolving, worn out by friction in their rush through the air. Most of these vanish a few hundred feet below the summit, changing to varied forms of cloud-like drapery. Near the bottom the width of the fall has increased from about twenty-five feet to a hundred feet. Here it is composed of yet finer tissues, and is still without a trace of disorder—air, water and sunlight woven into stuff that spirits might wear.

So fine a fall might well seem sufficient to glorify any valley; but here, as in Yosemite, Nature seems in nowise moderate, for a short distance to the eastward of Tueeulala booms and thunders the great Hetch Hetchy Fall, Wapama, so near that you have both of them in full view from the same standpoint. It is the counterpart of the Yosemite Fall, but has a much greater volume of water, is about 1700 feet in height, and appears to be nearly vertical, though considerably inclined, and is dashed into huge outbounding bosses of foam on projecting shelves and knobs. No two falls could be more unlike—Tueeulala out in the open sunshine descending like thistledown; Wapama in a jagged, shadowy gorge roaring and thundering, pounding its way like an earthquake avalanche.

Besides this glorious pair there is a broad, massive fall on the main river a short distance above the head of the Valley. Its position is something like that of the Vernal in Yosemite, and its roar as it plunges into a surging trout-pool may be heard a long way, though it is only about twenty feet high. On Rancheria Creek, a large stream, corresponding in position with the Yosemite Tenaya Creek, there is a chain of cascades joined here and there with swift flashing plumes like the one between the Vernal and Nevada Falls, making magnificent shows as they go their glacier-sculptured way, sliding, leaping, hurrahing, covered with crisp clashing spray made glorious with sifting sunshine. And besides all these a few small streams come over the walls at wide intervals, leaping from ledge to ledge with bird-like song and watering many a hidden cliff-garden and fernery, but they are too unshowy to be noticed in so grand a place.

The correspondence between the Hetch Hetchy walls in their trends, sculpture, physical structure, and general arrangement of the main rock-masses and those of the Yosemite Valley has excited the wondering admiration of every observer. We have seen that the El Capitan and Cathedral rocks occupy the same relative positions in both valleys; so also do their Yosemite points and North Domes. Again, that part of the Yosemite north wall immediately to the east of the Yosemite Fall has two horizontal benches, about 500 and 1500 feet above the floor, timbered with golden-cup oak. Two benches similarly situated and timbered occur on the same relative portion of the Hetch Hetchy north wall, to the east of Wapama Fall, and on no other. The Yosemite is bounded at the head by the great Half Dome. Hetch Hetchy is bounded in the same way, though its head rock is incomparably less wonderful and sublime in form.

The floor of the Valley is about three and a half miles long, and from a fourth to half a mile wide. The lower portion is mostly a level meadow about a mile long, with the trees restricted to the sides and the river banks, and partially separated

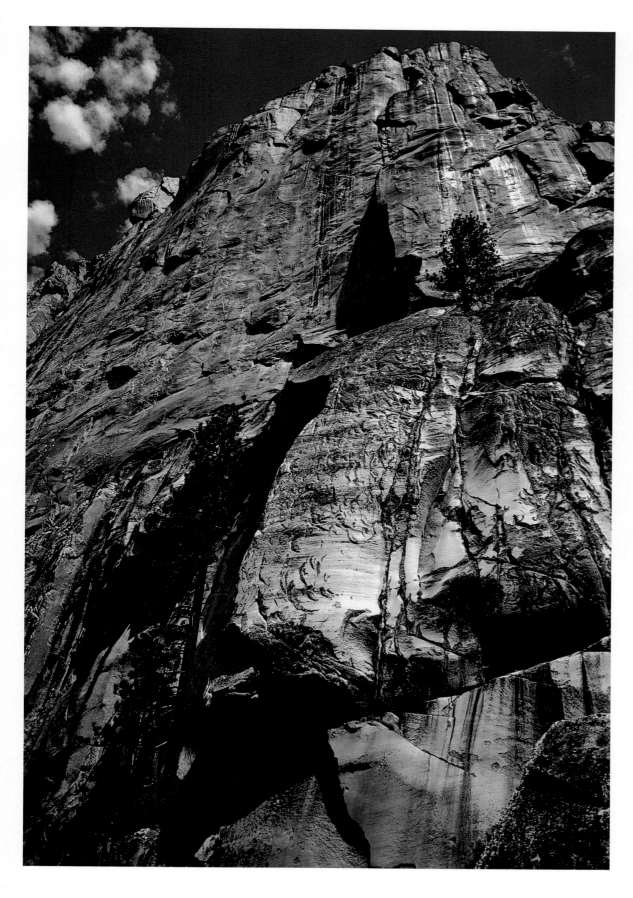

GLACIAL CHATTER MARKS ON
GRANITE, GRAND CANYON OF THE
TUOLUMNE, 1972.

"Clusters of peaks stand revealed
harmoniously correlated and
fashioned like works of art—
eloquent monuments of the ancient
ice rivers that brought them into
relief from the general mass of the
range. . . . Nature's poems carved
on tables of stone."

*The face of this dome above
California Falls shows not only the
high polish created by ice forced
through a narrow valley, but also
what are called chatter marks,
created when boulders imbedded in
the ice bumped against the wall.
Like poorly driven chisels, they
bounced and chipped rhythmic
patterns into the burnished cliffs.*

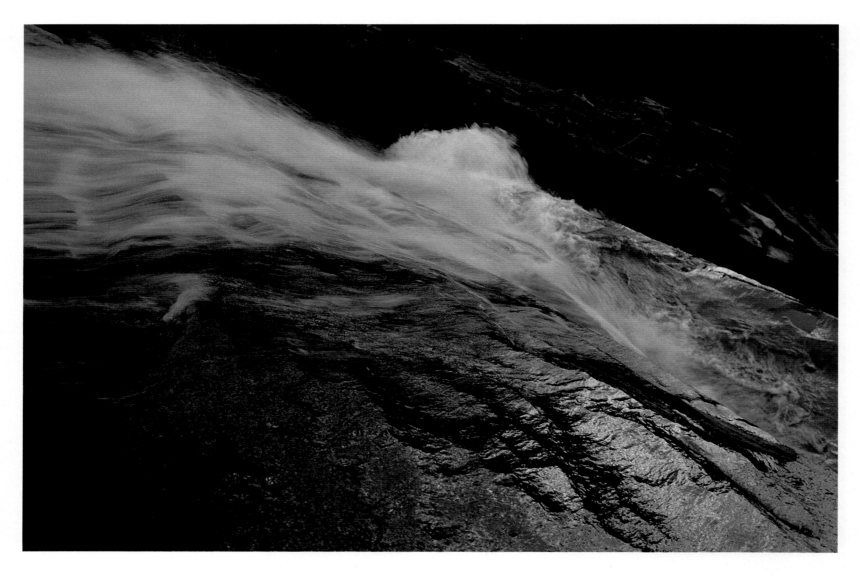

WATERWHEEL FALLS IN LATE
SUMMER, GRAND CANYON OF THE
TUOLUMNE, 1987.

"Down through the midst, the
young Tuolumne was seen pouring
from its crystal fountains, now
resting in glassy pools as if
changing back again into ice, now
leaping in white cascades as if
turning to snow."

*Running to Muir Gorge, I noticed
Waterwheel Falls in the deep early-
morning shadows. The rocks were
glassy and black, polished by the
passage of a great volume of water,
many times greater in the spring
than in late summer. Using a one-
second exposure, I tried to capture
the unusual wilderness textures:
white, silky water next to blue-
and-gold reflections on an inky
black surface.*

from the main, upper, forested portion by a low bar of glacier-polished granite across which the river breaks in rapids.

The principal trees are the yellow and sugar pines, digger pine, incense cedar, Douglas spruce, silver fir, the California and golden-cup oaks, balsam cottonwood, Nuttall's flowering dogwood, alder, maple, laurel, tumion, etc. The most abundant and influential are the great yellow or silver pines like those of Yosemite, the tallest over two hundred feet in height, and the oaks assembled in magnificent groves with massive rugged trunks four to six feet in diameter, and broad, shady, wide-spreading heads. The shrubs forming conspicuous flowery clumps and tangles are manzanita, azalea, spiræa, brier-rose, several species of ceanothus, calycanthus, philadelphus, wild cherry, etc.; with abundance of showy and fragrant herbaceous plants growing about them or out in the open in beds by themselves—lilies, Mariposa tulips, brodiaeas, orchids, iris, spraguea, draperia, collomia, collinsia, castilleja, nemophila, larkspur, columbine, goldenrods, sunflowers, mints of many species, honeysuckle, etc. Many fine ferns dwell here also, especially the beautiful and interesting rock-ferns—pellaea, and cheilanthes of several species—fringing and rosetting dry rock-piles and ledges; woodwardia and asplenium on damp spots with fronds six or seven feet high; the delicate maidenhair in mossy nooks by the falls, and the sturdy, broad-shouldered pteris covering nearly all the dry ground beneath the oaks and pines.

It appears, therefore, that Hetch Hetchy Valley, far from being a plain, common, rock-bound meadow, as many who have not seen it seem to suppose, is a grand landscape garden, one of Nature's rarest and most precious mountain temples. As in Yosemite, the sublime rocks of its walls seem to glow with life, whether leaning back in repose or standing erect in thoughtful attitudes, giving welcome to storms and calms alike, their brows in the sky, their feet set in the groves and gay flowery meadows, while birds, bees, and butterflies help the river and waterfalls to stir all the air into music—things frail and fleeting and types of permanence meeting here and blending, just as they do in Yosemite, to draw her lovers into close and confiding communion with her.

Sad to say, this most precious and sublime feature of the Yosemite National Park, one of the greatest of all our natural resources for the uplifting joy and peace and health of the people, is in danger of being dammed and made into a reservoir to help supply San Francisco with water and light, thus flooding it from wall to wall and burying its gardens and groves one or two hundred feet deep. This grossly destructive commercial scheme has long been planned and urged (though water as pure and abundant can be got from outside of the people's park, in a dozen different places), because of the comparative cheapness of the dam and of the territory which it is sought to divert from the great uses to which it was dedicated in the Act of 1890 establishing the Yosemite National Park.

The making of gardens and parks goes on with civilization all over the world, and they increase both in size and number as their value is recognized. Everybody needs beauty as well as bread, places to play in and pray in, where Nature may heal and cheer and give strength to body and soul alike. This natural beauty-hunger is made manifest in the little window-sill gardens of the poor, though perhaps only a geranium slip in a broken cup, as well as in the carefully tended rose and lily gardens of the rich, the thousands of spacious city parks and botanical gardens, and in our magnificent National Parks—the Yellowstone, Yosemite, Sequoia, etc.—Nature's sublime wonderlands, the admiration and joy of the world. Nevertheless, like anything else worth while, from the very beginning, however well guarded, they have always been subject to attack by despoiling gainseekers and mischief-makers of every degree from Satan to Senators, eagerly trying to make everything immediately and selfishly commercial, with schemes disguised in smug-smiling philanthropy, industriously, sham-piously crying, "Conservation, conservation, panutilization," that man and beast may be fed and the dear Nation made great. Thus long ago a few enterprising merchants utilized the Jerusalem temple as a place of business instead of a place of prayer, changing money, buying and selling cattle and sheep and doves; and earlier still, the first forest reservation, including only one tree, was likewise despoiled. Ever since the establishment of the Yosemite National Park, strife has been going on around its borders and I suppose this will go on as part of the universal battle between right and wrong, however much its boundaries may be shorn, or its wild beauty destroyed.

The first application to the Government by the San Francisco Supervisors for the commercial use of Lake Eleanor and the Hetch Hetchy Valley was made in 1903, and on December 22nd of that year it was denied by the Secretary of the Interior, Mr. Hitchcock, who truthfully said:

*Presumably the Yosemite National Park was created such by law because of the natural objects of varying degrees of scenic importance located within its boundaries, inclusive alike of its beautiful small lakes, like Eleanor, and its majestic wonders, like Hetch Hetchy and Yosemite Valley. It is the aggregation of such natural scenic features that makes the Yosemite Park a wonderland which the Congress of the United States sought by law to reserve for all coming time as nearly as practicable in the condition fashioned by the hand of the Creator—a worthy object of national pride and a source of healthful pleasure and rest for the thousands of people who may annually sojourn there during the heated months.*

In 1907 when Mr. Garfield became Secretary of the Interior the application was renewed and granted; but under his successor, Mr. Fisher, the matter has been referred to a Commission, which as this volume goes to press still has it under consideration.

The most delightful and wonderful camp-grounds in the Park are its three great valleys—Yosemite, Hetch Hetchy, and Upper Tuolumne; and they are also the most important places with reference to their positions relative to the other great features—the Merced and Tuolumne Cañons, and the High Sierra peaks and glaciers, etc., at the head of the rivers. The main part of the Tuolumne Valley is a spacious flowery lawn four or five miles long, surrounded by magnificent snowy mountains, slightly separated from other beautiful meadows, which together make a series about twelve miles in length, the highest reaching to the feet of Mount Dana, Mount Gibbs, Mount Lyell and Mount McClure. It is about 8500 feet above the sea, and forms the grand central High Sierra camp-ground from which excursions are made to the noble mountains, domes, glaciers, etc.; across the Range to the Mono Lake and volcanoes and down the Tuolumne Cañon to Hetch Hetchy. Should Hetch Hetchy be submerged for a reservoir, as proposed, not only would it be utterly destroyed, but the sublime cañon way to the heart of the High Sierra would be hopelessly blocked and the great camping-ground, as the watershed of a city drinking system, virtually would be closed to the public. So far as I have learned, few of all

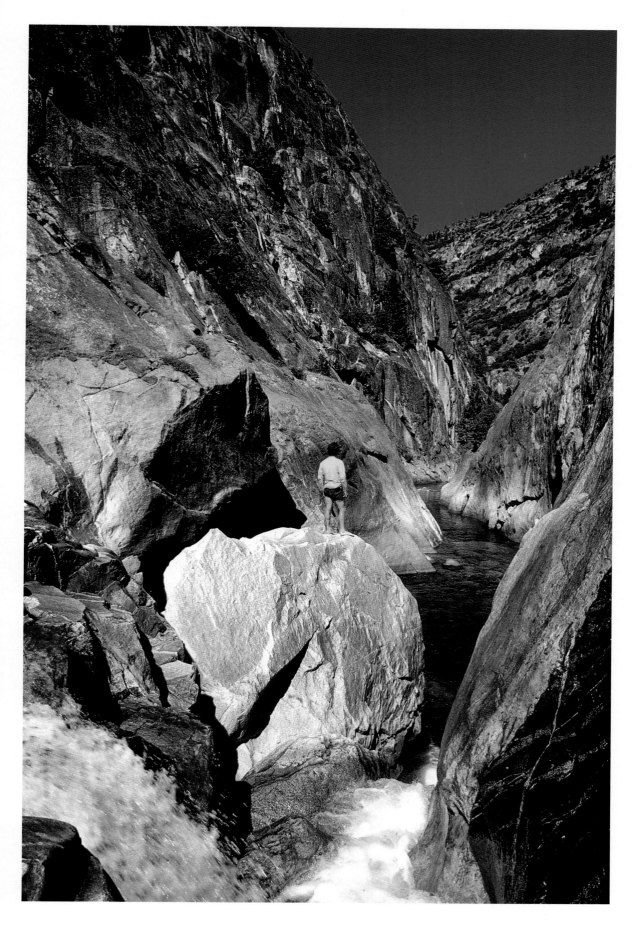

MUIR GORGE, GRAND CANYON OF THE TUOLUMNE, 1987.

"In the morning of the second day out from Hetch Hetchy we came to what is now known as 'Muir Gorge,' and Mr. [Galen] Clark without hesitation prepared to force a way through it, wading and jumping from one submerged boulder to another through the torrent . . . the savage, roaring, surging song it was singing was rather nerve-trying, especially to our inexperienced companion. . . . This hard trial, naturally enough, proved too much and he informed us, pale and trembling, that he could go no farther. I gathered some wood at the upper throat of the gorge, made a fire for him . . . and assured him that we would return some time in the night, although it might be late."

*More than half a century passed before anyone repeated the traverse of Muir Gorge. A trail through the canyon detours above and around it, and even today the gorge itself is considered impenetrable except late in low-water years. One August morning before dawn I set out with two friends from Tuolumne Meadows with a camera and some Ziploc bags. We ran sixteen miles to reach the start of the gorge just as the sun touched the river. With my camera triple-bagged, we scrambled over boulders and traversed steep rock walls until we were forced to swim a series of long, deep pools of icy water. At one point I climbed beside a waterfall to photograph the gorge from within, the way Muir and Clark saw it in 1872. After the gorge widened, we found the trail and ran several of the remaining eighteen miles, through Pate Valley to White Wolf, before our bodies were warm again.*

the thousands who have seen the Park and seek rest and peace in it are in favor of this outrageous scheme.

One of my later visits to the Valley was made in the autumn of 1907 with the late William Keith, the artist. The leaf-colors were then ripe, and the great god-like rocks in repose seemed to glow with life. The artist, under their spell, wandered day after day along the river and through the groves and gardens, studying the wonderful scenery; and, after making about forty sketches, declared with enthusiasm that although its walls were less sublime in height, in picturesque beauty and charm Hetch Hetchy surpassed even Yosemite.

That any one would try to destroy such a place seems incredible; but sad experience shows that there are people good enough and bad enough for anything. The proponents of the dam scheme bring forward a lot of bad arguments to prove that the only righteous thing to do with the people's parks is to destroy them bit by bit as they are able. Their arguments are curiously like those of the devil, devised for the destruction of the first garden—so much of the very best Eden fruit going to waste; so much of the best Tuolumne water and Tuolumne scenery going to waste. Few of their statements are even partly true, and all are misleading.

Thus, Hetch Hetchy, they say, is a "low-lying meadow." On the contrary, it is a high-lying natural landscape garden, as the photographic illustrations show.

"It is a common minor feature, like thousands of others." On the contrary it is a very uncommon feature; after Yosemite, the rarest and in many ways the most important in the National Park.

"Damming and submerging it 175 feet deep would enhance its beauty by forming a crystal-clear lake." Landscape gardens, places of recreation and worship, are never made beautiful by destroying and burying them. The beautiful sham lake, forsooth, would be only an eyesore, a dismal blot on the landscape, like many others to be seen in the Sierra. For, instead of keeping it at the same level all the year, allowing Nature centuries of time to make new shores, it would, of course, be full only a month or two in the spring, when the snow is melting fast; then it would be gradually drained, exposing the slimy sides of the basin and shallower parts of the bottom, with the gathered drift and waste, death and decay of the upper basins, caught here instead of being swept on to decent natural burial along the banks of the river or in the sea. Thus the Hetch Hetchy dam-lake would be only a rough imitation of a natural lake for a few of the spring months, an open sepulcher for the others.

"Hetch Hetchy water is the purest of all to be found in the Sierra, unpolluted, and forever unpollutable." On the contrary, excepting that of the Merced below Yosemite, it is less pure than that of most of the other Sierra streams, because of the sewerage of camp-grounds draining into it, especially of the Big Tuolumne Meadows camp-ground, occupied by hundreds of tourists and mountaineers, with their animals, for months every summer, soon to be followed by thousands from all the world.

These temple destroyers, devotees of ravaging commercialism, seem to have a perfect contempt for Nature, and, instead of lifting their eyes to the God of the mountains, lift them to the Almighty Dollar.

Dam Hetch Hetchy! As well dam for water-tanks the people's cathedrals and churches, for no holier temple has ever been consecrated by the heart of man.

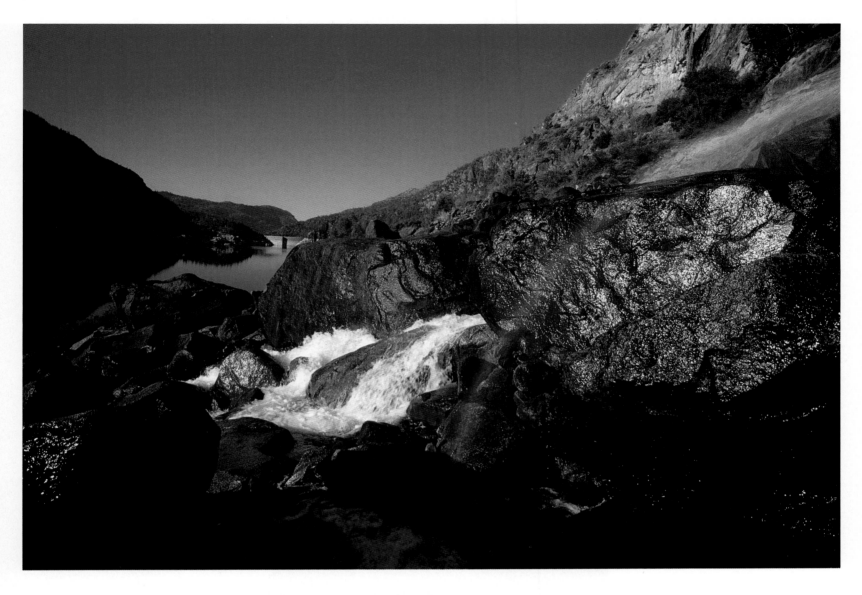

BASE OF WAPAMA FALLS, HETCH
HETCHY VALLEY, 1987.

"Everyone who is anything of a
mountaineer should go on through
the entire length of the [Tuolumne]
canyon, coming out by Hetch
Hetchy. There is not a dull step all
the way. With wide variations, it is
a Yosemite Valley from end to end."

*I don't share the common view of
Hetch Hetchy as merely a flooded,
ruined Yosemite. This image
purposely emphasizes Hetch
Hetchy's natural splendor and
diminishes perception of the
unnatural reservoir in the distance.
I see Hetch Hetchy this way
because of something that happened
one morning about twenty years
ago when I awoke there in the
middle of a sheer cliff during a first
ascent. Below me was the valley
floor, but with no roads, buildings,
campfires, or smoke. I heard no
horns, motors, or voices. I found
myself actually preferring Hetch
Hetchy's flood of water over
Yosemite Valley's flood of people.*

SUNRISE ON LENTICULAR CLOUDS,
TIOGA PASS, 1973.

"This grand show is eternal. It is
always sunrise somewhere; the dew
is never all dried at once; a shower
is forever falling; vapor is ever
rising. Eternal sunrise, eternal
sunset, eternal dawn and gloaming,
on sea and continents and islands,
each in its turn, as the round
earth rolls."

*Just before a storm closed Tioga
Pass for the winter, I slept near the
top hoping for an unusual sunrise.
A lenticular cloud display exceeded
my wildest expectations. Knowing I
had minutes at best to make
something more than just an image
of clouds, I found a clearing, set up
my camera with a self-timer, and
walked into the scene, taking my
personal dictum of photographing
landscapes as if I am a part of them
to its logical conclusion.*

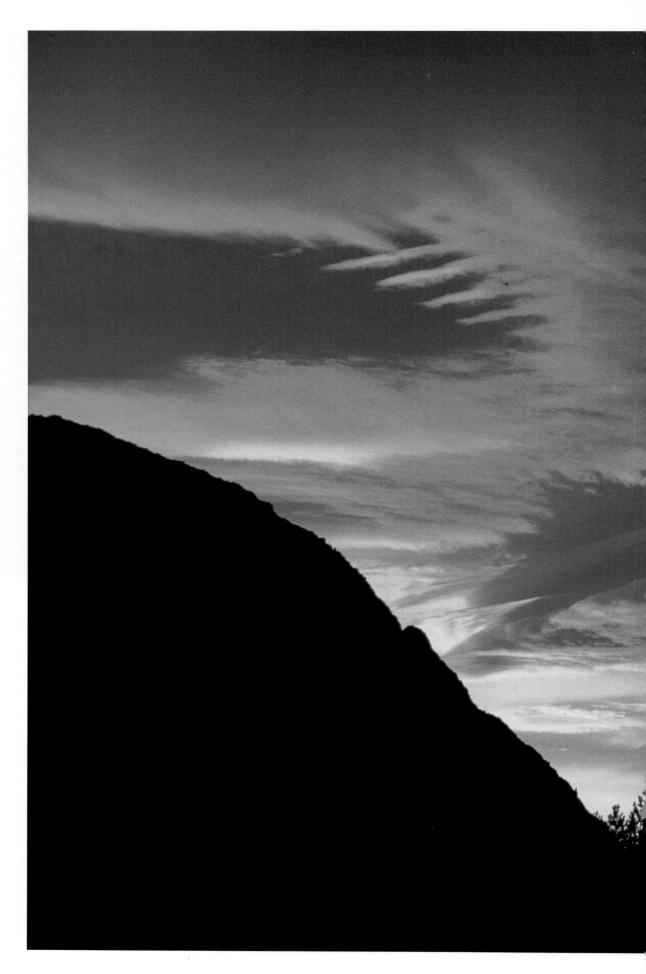

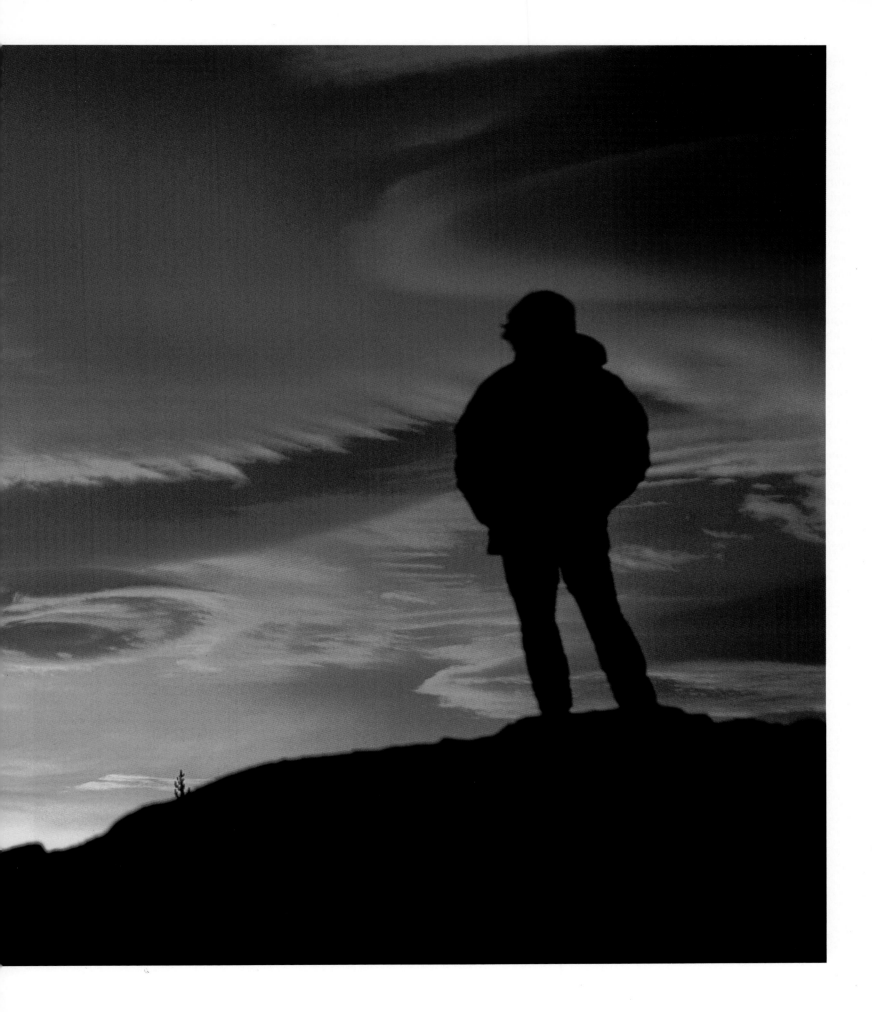

JULY WILDFLOWERS AND LEMBERT
DOME, 1987.

"Yosemite Park is a place of rest, a
refuge from the roar and dust and
weary, nervous, wasting work of the
lowlands, in which one gains the
advantages of both solitude and
society. Nowhere will you find more
company of a soothing peace-be-
still kind. . . . Every rock-brow and
mountain, stream, and lake, and
every plant soon come to be
regarded as brothers. . . . This one
noble park is big enough and rich
enough for a whole life of study and
aesthetic enjoyment. It is good for
everybody, no matter how
benumbed with care, encrusted
with a mail of business habits like a
tree with bark. None can escape
its charms."

*Despite more than a century of
visitation, Tuolumne Meadows
remains much the same carpet of
grass and flowers beneath sunlit
domes that Muir treasured during
his first summer in the Sierra in
1868. During most years, the
meadows are in their prime in early
July, after the June snow has fully
melted but before the August frosts
begin to bronze the grasses.*

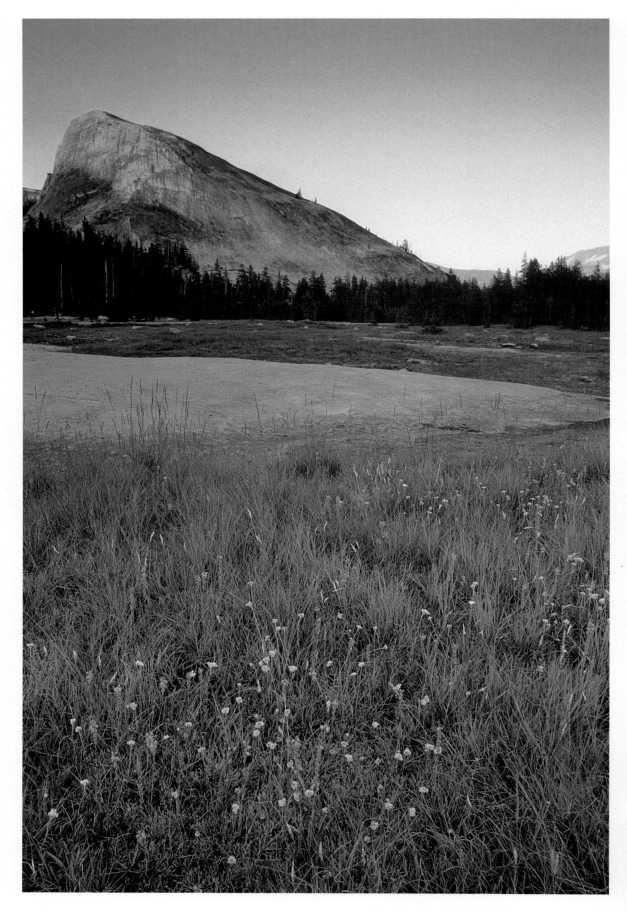

# List of Sources

The John Muir quotations accompanying the photographs in this book
are taken from the following works:

Page 14: John Muir, *The Yosemite*. 1912. Reprint, Garden City, NY:
Doubleday and Company and the Natural History Library, 1962.

Page 16: John Muir, *My First Summer in the Sierra*. 1911. Reprint,
Boston: Houghton Mifflin Company, 1979.

Page 20: *The Yosemite*.

Page 23: *The Yosemite*.

Page 26: *John of the Mountains: The Unpublished Journals of John Muir*,
ed. Linnie Marsh Wolfe. 1938. Reprint, Madison: University of
Wisconsin Press, 1979.

Page 28: *My First Summer in the Sierra*.

Page 32: *My First Summer in the Sierra*.

Page 35: *The Yosemite*.

Page 36: John Muir, *The Mountains of California*. 1894. reprint, Berkeley:
Ten Speed Press, 1979.

Page 38: *The Mountains of California*.

Page 41 and 42: *The Yosemite*.

Page 45: John Muir, *Studies in the Sierra*, ed. William E. Colby. San
Francisco: Sierra Club, 1969.

Page 46: *The Yosemite*.

Page 49: *The Yosemite*.

Page 50: *The Mountains of California*.

Page 52: *The Yosemite*.

Page 54: *The Yosemite*.

Page 57: *The Yosemite*.

Page 59: *The Yosemite*.

Page 60: *The Yosemite*.

Page 63: *John of the Mountains*.

Page 66: *The Yosemite*.

Page 68: *The Yosemite*.

Page 71: *The Yosemite*.

Page 72: *The Yosemite*.

Page 74: *The Yosemite*.

Page 77: *The Yosemite*.

Page 78: *The Mountains of California*.

Page 81: *Studies in the Sierra*.

Page 82: John Muir, "Cathedral Peak and the Tuolumne Meadows,"
*Sierra Club Bulletin*, January 1924.

Page 85: *My First Summer in the Sierra*.

Page 86: John Muir, *The Story of My Boyhood and Youth*. 1913. Reprint,
Madison: University of Wisconsin Press, 1965.

Page 89: *My First Summer in the Sierra*.

Page 90: *The Yosemite*.

Page 93: John Muir, *Mountaineering Essays*, ed. Richard F. Fleck. Salt
Lake City: Peregrine Smith Books, 1984.

Page 95: John Muir, "Our National Parks," *Atlantic Monthly*, April 1901.

Page 96: John Muir, "The American Forests," *Atlantic Monthly*,
August 1897.

Page 99: John Muir, "At East Cape," *San Francisco Daily Evening
Bulletin*, August 16, 1881.

Page 100: John Muir, "Save the Redwoods," *Sierra Club Bulletin*,
January 1920.

Page 103: *John of the Mountains*.

Page 106: John Muir, *To Yosemite and Beyond, Writings from the Years
1863 to 1875*, eds. Robert Engberg and Donald Wesling. Madison:
University of Wisconsin Press, 1980.

Page 109: *My First Summer in the Sierra*.

Page 111: *My First Summer in the Sierra*.

Page 115: John Muir. "The National Parks and Forest Reservations,"
*Sierra Club Bulletin*, January 1896.

Page 117: *Mountaineering Essays*.

Page 120: *John of the Mountains*.

Page 122: John Muir, "Flood-Storm in the Sierra," *The Overland
Monthly*, June 1875.

Page 125: *The Yosemite*.

Page 127: John Muir. "Alaska Gold Fields," *San Francisco Daily Evening
Bulletin*, January 10, 1880; revised version in the *San Francisco
Examiner*, October 11, 1897.

Page 130: *The Yosemite*.

Page 133: *My First Summer in the Sierra*.

Page 134: *John of the Mountains*.

Page 137: *Mountaineering Essays*.

Page 139: *Mountaineering Essays*.

Page 140: *The Mountains of California*.

Page 142: *The Yosemite*.

Page 144: *Picturesque California and the Region West of the Rocky
Mountains, from Alaska to Mexico*, ed. John Muir, two volumes. San
Francisco: J. Dewing, 1888.

Page 146: *Mountaineering Essays*.

Page 148: *The Yosemite*.

Page 151: *The Yosemite*.

Page 152: John Muir, "Living Glaciers of California," *Harper's New
Monthly Magazine*, November 1875.

Page 154: *My First Summer in the Sierra*.

Page 157: John Muir, *A Thousand-Mile Walk to the Gulf*, ed. William F.
Badè. 1916. Reprint, Boston: Houghton Mifflin, 1917.

Page 158: *Mountaineering Essays*.

Page 162: *John of the Mountains*.

Page 166: John Muir, "Yellowstone National Park," *Atlantic Monthly*,
April 1898.

Page 168: *My First Summer in the Sierra*.

Page 170: *John of the Mountains*.

Page 173: *My First Summer in the Sierra*.

Page 175: *The Yosemite*.

Page 179: *The Mountains of California*.

Page 180: *My First Summer in the Sierra*.

Page 183: *Mountaineering Essays*.

Page 184: *Picturesque California*.

Page 186: *Mountaineering Essays*.

Page 189: *To Yosemite and Beyond*.

Page 190: *The Mountains of California*.

Page 193: John Muir, "The Wild Parks and Forest Reservations of the
West," *Atlantic Monthly*, January 1898.

Page 194: *Picturesque California*.

Page 196: *The Mountains of California*.

Page 199: *The Yosemite*.

Page 200: *The Yosemite*.

Page 203: *The Yosemite*.

Page 204: John Muir, "The Discovery of Glacier Bay," *Century Magazine*,
June 1895.

Page 206: *John of the Mountains*.

Page 209: *Studies in the Sierra*.

Page 210: *Mountaineering Essays*.

Page 213: *The Yosemite*.

Page 214: *Mountaineering Essays*.

Page 217: *The Yosemite*.

Page 219: John Muir, Letter to his wife, July 1888. In William Frederick
Bade, ed., *The Life and Letters of John Muir*, two volumes. Boston:
Houghton Mifflin Company, 1923–24.

Page 220: *The Yosemite*.

Page 222: *John of the Mountains*.